5 STEPS TO A 5™

AP European History

2012-2013

Jeffrey Brautigam, Ph.D.

New York Chicago San Francisco Lisbon London Madrid Mexico City
Milan New Delhi San Juan Seoul Singapore Sydney Toronto

Copyright © 2011 by The McGraw-Hill Companies, Inc. All rights reserved. Printed in the
United States of America. Except as permitted under the United States Copyright Act of
1976, no part of this publication may be reproduced or distributed in any form or by any
means, or stored in a database or retrieval system, without the prior written permission of
the publisher.

2 3 4 5 6 7 8 9 10 11 12 13 14 15   QDB/QDB   1 9 8 7 6 5 4 3 2 1

ISBN 978-0-07-175160-5 (print book)
MHID   0-07-175160-2
ISSN 2150-6388

ISBN 978-0-07-175161-2 (e-book)
MHID   0-07-175161-0

Trademarks: McGraw-Hill, the McGraw-Hill Publishing logo, 5 Steps to a 5, and related
trade dress are trademarks or registered trademarks of The McGraw-Hill Companies and/or
its affiliates in the United States and other countries and may not be used without written
permission. All other trademarks are the property of their respective owners. The McGraw-
Hill Companies is not associated with any product or vendor mentioned in this book.

Credits:
Public domain Soviet cartoon, page 249: Wikipedia
Public domain *Punch* cartoon, page 253: John Leech Archive

Series editor was Grace Freedson, and the project editor was Del Franz.
Series design by Jane Tenenbaum.

AP, *Advanced Placement Program*, and *College Board* are registered trademarks of the
College Entrance Examination Board, which was not involved in the production of, and
does not endorse, this product.

McGraw-Hill books are available at special quantity discounts to use as premiums and
sales promotions, or for use in corporate training programs. To contact a representative,
please e-mail us at bulksales@mcgraw-hill.com.

CONTENTS

STEP 4   Review the Knowledge You Need to Score High

Unit 1   1450 to the French Revolutionary and Napoleonic Era   45

STEP 5   Build Your Test-Taking Confidence

PREFACE

Welcome to the world of Advanced Placement (AP) European History. Whether you are, or have been, enrolled in an AP European History course at your school or are just preparing on your own, this guide will help you to move smoothly and confidently from your individual starting point through a five-step process that will bring you the level of preparation you desire. Along the way, you will be evaluating your current level of preparation, evaluating your learning strategies, reading widely, analyzing primary documents, taking practice multiple-choice tests, and writing practice essays. As you go, you will be developing the strategies and confidence you need to score a 5 on the AP European History exam.

The five-step process is described in detail in the Introduction to this guide. Here, I simply want to urge you to enter into your preparation with enthusiasm. The intricate story of European history is dramatic, fascinating, and extremely relevant to the world in which you live. The information, understanding, and skills that you learn by working through this guide will help you to do well on the AP European History exam, but they will also help you to excel in college and to become a well-informed, critically thinking human being.

As you begin, it is important that you not think of this guide as some large book to "get through." This guide is a tool, and, like many tools, it can be used in a number of different ways. You can follow it through from beginning to end, or you can jump around, using the information and exercises contained in it in any way that suits you best. So take some time to familiarize yourself with the contents of this guide; get a feel for how it "works." Then, when you are ready, read Chapters 1 and 2; they will help you to choose the mode of preparation that is right for you.

Good luck and enjoy your journey!

ACKNOWLEDGMENTS

I would like to thank Eric Dodge for putting me in touch with Grace Freedson, and Grace Freedson for connecting me with McGraw-Hill. I would also like to thank all those who assisted me in the preparation of this book: Ruth Mills for her superior editing of the first edition and Del Franz for his efforts on the second; Robyn Ryle for her critical reading and support; and my daughter, Grace Brautigam, for all the times she patiently waited for daddy to "finish his book."

ABOUT THE AUTHOR

JEFFREY BRAUTIGAM is professor of history in the Department of History at Hanover College in Hanover, Indiana, where he evaluates all requests for AP college credit and placement in history. A recipient of a Ph.D. in history from the University of Florida, he has taught European History at the college level for 15 years. He is the coauthor of *A Student Introduction to Charles Darwin* (Kendall/Hunt, 1999, ISBN 0-7872-6311-7). Professor Brautigam is a historian who writes for students and general audiences. He is a member of the American Historical Association and the Association of Core Texts and Courses.

INTRODUCTION: THE FIVE-STEP PROGRAM

The Basics

If you are looking at this book, it is because you are considering taking the AP European History exam. Maybe you are enrolled in an AP European History class in your high school, or maybe you are planning a course of study on your own. Either way, you need some help, and you have come to a bookstore or are shopping online to find it. Right now, there are a number of guides either on the shelf or on the screen in front of you, and you are wondering about the differences between them. The fact is, all the guides in front of you are similar in a number of ways: Each is written by an experienced history instructor who is intimately familiar with the AP European History exam; each contains a concise review of the material you will need to master in order to do well on the exam; and each contains a number of practice exams and exercises to assist you in that preparation.

There is, however, one crucial difference: This book is based upon the highly successful "5 Steps to a 5" program. If you are like the thousands of students who have used the *5 Steps to a 5* program to successfully prepare for AP exams, it is a difference worth exploring.

Introducing the Five-Step Preparation Program

This book is organized as a five-step program to prepare you for success on the AP European History exam. These steps are designed to provide you with the skills and strategies vital to the exam and the practice that can lead you to that perfect 5. Here are the five steps:

Step 1: Set Up Your Study Program

In this step, you will read a brief overview of the AP European History exam and be guided through a process to help determine which of the following preparation programs is right for you:

- full school year: September through May
- one semester: January through May
- six weeks: basic training for the exam

This is covered in Chapters 1 and 2.

Step 2: Determine Your Test Readiness

In this step, you will work through a series of diagnostic exercises and questions that will evaluate your current level of preparation and help you to devise new strategies for success.

- Go through each diagnostic exercise step by step and question by question to build your confidence level.
- Review the correct answers and explanations so that you see what you do and do not yet fully understand.
- Evaluate your level of preparation and your current preparation strategies.

All of this is provided in Chapter 3.

Step 3: Develop Strategies for Success

In this step, you will learn strategies that will help you do your best on the exam. These strategies cover both the multiple-choice and free-response sections of the exam:

- Learn to read multiple-choice questions: see Chapter 4.
- Learn how to answer multiple-choice questions, including whether or not to guess: see Chapter 4.
- Learn how to plan and write the free-response questions, which include both document-based questions, covered in Chapter 5, and the thematic essay questions, which are covered in Chapter 6.

Step 4: Review the Knowledge You Need to Score High

In this step, you will learn or review the material you need to know for the test. This review section takes up the bulk of this book and covers the material covered on the AP European History exam:

- 1450 to the French Revolutionary and Napoleonic Era: see Chapters 7–14 and the Unit I summary
- the Napoleonic Era to the present: see Chapters 15–22 and the Unit 2 summary

At first glance, it may look like there is a lot of material to cover, enough to summarize a yearlong experience in an AP European History course. Some AP courses will have covered more material than yours, and some will have covered less, but the bottom line is that if you thoroughly review this material, you will have studied the great majority of the material that is tested on the exam, and you will have significantly increased your chances of scoring well. But even more important, you will have developed successful strategies for testing well in the field of history that will help you on both the exam and in your future college history classes.

Step 5: Build Your Test-Taking Confidence

In this step, you will complete your preparation by testing yourself on practice exams. This guide contains *two* complete exams in European History, each with full answers and explanations for the multiple-choice questions and suggestions and possible outlines for answers to the free-response essay questions. Be aware that these practice exams are *not* reproduced questions from actual AP European History exam, but they mirror both the material tested by AP and the way in which it is tested.

Appendixes of Other Helpful Information

Finally, at the end of this book, you will find additional resources to aid your preparation:

- a glossary of key terms you are likely to encounter in your reading and on the AP European History exam
- a list of Web sites related to the AP European History exam
- a brief bibliography

Introduction to the Graphics Used in This Book

To emphasize particular skills and strategies, several icons are used throughout this book. An icon in the margin will alert you that you should pay particular attention to the accompanying text. The three icons are:

This icon indicates a very important concept or fact that you should not pass over.

This icon calls your attention to something you might want to try when attempting to answer a particular type of question.

This icon indicates other useful information you might want to keep in mind about the exam.

Finally, *italic* words indicate terms that are included in the glossary at the end of this book.

STEP 1

Set Up Your Study Program

CHAPTER 1

What You Need to Know About the AP European History Exam

IN THIS CHAPTER

Summary: Familiarize yourself with the exam and get answers to frequently asked questions.

Key Ideas

○ The AP European History exam offers high school students the opportunity to earn college credit.

○ You should check with the colleges you are considering for their AP-credit policies.

○ The AP coordinator at your school is your contact person for the exam.

○ The exam is divided into multiple-choice and free-response sections; each is worth 50 percent of the total grade.

○ The free-response section consists of three essays: a document-based question and two thematic questions.

Background Information

The Advanced Placement Program is overseen by an organization known as the College Board, which is involved in many facets of the college admissions process. The program offers highly motivated high school students the opportunity to take college-level courses while they are still in high school, and the opportunity to earn credit or advanced standing at college or university by taking the Advanced Placement exams. The European History program is just one of many offered in the social studies area.

Frequently Asked Questions About the AP European History Exam

Why Take the AP European History Exam?

Most students take the exam with the hope of earning college credit. Most schools will give you college credit for a score of 4 or 5, and some will give credit for a 3. However, the policies of individual colleges and universities vary, so you should check with the schools you are interested in attending for their specific policies.

One advantage of having a college credit in European History is that you are one class closer to graduation, but there are a couple of other good reasons to take the exam:

- First, getting a college credit for AP European History will mean that you will be able to opt out of either a required, introductory course in European History or an elective course. Either way, you will have greater flexibility in choosing your courses, and you will be able to move on to the more advanced and specific courses (either in history or in some other field) that interest you.
- Second, having AP credit on your transcript can increase your chances of getting into the school you want because it tells college admissions officers that you are a serious student who has some experience with college-level work.

Do I Have to Take an AP European History Class to Take the Exam?

No. Taking an AP European History class at your high school is a great way to prepare, but it is not required. The College Board simply urges students to study the kinds of skills and subjects outlined in the AP European History Course Description. The Course Description is available online from the College Board (www.collegeboard.com). The McGraw-Hill five-step program is based on both the College Board Course Description for AP European History and the Exam Guidelines, so working through this guide will help you both to develop the relevant skills and to familiarize yourself with the relevant subject material.

Who Writes and Grades the AP European History Exam?

The exam is written by a team of college and high school history instructors called the AP European History Test Development Committee. The Committee is constantly evaluating the test and field-testing potential questions. The exam is graded by a much larger group of college and high school teachers who meet at a central location in early June to evaluate and score exams that were completed by students the previous month.

What Is on the Exam?

The format of the AP European History exam is shown in Table 1.1. The multiple-choice questions cover European history from the High Renaissance period to the present. About half of the questions cover the period from 1450 to the French Revolutionary and Napoleonic era, with

Table 1.1   AP European History Exam Format

SECTION	TEST ITEMS	TIME LIMIT	PERCENTAGE OF TOTAL GRADE
Multiple-choice	80 questions	55 minutes	50%
15-minute Break			
Free-response	3 essays	130 minutes	50%

Table 1.2 The Free-Response Section

PART	TEST ITEM	SUGGESTED TIME LIMIT
A	Document-based question (DBQ)	60 minutes (includes 15-minute reading period)
B	First thematic essay question	35 minutes
C	Second thematic essay question	35 minutes

the second half covering the French Revolutionary and Napoleonic era to the present. Within the 80 questions, there is a thematic breakdown:

- about one-third of the questions covers cultural and intellectual themes
- about one-third covers political and diplomatic themes
- about one-third covers social and economic themes

We will discuss strategies for doing well on the multiple-choice section in Chapter 4. The free-response section is composed of three parts, as shown in Table 1.2. The document-based question (DBQ) requires you to read a series of excerpts from historical documents and respond to a question about them. The thematic essay questions each ask you to choose one question from each of two groups of three questions. Once the 15-minute reading period for the DBQ is over, you are free to use the rest of the 130-minute time period any way you wish.

We will discuss strategies for doing well on the DBQ in Chapter 5, and on the thematic essays in Chapter 6.

How Is the Exam Evaluated and Scored?

The multiple-choice section, worth 50 percent of the total grade, is scored by computer. The three essays that make up the free-response section are, together, worth 50 percent of the total score. The DBQ essay is worth 45 percent of the free-response score; the two thematic essays together make up 55 percent of the free-response score. All free-response essays are scored by "readers" (the college and high school teachers who are hired to do the job), who have been trained to score the responses in accordance with a set of guidelines. The scoring guidelines for each question are drawn up by a team of the most experienced readers. (We will discuss what kinds of things the guidelines tell the readers to look for in Chapters 5 and 6.) Evaluation and scoring are monitored by the chief reader and table leaders and are periodically analyzed for consistency.

The scores for the multiple-choice and free-response sections are combined into composite scores; the Chief Faculty Consultant then converts the range of composite scores to the 5-point scale of the AP grades:

- Grade 5 is the highest possible grade; it indicates that you are extremely well qualified to receive college credit.
- Grade 4 indicates that you are well qualified.
- Grade 3 indicates that you are qualified.
- Grade 2 indicates that you are possibly qualified.
- Grade 1 indicates that you are not qualified to receive college credit.

How Do I Register?

Whether you are enrolled in a high school AP course or preparing for the test on your own, the best thing to do is see your guidance counselor. He or she will direct you to the AP coordinator for your school. You will need the coordinator because that is the person who collects

› Multiple-Choice Questions Exercise

Directions: Choose the best answer for each question. Circle the answer of your choice. As you choose, make notes about the process of elimination you used to arrive at your answer. When you are finished, compare your answers and your reasoning with the Answers and Explanations section that follows.

1. Which of the following were effects of the Hundred Years War on England and France?
   - (A) It disrupted agriculture, causing famine, disease, and a significant decrease in the population.
   - (B) It created an enormous tax burden that led to a series of peasant rebellions.
   - (C) It left France an economically devastated but more politically unified kingdom.
   - (D) It weakened England economically but led to the beginning of a textile industry upon which it would rebuild its economic strength.
   - (E) All of the above.

2. The goal of the Conciliar Movement was
   - (A) the end of the Hundred Years War
   - (B) to heal the rift between Catholics and Protestants
   - (C) to select a new pope
   - (D) to reform, reunite, and reinvigorate the Church
   - (E) to allow secular governments to gain some measure of control of the Church in their kingdoms

3. In the fifteenth century, which of the following were increasing their power?
   - (A) the Church
   - (B) secular monarchs
   - (C) the nobility
   - (D) the peasantry
   - (E) artisans

4. An unprecedented era of exploration and discovery in the late-fifteenth and early-sixteenth centuries was spurred by
   - (A) the desire for precious metals and competition for the spice trade
   - (B) the need for markets to sell manufactured goods
   - (C) the need to find space for an expanding population
   - (D) the missionary work of the Church
   - (E) the Hundred Years War

5. The most outstanding characteristic of Renaissance Italian society was
   - (A) the strength of the monarchy
   - (B) the power of the traditional nobility
   - (C) the degree to which it was urban
   - (D) the freedom allowed to women
   - (E) the development of cash-crop agriculture

6. "Humanism," in early-Renaissance Italy, refers primarily to
   - (A) renewed interest in the scientific method
   - (B) scholarly interest in and the study of classical cultures of Greece and Rome
   - (C) an anti-Christian attitude
   - (D) a focus on the qualities and strategies necessary for attaining and holding power
   - (E) the study of the works of Aristotle

7. Giotto is often referred to as a transition figure between medieval art and the Renaissance style because
   - (A) his subject matter was secular
   - (B) of the scale of his *David*
   - (C) his works were commissioned by patrons
   - (D) his subject matter was religious but his concern was for the human experience
   - (E) he specialized in nudes

8. Nineteenth-century conservatism tended to be supported by
   - (A) traditional, landed aristocracy
   - (B) the merchant class
   - (C) industrial barons
   - (D) the working class
   - (E) women

› Answers and Explanations

1. **E.** All of the above are correct. Choice A is correct because the continual fighting made it difficult for peasant farmers to cultivate the land, resulting in frequent famine. Famine and the many corpses lying around led to disease; famine and disease combined to decrease the population. Choice B is correct because money had to be raised to field armies; the nobility and Church were largely exempt so the burden fell on the peasants, who frequently rebelled. Choice C is correct because the war brought economic devastation, but that devastation broke the power of regional nobility, allowing the king to politically unify the kingdom. Choice D is correct because the war similarly weakened England economically, but the difficulty of keeping trade lines open led the English to begin producing textiles for clothing.

2. **D.** The goal of the Conciliar Movement of the fifteenth century, led by various councils of cardinals, was to reform, reunite and reinvigorate the Church, which was deeply divided by the Avignon Papacy (1309–1377) and the Great Schism (1378–1417). Choice A is incorrect because the Conciliar Movement was not related in any direct way to the Hundred Years War. Choice B is incorrect because the Conciliar Movement predated the Reformation and the creation of a Protestant movement. Choice C is incorrect because the Conciliar Movement was concerned with reforming the Church, not selecting a pope. Choice E is incorrect because the gains secular governments made over the Church in their kingdoms were a result of the Conciliar Movement, not a goal.

3. **B.** Secular monarchs, such as Isabella and Ferdinand of Spain, were increasing their power in the fifteenth century because traditional institutions seemed powerless in the face of calamities such as the Hundred Years War and the Black Death. Choices A and C are incorrect because the Church and the nobility were traditional institutions whose power had been weakened; the Church was additionally weakened by internal divisions. Choices D and E are incorrect because both the peasantry and the artisans still

lacked any basis for political power in the fifteenth century.

4. **A.** It was the desire for precious metals and the competition for the spice trade that led the monarchies of Spain and Portugal to invest large sums of capital in voyages of exploration. Choice B is incorrect because manufacturing in Europe had not yet reached a stage that demanded new markets. Choice C is incorrect because the population of Europe was still recovering from the plague and was not large enough to create pressure for new land. Choice D is incorrect because, while it is true that missionaries accompanied the voyages, the monarchies would not have invested huge sums without hope of financial return. Choice E is incorrect because the Hundred Years War preceded the era of great voyages.

5. **C.** Renaissance Italy was uniquely urban. By 1500, seven of the ten largest cities in Europe were in Italy. Choice A is incorrect because unlike the majority of Western Europe, which was characterized by large kingdoms with powerful monarchs, the Italian peninsula was made up of numerous independent city-states, such as Milan, Florence, Padua, and Genoa. Choice B is incorrect because the urban nature of Renaissance Italy meant that the traditional landed nobility were less powerful than elsewhere in Europe. Choice D is incorrect because the social conventions of Renaissance Italy were as restrictive as elsewhere in Europe. Choice E is incorrect because cash-crop agriculture did not develop to any significant degree in Renaissance Italy.

6. **B.** Early-Renaissance humanism is best understood as a scholarly interest in and the study of classical Greece and Rome for the purpose of learning how to succeed in life and live a good life. Choice A is incorrect because the notion of a scientific method is a seventeenth-century invention. Choice C is incorrect because humanism was never anti-Christian. Choice D is incorrect because a focus on the qualities and strategies necessary for attaining and holding power was a characteristic of the "princely ideal" of *late*-Renaissance humanism. Choice E is

incorrect because the myopic focus on the works of Aristotle was a characteristic of medieval scholasticism.

7. **D.** The combination of a concern for the human experience with a religious subject matter that characterizes the transitional nature of Giotto's work can be seen in his frescos depicting the life of St. Francis, where the human characters are depicted in realistic detail and with clear concern for their psychological reaction to the saint's life. Choice A is incorrect because Giotto's subject matter was not secular, but religious. Choice B is incorrect because Giotto did not do a version of *David*. Choice C is incorrect because both medieval and Renaissance Italian art was commissioned by patrons. Choice E is incorrect because Giotto did not specialize in nudes.

8. **A.** Conservatism was the ideology that asserted that tradition is the only trustworthy guide to social and political action, and held that the monarchy, the hierarchical class system, and the Church were crucial institutions. Accordingly, they drew their support from the traditional elites of Europe, the landed aristocracy and the Church. Choices B and C are incorrect because the merchant class and industrial barons, who did not have a comfortable place in the traditional hierarchy, tended to support liberalism and its platform of reform. Choice D is incorrect because the working classes of the nineteenth century looked first to liberalism and then, increasingly, to socialism as the best hope for representation of their interests. There were women who supported conservatism, though not in a political sense, since they were excluded from political participation. But women who supported the women's rights movements tended to support the notions of individual liberty promoted by liberalism; thus, choice A is a better answer.

The Document-Based Question

The second part of the AP European History exam is the document-based question, also known as the DBQ. The DBQ is simply an essay question about primary sources. It asks you to respond to a question by interpreting a set of excerpts (typically 10–12) from documents that were written in a particular historical period. The set of excerpts will come from sources like newspaper articles or editorials, classic texts, pamphlets, speeches, diaries, letters, and other similar sources. The DBQ will also give you a paragraph of information that identifies the historical context that connects the documents.

Below you will find a DBQ of the sort that might appear on the AP European History exam, giving the question, the historical background, and a set of excerpted documents (for this exercise, we will start with five instead of the usual 10–12). If you have written essays like this before, take a shot at writing one here. Time yourself the way you will be timed in the exam, giving yourself 15 minutes to read the question and the documents (you may not write during this period) and then writing for no more than 45 minutes (the amount of time suggested by the exam). When you are finished, compare your essay with the Suggestions and Possible Outline of a Response to the DBQ Exercise at the end of this section.

If you have not written many essays of this type, then simply construct an outline of a possible answer to the question. As you do so, make some notes about your thought processes. How did you begin? What did you do with the documents? Then, compare your outline and notes with the Suggestions and Possible Outline that appear at the end of this section. *If you struggle or do not get very far in your attempts to make an outline, do not worry; Chapter 5 will teach you how to develop strategies for doing this quickly, efficiently, and well.* If you feel good about your essay or outline, you may want to go to the back of this guide and take the DBQ section of Practice Test 1. Then compare your essay with the outline and comments that appear at the end of the test.

Document-Based Question Exercise

Directions

A. Give yourself 15 minutes to read the question, historical background, and documents. Then, on separate sheets of paper, write an essay that responds to the question (take no more than 45 minutes). When you are finished, compare your essay with the Suggestions and Possible Outline that follow. If you wish, proceed to the DBQ section of Practice Test 1.

or

B. Read the question and, historical, background, and documents. Then, on a separate sheet of paper, make an outline of an essay that responds to the question and take some notes about your thought processes. When you are finished, compare your essay with the Suggestions and Possible Outline that follow.

1. Discuss the competing notions concerning the origin and nature of political sovereignty and the proper role of government that were developed in the seventeenth and eighteenth centuries.

Historical Background: Throughout the seventeenth and eighteenth centuries, European political philosophers argued about the origin and nature of political sovereignty and the proper role of government. In seventeenth-century Britain, the argument became part of a civil war and revolution that pitted the Stuart monarchy and its supporters against the forces of Parliament. In eighteenth-century France, the Bourbon monarchy, the aristocracy, and the Church all found themselves faced with an increasingly radical revolution.

Document 1

> **Source:** James I, speech to the English Parliament, 1610.
> The state of monarchy is the supremest thing upon the earth: for kings are not only God's lieutenants upon earth and sit upon God's throne, but even by God himself they are called gods . . . In the Scriptures kings are called gods, and so their power after a certain relation compared to the Divine power. Kings are also compared with fathers of families; for a king is truly *parens patriae* [parent of the country], the politic father of his people. And lastly, kings are compared to the head of this microcosm of the body of man.

Document 2

> **Source:** Thomas Hobbes, *Leviathan*, London, 1651.
> The only way to erect such common power, as may be able to defend them from the invasion of foreigners, and the injuries of one another, and thereby to secure them in such sort, as that by their own industry, and by the fruits of the earth, they may nourish themselves and live contentedly, is to confer all their power and strength upon one man, or upon one assembly of men, that may reduce all their wills, by plurality of voices, unto one will . . . This is more than consent or concord; it is a real unity of them all, in one and the same person, made by covenant of every man . . .

Document 3

> **Source:** John Locke, *The Second Treatise of Government*, London, 1690.
> The only way whereby anyone divests himself of his natural liberty and puts on the bonds of civil society, is by agreeing with other men to join and unite into a community for their comfortable, safe and peaceable living one among another, in a secure enjoyment of their

properties, and a greater security against any that are not of it ... And thus every man, by consenting with others to make one body politic under one government, puts himself under obligation to every one of that society to submit to the determination of the majority, and to be concluded by it ... [But]When the governor, however entitled, makes not the law but his will the rule, and his commands and actions are not directed to the preservation of the properties of his people, but the satisfaction of his own ambition, revenge, covetousness, or any other irregular passion, ... there it presently becomes tyranny.

Document 4

Source: M. de Montesquieu, *Spirit of the Laws*, Paris, 1748.
Law in general is human reason, inasmuch as it governs all the inhabitants of the earth; the political and civil laws of each nation ought to be only the particular cases in which human reason is applied ... Democratic and aristocratic states are not in their own nature free. Political liberty is to be found only in moderate governments; and even in these it is not always found. It is there only when there is no abuse of power ... To prevent this abuse, it is necessary, from the very nature of things, power should be a check to power. A government must be so constituted as no man shall be compelled to do things to which the law does not oblige him, nor forced to abstain from things which the law permits.

Document 5

Source: Emmanuel Joseph Sieyès, *What Is the Third Estate?* Paris, 1789.
Public functions may be classified equally well, in the present state of affairs, under four recognized heads: the sword, the robe, the church, and the administration. It would be superfluous to take them up one by one, for the purpose of showing that everywhere the Third Estate attends to nineteen-twentieths of them, with this distinction; that it is laden with all that which is really painful, with all the burdens which the privileged classes refuse to carry ... Who then shall dare to say that the Third Estate has not within itself all that is necessary for the formation of a complete nation?

Suggestions and Possible Outline of a Response to the DBQ Exercise

Suggestions

Begin by finding a way to group the documents. Notice that James I and Thomas Hobbes believed in an all-powerful ruler, while Locke and Montesquieu argued for a more limited government. On the issue of origins, note that James I believed in Divine Right Monarchy. Hobbes actually agreed with Locke and Montesquieu that power is derived from the people, but rejected the notion of "consent" introduced by Locke. Notice how Sieyès places sovereignty in the "nation" at all times.

Next, address the relationship between the groups of documents; here it would be a good idea to see them as an evolution from notions of an all-powerful, Divine Right monarch to the more modern notion of a nation. Topic sentences should make clear claims about that evolution.

The body of the essay's paragraphs must present historical evidence that supports and illustrates the topic sentences and, therefore, the thesis. An outline of such an essay might look like this.

Outline

Thesis: The documents, taken in chronological order, reflect an evolution of political thought from Divine Right Monarchy to the notion of a sovereign nation.

Topic sentence A: Documents 1 and 2 both argue for a sovereign with unlimited power, but demonstrate a shift away from Divine Right Monarchy.

Specific examples: James I, who was attempting to reestablish Divine Right Monarchy in England, is lecturing an uppity Parliament. He emphasizes: scripture, kings as gods, paternalism, and the king as head of the body politic. Hobbes, who supported the monarchy in the English Civil War, is arguing the necessity an all-powerful ruler. He allows that a ruler is chosen by the people, but he emphasizes "real unity" and a covenant, not consent. The meaning of *Leviathan* summarizes his point.

Topic sentence B: Documents 3 and 4 argue for limited government, by consent, according to the laws of reason.

Specific examples: Locke, a supporter of Parliament and writing immediately after the Glorious Revolution in England, emphasizes "natural liberty"; indicates consent as the origin of legitimate power; and gives a definition of tyranny (it does not exist in Hobbes) that must be opposed. Montesquieu, of the Enlightenment period, argues from a notion of natural law. He argues that power is always limited by reason. The meaning of "spirit of the laws" summarizes his point.

Topic sentence C: Document 5 illustrates the new concept of a "nation" as the home of sovereignty.

Specific examples: Sieyès, leader of the moderate phase of the French Revolution, is justifying the revolt of the Third Estate. He argues that "Third Estate" (define) executes the functions of administration; the burden of administration equals the right to rule.

Conclusion (if time): There was a clear evolution of political thought from Divine Right Monarchy to the notion of a sovereign nation.

The Thematic Essay Questions

The thematic essay questions make up the remainder of the 130-minute, free-response section of the AP European History exam. You will be presented with two groups of three questions (six total). The first group will present questions that ask about the period from roughly 1450 to the Napoleonic Era, and the second group will present three questions that ask about the period from the Napoleonic Era to the present. You must respond to one question from each group. Remember that the exam instructions recommend that you divide your time as follows:

- Part A (the DBQ)—15 minutes reading time, 45 minutes writing time
- Part B (first thematic essay)—35 minutes writing time
- Part C (second thematic essay)—35 minutes writing time

Your goal is to quickly choose the two questions you will answer and construct a short history essay of high quality in the approximately 35 minutes allotted for each. Below you will find a thematic essay question similar to the ones that appear on the AP European History exam. If you have written essays like this before, take a shot at writing one that answers the question. Time yourself the way you will be timed in the exam, giving yourself 35 minutes to compose and write your essay. When you are finished, compare your essay with the Suggestions and Possible Outline of a Response to the Thematic Essay Questions Exercise at the end of this section.

If you have not written many of these kinds of essays, then begin by constructing an outline of a possible answer to the question and taking some notes about your thought processes. How did you begin? How did you organize your thoughts? Then, compare your outline and notes with the outline and comments that appear at the end of this section. *If you struggle or do not get very far in your attempts to make an outline, do not worry; Chapter 6 will teach you how to develop strategies for doing this quickly, efficiently, and well.* If you feel good about your essay or outline, you may want to go to the back of this guide and complete the thematic essay questions section of Practice Test 1. Then compare your essays with the Suggestions and Possible Outline that appear at the end of the test.

Thematic Essay Question Exercise

Directions

A. Write an essay that responds to the question (take no more than 35 minutes). Write your essay on separate sheets of paper. When you are finished, compare your essay with the Suggestions and Possible Outline that follow. If you want to, proceed to the thematic essay questions section of Practice Test 1.

or

B. Read the question and make an outline of an essay that responds to the question, and take some notes about your thought processes. Write your outline and notes on a separate sheet of paper. When you are finished, compare your essay with the Suggestions and Possible Outline that follow.

1. Analyze the factors that led to World War I and determine which were decisive.

Suggestions and Possible Outline of a Response to the Thematic Essay Question Exercise

Suggestions

Make a quick list of the "causes" of World War I as they were covered in your class and your readings. Rank them in order of importance and select one or two as "decisive" (i.e., most directly responsible for the outbreak of war). Compose a thesis stating clearly your argument for ranking them the way you do. Write three topic sentences making three clear points that add up to your thesis. Underneath each of the topic sentences, list specific examples that illustrate and support your topic sentences. From that outline write a clear, concise essay.

Outline

Thesis: The determination of Germany to expand and the requirements of the Schlieffen Plan were the most decisive factors in bringing about World War I.
Topic sentence A: Since unification in 1871, Imperial Germany was fearful of encirclement and determined to gain *lebensraum* (room to live).
Specific examples: German unification was itself expansionist in nature; the concept of *lebensraum* was prevalent in German culture; the fear of encirclement led to the German belief that war was inevitable and, thus, to the drawing up of the Schlieffen Plan, a plan to win a two-front war.
Topic sentence B: The Anglo-German rivalry, the Nationalities Problem in the Hapsburg Empire, and the Alliance System were all factors, but none was decisive.

Specific examples: Britain and Germany engaged in an arms race in the decades before the war; but they were also each other's largest trading partners; past examples of ethnic-nationalist agitation inside the Hapsburg Empire were handled without war; details of the alliance system did restrict diplomatic options and seemed to guarantee military response, but such alliances were broken when necessary, for example, Italy's initial neutrality.

Topic sentence C: The assassination of the Archduke Franz Ferdinand was the fuse, but the Schleiffen Plan, born of Germany's belief that war was inevitable, was a more decisive factor.

Specific examples: Serbia agreed to the Hapsburg ultimatum, but Austrian aggression was spurred on by Germany's "blank check"; Russian troop mobilization was a standard "show of support"; the Schleiffen Plan's existence shows Germany's preparation for war (no other country was thus prepared), and its logic guaranteed large-scale military movement at the first sign of Russian mobilization.

Conclusion (if time): Of the many factors that led to World War I, Germany's determination to expand and the iron logic of the Schlieffen Plan were decisive.

STEP 3

Develop Strategies for Success

CHAPTER 4

The Multiple-Choice Questions

IN THIS CHAPTER

Summary: Develop a successful strategy for the multiple-choice section.

Key Ideas

✪ Multiple-choice questions test passive knowledge.
✪ The question always provides clues to the answer.
✪ The key is to quickly devise a process of elimination.

Introduction

Section I of the AP European History exam consists of 80 multiple-choice questions. The directions are straightforward, and they resemble the directions for every multiple-choice test you have ever taken. They read:

> **Directions:** Each of the questions or incomplete statements below is followed by five suggested answers or completions. Select the one that is best in each case and then fill in the corresponding oval on the answer sheet.

So, you know the drill; you select the best answer of the five and fill in your choice. And you have probably taken enough multiple-choice tests to know that there is an important question you should ask: "If I am not sure of the best answer, should I guess?" The answer is yes but we will get to that in a minute. Right now, ask yourself a few more questions: What does a multiple-choice question test? How did the authors of the exam come up with the 80 questions? Are there different kinds of multiple-choice question? How did they decide what order to put them in? Knowing the answers to these questions can help you develop a successful strategy for approaching them.

Passive Knowledge and the Premise

All multiple-choice exams test *passive knowledge*. The multiple-choice section of the AP European History exam will test your passive knowledge of European history from roughly 1450 to the present. That is, it will test your ability to *recognize* the best answer from a group of possible answers to a specific historical question. The word "best" is important. It means that all multiple-choice questions are answered through a *process of elimination*; you begin by eliminating the one that is most clearly not the "best" and continue until you have a "survivor."

Additionally, a multiple-choice question and its answer try to say something meaningful about history in a single sentence. That is a very difficult thing to do. In order to do it, the question creates a *premise* which the test taker must accept. For example, look at the following question:

1. The most outstanding characteristic of Renaissance Italian society was
    (A) the strength of the monarchy
    (B) the power of the traditional nobility
    (C) the degree to which it was urban
    (D) the freedom allowed to women
    (E) the development of cash-crop agriculture

The question proceeds from the premise that there was a single most outstanding characteristic of Renaissance Italian society. That is a debatable premise (was there really one that was more "outstanding" or noteworthy than all the other characteristics?), and a sophisticated student of history could debate (and indeed write a doctoral dissertation debating) the merits of several possible answers. Doing so would make you seem very sophisticated and knowledgeable, but it would be both silly and counterproductive on an exam.

The people who wrote the question realize that the premise is debatable, but they have constructed the question so that, *if* you accept the premise (and for the purpose of the exam, they insist that you do), there is an internal, historical logic that will lead you to the *best* answer, provided you have some knowledge of the significant aspects of Renaissance Italian history (and that is what the question tests).

Organizational Keys

How did they come up with the 80 questions? The high school and college teachers who created the AP European History exam followed these organizational principles:

1. The questions are broken down by era:
    • Forty questions cover the era from roughly 1450 to 1815.
    • Forty questions cover the era from 1815 to the present.

2. The questions are also broken down by general subject:
    • Roughly 30–40 percent (or 24–32 questions) cover political and diplomatic themes.
    • Roughly 20–30 percent (or 16–24 questions) cover cultural and intellectual themes.
    • Roughly 30–40 percent (or 24–32 questions) cover social and economic themes.

Knowing these two organizing principles of the exam helps you only in a general sense; they let you know that you have to devote about equal preparation time for the questions on the period from 1450 to 1815 and from 1815 to the present, and about equal time for the three thematic categories. But knowing some other guiding principles can actually help you to answer specific questions.

3. The questions test basic principles and general trends, *not* memorization and trivia. Knowing that the exam seeks to test basic principles and general trends tells you that you do not need to memorize loads of dates and facts; rather you can use your knowledge to reason your way to the best answer. It also tells you that the best answer will *not* be an exception or an obscure fact, but rather an illustration of the basic principle or general trend.

4. The questions appear in groups of four to seven questions that are in chronological order. You should be able to tell where the breaks between groups are. When, for example, you see a question about World War I followed by a question about the Renaissance, you have come upon a break between groups. Identifying the groups of questions can be helpful; if you come upon a question that lies between a question about the Renaissance and one about the Scientific Revolution, you know that the event or process that it asks about occurred between those two eras.

5. The questions get progressively more difficult. Therefore the early questions have easy, straightforward answers. Do not read too much complexity into the early questions. Choose the most obvious answers.

The Kinds of Questions

There are several kinds of multiple-choice questions on the AP European History exam. Most of the questions are straightforward, such as find-the-best-answer questions like the one about the outstanding characteristic of the Renaissance above. However, there are two other types worth watching out for:

- There are questions that include the words NOT or EXCEPT. These questions give you five choices and ask you to pick the one that is not true or, following the premise of the question, the worst answer. In these questions, the words NOT or EXCEPT are always capitalized, so you will not miss them. Just be sure to remember that you are looking for the worst answer when you analyze the choices.

- Once in a while, there are questions that ask you to interpret an *illustration*. The illustration may be a map, a graph, a chart, or perhaps a poster or cartoon from a particular period of history. You will almost certainly not have seen the illustration before, and the authors of the exam do not expect you to have seen it. What they are looking for is your ability to "get" the illustration based on your knowledge of the period.

About Guessing

Should you guess? The AP administration has recently changed its policy regarding scoring for wrong answers. Effective with the 2011 AP exams, total scores on the multiple-choice section are based solely on the number of questions answered correctly. Points are no longer deducted for incorrect answers, and no points are awarded for unanswered questions. In other words, there is no longer any guessing penalty. If you are unsure of an answer, by all means take a guess.

Developing a Strategy

OK. Let us put what we have learned into practice to answer that question about the Renaissance.

1. The most outstanding characteristic of Renaissance Italian society was
   (A) the strength of the monarchy
   (B) the power of the traditional nobility
   (C) the degree to which it was urban
   (D) the freedom allowed to women
   (E) the development of cash-crop agriculture

Step 1: Identify the context

In this case, that is easy. The question tells us it is about Renaissance Italy. If the question were about a specific document, say Pico's *Oration on the Dignity of Man*, we could figure out that the context was Renaissance Italy by remembering that Renaissance humanism stressed the dignity of man, or by noticing that the question started a chronological "group" of questions and was followed by a question about the Reformation.

Step 2: Identify the premise

As we noted earlier, the premise of this question is that there was one social characteristic of Renaissance Italian society that stood out more prominently than the rest.

Step 3: Decide whether you are working from a good knowledge base or a weak one, and begin the process of elimination

When you read the question, was your reaction something like: "Excellent, I know the Renaissance"? Or was it more like, "Aargh! I should have studied the Renaissance"?

If you had the "Excellent" reaction, then you are working from a good knowledge base, and your process of elimination would work something like this: "I know that Renaissance Italy, unlike the rest of Europe, was organized into independent *city*-states rather than large kingdoms, so the best answer is probably choice C, 'the degree to which it was urban,' because urban means lots of *cities*." All that is left to do now is quickly scan the other answers to make sure there are no other contenders: "I know choices A and B are no good because strong monarchies and powerful traditional nobility are the characteristics of the rest of Europe at this time. Choice E is no good because agriculture is a rural characteristic, and Renaissance society is urban. And choice D is out because Renaissance women were no better off than women anywhere else in Europe. My first instinct was correct, the answer is choice C."

If you had the "Aargh!" reaction, you will have to operate something like this: "OK, I know zip about the Renaissance, but I am throwing out choices A and B because I am pretty sure there were lots of strong kings and powerful nobility. How about choice D? Were women better off in Renaissance Italy? I have no idea, but I do remember that women were still fighting for equal rights in the twentieth century, so it is not very likely that they had it great in the Renaissance. That leaves choices C and E, which are opposites; either Renaissance Italy was really urban or it was on the cutting edge of agricultural development. Urban? Hmmmm. Rome, Venice, yeah, Italy has lots of famous cities with a lot of famous old buildings; I am going with choice C."

Both processes of elimination produce the same, correct answer. The outstanding characteristic of Renaissance Italy was the degree to which it was urban. Now, before you go on to the next chapter, look at your notes regarding the processes of elimination you used to answer the multiple-choice questions in Chapter 3. For the ones you got wrong, construct a process of elimination that leads to the right answer. If you feel ready, go to the back of the guide and do the multiple-choice section of Practice Test 1.

CHAPTER 5

The Document-Based Question (DBQ)

IN THIS CHAPTER

Summary: Learn how to write a short history essay of high quality and how to adapt the process for the DBQ.

Key Ideas
- ✪ There are three basic components to a short history essay of high quality.
- ✪ Writing a short history essay of high quality can be done in five simple steps.
- ✪ The DBQ requires you to write a short history essay about primary source documents.
- ✪ The five-step process for writing a short history essay of high quality is easily adapted for the DBQ.

Introduction

In this chapter, we discuss the nature of the document-based question and develop strategies for doing well on that section of the exam. In Chapter 6, we look at the thematic essay questions. But before we do either, we would do well to remember that, in essence, your task is to write a short history essay of high quality. I have seen a lot of gibberish written about how to "crack" AP essay questions that dwells far too much on "what the graders are looking for" and gives misguided advice like, "Throw in a few big words." In this chapter, I *do* discuss the guidelines that are given to those who grade the AP European History exam essays, but only to give you a sense of the purpose of the questions.

In reality, those who grade the AP essay exams are "looking for" the thing that all history instructors look for and, I dare say, hope for when they read student essays: a reasonably well-written essay that answers the question, makes an argument, and supports the argument with evidence. In short, the key to "cracking" the AP essay questions is to know how to write a short history essay of high quality. Learn that skill now, and you will not only do well on the AP exam, but you will also do well in your history classes in college.

The Quality History Essay

There are three basic components to a short history essay of high quality:

1. a clear thesis that answers the question
2. three to five topic sentences that, taken together, add up logically to the thesis
3. evidence that supports and illustrates each of the topic sentences

Thesis

In a short history essay, the thesis is a sentence that makes a clear assertion in response to the question. It is, therefore, also a statement of what your reader will believe if your essay is persuasive.

Topic Sentences

The topic sentences should appear at the beginning of clearly marked paragraphs. Each topic sentence makes a clear assertion that you will illustrate and support in the body of the paragraph. All of your topic sentences together should add up logically to your thesis. That is, if you were to successfully persuade your reader of the truth (or at least plausibility) of your topic sentences, they would have no choice but to admit the plausibility of your thesis.

Evidence

This is the part that makes your essay historical. In a history essay, the evidence is made up of specific examples explained to support and illustrate your claim.

Five Steps to Outlining a Short History Essay

Before you begin writing a short history essay, you should always make an outline. You probably know that but, when you keep the three components of the high-quality short history essay in mind, you can produce an outline quickly and efficiently by following a very simple five-step process.

Step 1: Find the Action Words in the Question and Determine What the Question Wants You to Do

Too many essays respond to the topic instead of the question. In order to answer a question, you must do what it asks. To determine, specifically, what a question is asking you to do, you must pay attention to the action words—the words that give you a specific task. Look at the following question; notice the action words and go to Step 2.

Compare and contrast the roles played by the various social classes in the unification of Italy and Germany in the 1860s and 1870s.

Step 2: Compose a Thesis That Responds to the Question and Gives You Something Specific to Support and Illustrate

Compare the following two attempts at a thesis in response to our question:

A. German and Italian unifications have a lot in common but also many differences.
B. The unifications of both Italy and Germany were engineered by the aristocracy.

Alas, attempts at a thesis statement that resemble example A are all too common. Notice how example A merely makes a vague claim about the topic and gives the author nothing specific to do next. Example B, in contrast, makes a specific assertion about the role of a social class in the unifications of Italy and Germany; it is responding directly to the question. Moreover, example B is a thesis because it tells its readers what they will accept if the essay is persuasive. Finally, example B gives the author something specific to do, namely, build and support an argument that explains why we should conclude that the unifications of Italy and Germany were engineered by the aristocracy.

Step 3: Compose Your Topic Sentences and Make Sure That They Add Up Logically to Your Thesis

In response to our question, three good topic sentences might be:

A. The architects of both Italian and German unification were conservative, northern aristocrats.
B. The middle classes played virtually no role in Italian unification and, in the south, initially opposed the unification of Germany.
C. The working classes and peasantry followed the lead of the aristocracy in both the unification of Italy and that of Germany.

Notice how the topic sentences add up logically to the thesis and how each gives you something specific to support in the body of the paragraph.

Step 4: Support and Illustrate Your Thesis with Specific Examples

The paragraphs that follow the topic sentences should present specific examples that illustrate and support its point. That means that each paragraph is made up of two things: factual information and your explanation of how that factual information supports the topic sentence. When making your outline, you can list the examples you want to use. For our question, the outline would look something like this:

Thesis: The unifications of both Italy and Germany were engineered by the aristocracy.

Topic sentence A: The architects of both Italian and German unification were conservative, northern aristocrats.

Specific examples: Cavour, conservative aristocrat from Piedmont; Bismarck, conservative aristocrat from Prussia. Both took leadership roles and devised unification strategies.

Topic sentence B: The middle classes played virtually no role in Italian unification and, in the south, initially opposed the unification of Germany.

Specific examples: Italy—mid-century *Risorgimento*, a middle-class movement, failed, and played virtually no role in subsequent events. Germany—middle-class liberals in the Frankfort Parliament were ineffective; middle-class liberals in southern Germany were initially wary of Prussian domination; they rallied to the cause only when Bismarck engineered the Franco-Prussian War.

Topic sentence C: The working classes and peasantry followed the lead of the aristocracy in the unification of both Italy and Germany.

Specific examples: Italy—the working classes played no role in the north; the peasantry of the south followed Garibaldi, but shifted without resistance to support of Cavour and the king at the crucial moment. The working classes in Germany supported Bismarck and Kaiser Wilhelm I of Prussia; the socialists, supposedly a working-class party, rallied to the cause of war.

Step 5: *If You Have Time,* Compose a One-Paragraph Conclusion That Restates Your Thesis

A conclusion is *not* necessary, and you will get little or no credit for one. If you have time remaining and you are happy with all the other aspects of your essay, then you can write a one-paragraph conclusion that restates your thesis.

Things to Avoid

There are some things that sabotage an otherwise promising essay and should be avoided. Follow these guidelines:

- *Avoid long sentences with multiple clauses.* Your goal is to write the clearest sentence possible; most often the clearest sentence is a relatively short sentence.
- *Do not get caught up in digressions.* No matter how fascinating or insightful you find some idea or fact, if it does not directly support or illustrate your thesis, do not put it in.
- *Skip the mystery.* Do not ask a lot of rhetorical questions, and do not go for a surprise ending. The readers are looking for your thesis, your argument, and your evidence; give these to them in a clear, straightforward manner.

Characteristics of the DBQ

As we learned in Chapter 3, the document-based question is simply an essay question about primary sources. It asks you to respond to a question by interpreting a set of excerpts (typically 10–12) from documents that were written in a particular historical period. The DBQ is the second part of the AP European History exam. It is administered after the short break which follows the multiple-choice section of the exam. Because the DBQ involves reading and organizing short excerpts from documents, it begins with a 15-minute reading period. Following the reading period, you will have 45 minutes to write your essay.

The directions for the DBQ are straightforward and instructive:

> **Directions:** The following question is based on the accompanying Documents 1–11. (The documents have been edited for the purpose of this exercise.) Write your answer on the lined pages of the Section II free-response booklet.
>
> This question is designed to test your ability to work with and understand historical documents. Write an essay that:
>
> - has a relevant thesis and supports that thesis with evidence from the documents
> - uses the majority of the documents
> - addresses all parts of the question
> - analyzes the documents by organizing them in as many appropriate ways as possible and **does not simply summarize the documents individually**
> - takes into account both the sources of the documents and the authors' points of view
>
> You may refer to relevant historical information not mentioned in the documents.

Notice that the first and third of the bulleted instructions will be taken care of automatically if you follow the five-step guide to writing a short history essay of high quality. The key instructions that are specific to the DBQ are: Use the majority of the documents; analyze (not summarize individually); and take into account sources and authors' points of view.

The key to the first two DBQ-specific instructions is to remember to *group the documents*. You do not want to take them one by one, because that will take too long and will lead you to simply repeat what each document says (the individual summarizing that the instructions tell you to avoid). If you force yourself to group them at the beginning, you will be forcing yourself to *analyze* them because the way you group them will automatically say something about the relationship between them.

The way to make sure that you are taking the sources and authors' point of view into account is to *bring your knowledge of the historical context into your analysis*. Remember the last line of the instruction: "You may refer to relevant historical information not mentioned in the documents." That is the examiner's way of telling you that you need to do more than talk about the documents; you need to talk about the context too.

Applying the Principles of the Quality History Essay to the DBQ

By keeping the couple of special instruction of the DBQ in mind, the five steps to outlining a short history essay can easily be modified for the DBQ:

Step 1: As you read the documents, decide how you are going to group them.
Step 2: Compose a thesis that explains why the documents should be grouped in the way you have chosen.
Step 3: Compose your topic sentences and make sure that they add up logically to your thesis.
Step 4: Support and illustrate your thesis with specific examples that contextualize the documents.
Step 5: *If you have time*, compose a one-paragraph conclusion that restates your thesis.

Now, review the Suggestions and Possible Outline for a Response to the DBQ Exercise in Chapter 3 and notice how it was produced by following the five steps to outlining a quality history essay.

Scoring of the DBQs

The high school and college instructors who score the DBQ work from a set of scoring guidelines. Those guidelines are tweaked a bit each year, but so far they continue to follow a "core-point" method, where they look to see, and assign points for, your ability to do the following:

1. Provide a clearly stated and appropriate thesis that addresses all points of the question.
2. Discuss the majority of the documents.
3. Demonstrate an understanding of the basic meaning of the documents.
4. Support the thesis with an appropriate interpretation of the majority of the documents.
5. Show the point of view of at least three documents.
6. Analyze documents by organizing them into a least three appropriate groups.

After the readers look for those six objectives, they can award additional points for sophistication in any of those areas. The main thing to notice here is that *there are no tricks* to the scoring and the best way to get the highest score is to simply *write a short history essay of high quality* using the five-step process adapted for the DBQ.

Thematic Essay Questions

IN THIS CHAPTER

Summary: Learn how to write a short history essay of high quality in response to the thematic essay questions.

Key Ideas

✪ The thematic essay questions test your ability to use your knowledge of European history to make a historical argument.

✪ Choose the two questions (one from each group) based on your ability to make and support an argument.

✪ Apply the five-step process to writing a short history essay of high quality in response to the thematic essay questions.

Introduction

The thematic essay questions test your ability to use your knowledge of European history to create a historical argument. The keys to success are choosing properly the questions you will answer and following the five steps to a short history essay of high quality.

Characteristics of the Thematic Essay Questions

You are allowed to read the thematic essay questions during the 15-minute reading time, but there are 10–12 documents to read for the DBQ, so you will probably not be able to do anything more than glance at the thematic questions. That means that you will have 35 minutes to choose your questions, compose your answers, and write your essays. The good news is that both the authors and the readers of the exam know that you only have 35 minutes, and they adjust their expectations accordingly.

The two thematic essays together contribute only 55 percent of the free-response score (the DBQ essay by itself is worth 45 percent of the free-response score), so do not rush through the DBQ to get to the thematic essays. It is also important that you divide your time roughly equally between the two thematic essay questions; a few additional lines on one of the essays will not add much to your score, but an essay that is too short will hurt your score.

Like those for the DBQ, the directions for the thematic essay questions are straightforward and instructive:

> **Directions:** You are to answer TWO questions, one from each group of three questions below. Make your selections carefully, choosing the questions that you are best prepared to answer thoroughly in the limited time permitted. You should spend five minutes organizing or outlining your answer. In writing your essays, use specific examples to support your answer.

The instructions then conclude by telling you where in the test booklet to write your answers and to remember to indicate in the appropriate place which questions you have chosen. Notice that the directions can be summarized in two crucial directives: Choose well and write a short history essay of high quality.

The key to choosing properly is to understand that you are *not* looking for the "easiest" questions to answer; each of the questions you encounter on the exam will take an equal amount of knowledge and effort. The key (as the directions indicate) is to recognize the questions for which you are best prepared to respond. Thinking about the five-step process to writing a short history essay of high quality, means that you should look at each question and ask yourself: "To which of these can I quickly write a clear thesis and three topic sentences that I can illustrate and support with several specific examples?"

Applying the Principles of the Quality History Essay to the Thematic Essay Questions

Once you have chosen your question, simply follow the five-step formula to constructing a short history essay of high quality:

Step 1: Find the action words in the question and determine what the question wants you to do.

Step 2: Compose a thesis that responds to the question and gives you something specific to support and illustrate.

Step 3: Compose your topic sentences and make sure that they add up logically to your thesis.

Step 4: Support and illustrate your thesis with specific examples.

Step 5: *If you have time*, compose a one-paragraph conclusion that restates your thesis.

And remember these writing guidelines:

- *Avoid long sentences with multiple clauses.* Your goal is to write the clearest sentence possible; most often the clearest sentence is a relatively short sentence.
- *Do not get caught up in digressions.* No matter how fascinating or insightful you find some idea or fact, if it does not directly support or illustrate your thesis, do not put it in.

- *Skip the mystery.* Do not ask a lot of rhetorical questions, and do not go for a surprise ending. The readers are looking for your thesis, your argument, and your evidence; give these to them in a clear, straightforward manner.

Now, review the Suggestions and Possible Outline of a Response to the Thematic Essay Questions Exercise in Chapter 3 and notice how it was produced by following the five steps to outlining a quality history essay.

Scoring of the Thematic Essays

Like the DBQs, the thematic essays are scored on a point system, but, again, *there are no tricks to the scoring and the best way to get the highest score is to simply write a short history essay of high quality*. If your essay answers the question with a clear thesis and develops and supports your thesis with paragraphs made up of clear topic sentences and specific examples, you will get the maximum number of points.

STEP 4

Review the Knowledge You Need to Score High

provided the inspiration for the era of daring exploration and discovery at the end of the fifteenth and beginning of the sixteenth centuries. Choice A is incorrect because the Reformation's focus was internal to Europe and had nothing to do with exploration outside European borders. Choice B is incorrect because the steam engine was not widely used to power ships until the nineteenth century, not in the fifteenth and sixteenth centuries. Choice C is also incorrect not only because the timing is wrong—the Black Death was a fourteenth-century phenomenon that had ended by the fifteenth- to sixteenth-century time period mentioned in the question—but also because it was a sickness that killed much of the population of Europe and crippled Europe's economy and had nothing to do with exploring the rest of the world beyond Europe. Finally, choice E is incorrect because the successful circumnavigation of the globe by the Magellan expedition was an *example* and, in some ways, *a culmination* of the era of exploration and discovery, but it was *not* its inspiration.

8. **D.** The hierarchical social structure of Europe was *not* a result of the creation of a Spanish Empire in the New World; that social structure dates back to the early medieval period. Choice A is incorrect because the influx of new wealth from Spain's New World Empire *did* cause inflation in Europe. Choice B is incorrect because the creation of Spain's New World Empire also involved missionaries who firmly established Christianity there. Choice C is incorrect because the wealth gained in trade with the New World Empire did lead to the rise of a wealthy merchant class. Choice E is incorrect because it *did* foster economic dependence between Europe and the New World.

CHAPTER 8

The Renaissance, 1350–1550

IN THIS CHAPTER

Summary: Between 1350 and 1550, Europe experienced a rebirth (renaissance) of commerce, interest in the classical cultures of ancient Greece and Rome, and confidence in human potential.

KEY IDEA

Key Ideas

✪ The Renaissance began on the Italian peninsula because of its location as the gateway to Eastern trade.

✪ The outstanding feature of Renaissance Italian society was the degree to which it was urban.

✪ Renaissance values were based on the revival of humanism—that is, an interest in an education program based on the languages and values of Classical Greek and Roman cultures.

✪ In the fifteenth century, Renaissance values spread northward to the rest of Europe.

Key Terms

guilds
doge
humanism
studia humanitas
Oration on the Dignity of Man

The Prince
neoplatonism
Florentine Academy
frescos
Michelangelo's *David*
Treaty of Lodi

Colloquies
lay piety
On the Fabric of the Human Body
De Revolutionibus Orbium Caelestum

Introduction

The word *Renaissance* means "rebirth." Historically, it refers to a time in Western civilization (1350–1550) that was characterized by the revival of three things: commerce, interest in the Classical world, and belief in the potential of human achievement. For reasons that are both geographical and social, the Renaissance began in Italy where renewed trade with the East flowed into Europe via the Mediterranean Sea and, therefore, through the Italian peninsula. The Italian Renaissance flowered for approximately a century until, as a result of invasions from France and Great Britain, it flowed north into the rest of Western Europe.

Renaissance Italian Society

The society of the Italian peninsula between 1350 and 1550 was unique in Western civilization. The most outstanding characteristic of Italian society was the degree to which it was urban. By 1500, seven of the ten largest cities in Europe were in Italy. Whereas most of Western Europe was characterized by large kingdoms with powerful monarchs and increasingly centralized bureaucracies, the Italian peninsula was made up of numerous independent city-states, such as Milan, Florence, Padua, and Genoa. These city-states were, by virtue of their location, flourishing centers of commerce in control of reviving networks of trade with Eastern empires.

Social status within these city-states was determined primarily by occupation, rather than by birth or the ownership of land, as was common in the rest of Europe during this period. The trades were controlled by government-protected monopolies called *guilds*. Members of the manufacturing guilds, such as clothiers and metalworkers, sat at the top of the social hierarchy. The next prestigious were the professional groups that included bankers, administrators, and merchants. They were followed by skilled labor, such as the stone masons.

Because the city-states of Italy developed as commercial centers, wealth was not based on the control of land as it was in the rest of Europe during this period. Instead, wealth was in the form of capital, and power was the ability to lend it. Accordingly, the traditional landed aristocracy of the Italian peninsula was not as politically powerful as their other European counterparts. Rather, powerful merchant families dominated socially and politically. Their status as the holders of capital also made the commercial elites of Italy powerful throughout Europe as the monarchs of the more traditional kingdoms had to come to them when seeking loans to finance their wars of territorial expansion.

The city-states of Renaissance Italy were set up along a variety of models. Some, like Naples, were ruled by hereditary monarchs; others were ruled by powerful families, such as the Medicis of Florence; still others, like Venice, were controlled by a military strongman known as a *doge*.

Renaissance Values

Prior to the Renaissance, the values of European civilization were based on the codes of honor and chivalry that reflected the social relations of the traditional feudal hierarchy. During the Renaissance, these traditional values were transformed to reflect both the ambition and the pride of the commercial class that dominated Renaissance Italian society. In contrast to traditional European noblemen, who competed for prestige on the battlefield or in jousting and fencing tournaments, successful Renaissance men competed via the displays of civic duty that included patronage of philosophy and the arts.

At the center of the Renaissance system of values was *humanism*. Renaissance humanism combined an admiration for Classical Greek and Roman literature with a new-found confidence in what modern men could achieve. Accordingly, Renaissance humanism was characterized by the *studia humanitas*, an educational program founded on knowledge of the Classical Latin and Greek languages. Once these languages had been mastered, the Renaissance humanist could read deeply in the Classical works of the ancient Greek and Roman authors, absorbing what the philosophers of the last great Western civilization had to teach them about how to succeed in life and how to live a good life.

To the Renaissance humanist, the ancient Greek and Roman philosophers were guides, but guides whose achievements could be equaled and eventually improved upon. The ultimate goal of the Renaissance humanist program was the truly well-rounded citizen, one who excelled in grammar, rhetoric, poetry, history, politics, and moral philosophy. These scholarly achievements were valued in their own right, as a testament to the dignity and ability of man, but also for the way in which they contributed to the glory of the city-state.

Prime examples of early Renaissance humanism were Petrarch, who celebrated the glory of ancient Rome in his *Letters to the Ancient Dead*, and Boccaccio, who compiled an encyclopedia of Greek and Roman mythology. The best articulation of the belief in the dignity and potential of man that characterized Renaissance humanism was Pico della Mirandola's *Oration on the Dignity of Man* (1486). In the *Oration*, Pico argued that God endowed man with the ability to shape his own being, and that man has the obligation to become all that he can be.

By the late Renaissance, humanism lost some of its ideal character, where scholarly achievements were valued for their own sake, and took on a more cynical quality that promoted only individual success. This shift is sometimes characterized as a shift from a "civic ideal" to a "princely ideal," as texts like Castiglione's *The Book of the Courtier* (1513–1518) and Machiavelli's *The Prince* (1513) focused on the qualities and strategies necessary for attaining and holding social and political power.

Neoplatonism

Another aspect of Renaissance thought that had profound implications for the intellectual development of Western civilization was neoplatonism. At the core of Renaissance neoplatonism is a rediscovery and reinterpretation of the works of the ancient Greek philosopher Plato. Medieval scholastics had found the world view of the ancient Greek philosopher Aristotle to be most compatible with Christianity. Accordingly, they made his philosophy the centerpiece of medieval scholasticism. After the fall of Constantinople in 1453, however, ancient Greek manuscripts and accompanying Greek scholars flowed into Italy. Led by the Florentine humanist Marsilio Ficino, Renaissance scholars translated the works of Plato and made a version of his thought central to their own philosophy.

Plato's writings distinguished between a changeless and eternal realm of being or form and the temporary and perishable world we experience. Crucially for Renaissance humanists, Plato contended that both human reason and love belonged to the world of forms. The implication for the Renaissance humanists was that, by cultivating the finest qualities of their being, humans could commune with God in an eternal realm of form and soul. In order to cultivate these human qualities, Ficino persuaded the Florentine merchant-prince Cosimo de Medici to fund the *Florentine Academy*, an informal gathering of humanists devoted to the revival and teachings of Plato.

The Renaissance Artistic Achievement

The unique structure of Renaissance society and the corresponding system of Renaissance values combined to give birth to one of the most amazing bursts of artistic creativity in the history of Western civilization. The wealthy and powerful elite of Renaissance society patronized the arts for the fame and prestige that it brought them. The competitive spirit of the elite both within and among the Italian city-states meant that artists and craftsmen were in almost constant demand.

For example, Lorenzo de Medici, who led the ruling family of Florence from 1469 until his death in 1492, commissioned work by almost all of the great Renaissance artists. As an art patron, he was rivaled by Pope Julius II, whose patronage of the arts during his papacy (1503–1513), including the construction of St Peter's Basilica, transformed Rome into one of Europe's most beautiful cities.

The artists themselves usually hailed not from the elite class but from the class of guild craftsmen. Young men with skill were identified and apprenticed to guild shops run by master craftsmen. Accordingly, there was no separation between the "artistic" and "commercial" sides of the Renaissance art world. All works were commissioned, and the artist was expected to give the patron what he ordered. The Renaissance artist demonstrated his creativity within the bounds of explicit contracts that specified all details.

Another aspect of the guild culture that contributed to the brilliant innovations of the Renaissance period was the fact that the various media, such as sculpture, painting, and architecture, were not viewed as separate disciplines; instead, the Renaissance apprentice was expected to master the techniques of each of these areas. As a result, mature Renaissance artists were able to work with a variety of materials and to apply ideas and techniques learned in one medium to projects in another.

Whereas medieval art had been characterized by religious subject matter, the Renaissance style took the human being and the human form as its subject. The transition can be seen in the series of *frescos* painted by Giotto in the fourteenth century. Although he still focused on religious subject matter (i.e., the life of St Francis), Giotto depicted the human characters in realistic detail and with a concern for their psychological reaction to the events of St Francis's life. The Renaissance artist's concern for the human form in all its complexity is illustrated by two great sculptures, each nominally depicting the biblical character of David:

- One is Donatello's version (completed in 1432), the first life-size, free-standing nude sculpture since antiquity, which depicts David in a completely naturalistic way and casts him as a young Florentine gentleman.
- The second version was sculpted by Michelangelo Buonarroti (completed in 1504) and is characteristic of the last and most heroic phase of Renaissance art. Sculpted from a single piece of marble, *Michelangelo's David* is larger than life and offers a vision of the human body and spirit that is more dramatic than real life, an effect that Michelangelo produced by making the head and hands deliberately too large for the torso. Upon its completion, the rulers of Florence originally placed Michelangelo's *David* at the entrance to the city hall as a symbol of Florentine strength.

Knowledge of the Natural World

The same spirit that produced the Renaissance's artistic achievement brought advances in Europeans' understanding of the natural world. The desire to restore what the ancients knew about the natural world led Renaissance natural philosophers to both reexamine ancient texts and observe the natural world for themselves.

During this period, great strides were made in the accurate understanding and depiction of human anatomy. In 1536, Johannes Guinther published an anatomy textbook based on a new translation of the work of the ancient Greek philosopher Galen. The new textbook, titled *Anatomical Institutions According to the Opinions of Galen for Students of Medicine*, provided accurate information, previously unknown to European physicians, about the human skeleton, muscles, cardiovascular system, and internal organs. One of Guinther's students, Andreas Vesalius, produced an exhaustive study of human anatomy that was based on first-hand dissection of human cadavers. Vesalius's *On the Fabric of the Human Body*, published in seven volumes beginning in 1543, became the standard text for medical students and greatly improved the medical profession's understanding of human anatomy.

The Renaissance spirit of inquiry also produced new knowledge in the field of natural history. Georg Bauer, who published under the pen name Agricola, published *On the Nature of Fossils* in 1546. In addition to providing valuable summaries of what the ancient philosophers knew about fossils, Agricola's text classified fossils according to their physical properties.

The greatest scientific achievement of the Renaissance came in the field of astronomy. The need to produce a more accurate calendar led to both a reexamination of ancient astronomical tables and new observations of the regular movements of the stars and planets. The culmination of this effort was the publication of Nicolas Copernicus's *De Revolutionibus Orbium Caelestum (On the Revolutions of the Heavenly Spheres)* in 1543. Copernicus's *De Rev* (as it is often called) proposed the shift from a geocentric (earth-centered) model of the cosmos to a heliocentric (sun-centered) model. While Copernicus's work was known only among the educated elite during the Renaissance, his theories would become a touchstone of the Scientific Revolution in the seventeenth century.

The Spread of the Renaissance

In the late fifteenth and sixteenth centuries, the Renaissance spread to France, Germany, England, and Spain. The catalyst for this spread was the breakup of the equilibrium that characterized the politics of the Italian peninsula. An internal balance of power had been established by the *Treaty of Lodi* (1454–1455), which brought Milan, Naples, and Florence into an alliance to check the power of Venice and its frequent ally, the Papal States. The balance of power was shattered in 1494 when Naples, supported by both Florence and the pope, prepared to attack Milan. The Milanese despot, Ludovico il Moro, appealed to King Charles VIII of France for help, inviting him to lead French troops into Italy and to revive his old dynastic claims to Naples, which the French had ruled from 1266 to 1435. French troops invaded the Italian peninsula in 1494 and forced Florence, Naples, and the Papal States to make major concessions. In response, the pope and the Venetians persuaded King Ferdinand of Aragon to bring troops to Italy to help resist French aggression. From the late 1490s through most of the sixteenth century, Italy became a battleground in a war for supremacy between European monarchs.

Once the isolation of the Italian peninsula was shattered, the ideals and values of the Renaissance spread through a variety of agents:

- teachers migrating out of Italy
- students who came to study in Italy and then returned home
- European merchants whose interests now penetrated the peninsula
- various lay groups seeking to spread their message of piety

However, the major cause of the spread of Renaissance ideals and values was the printing press. Invented by Johann Gutenberg in the German city of Mainz in about 1445 in response to increased demand for books from an increasingly literate public, the movable type printing press allowed for faster, cheaper, mass-produced books to be created and distributed throughout Europe. By 1500, between 15 and 20 million books were in circulation. Among the ideas that spread with the books were the thoughts and philosophies of the Renaissance humanists, which were both adopted and transformed in northern Europe.

The most important and influential of the northern humanists was Desiderius Erasmus, sometimes referred to as "the prince of the humanists." Spreading the Renaissance belief in the value of education, Erasmus made his living as an educator. He taught his students both the Latin language and lessons on how to live a good life from Latin dialogues that he wrote himself. Published under the title of *Colloquies*, Erasmus's dialogues also displayed the humanist's faith in both the power of learning and the ability of man by satirizing the old scholastic notions that the truth about God and nature could be discerned only by priests. Erasmus argued instead that, by mastering ancient languages, any man could teach himself to read the Bible and an array of ancient philosophers, thereby learning the truth about God and nature for himself.

In France, England, and Spain, the existence of strong monarchies meant that the Renaissance would be centered in the royal courts. In the smaller, independent German provinces, the characteristics of the Renaissance were absorbed into a tradition of *lay piety*, where organized groups, such as the Brethren of Common Life, promoted pious behavior and learning outside the bureaucracy of the Church. In that context, German scholars, such as Martin Luther, who were educated in a context that combined the humanistic and lay piety traditions, would be prominent in the creation of the Reformation.

› Rapid Review

The revival of commerce, interest in the Classical world, and belief in the potential of human achievement that occurred on the Italian peninsula between 1350 and 1550 is known as the Renaissance. Within the independent, urban city-states of Renaissance Italian society, the successful merchant class sought a well-rounded life of achievement and civic virtue which led its members to give their patronage to scholars and artists. Accordingly, both scholarship and artistic achievement reached new heights, and new philosophies like humanism and neoplatonism were fashioned.

In 1494, mounting jealousy and mistrust between the Italian city-states caused the leaders of Milan to invite intervention by the powerful French monarchy, thereby breaking a delicate balance of power and causing the Italian peninsula to become a battleground in a war for supremacy between European monarchies. The destruction of the independence of the Italian city-states caused the spread and transformation of Renaissance ideals and values. A northern European humanism, less secular than its Italian counterpart, developed and served as the foundation of the Reformation.

› Chapter Review Questions

1. Reasons that the Renaissance originated on the Italian peninsula include all of the following EXCEPT the peninsula's
   (A) geographic location
   (B) political organization
   (C) religion
   (D) social structure
   (E) economic structure

2. Which of the following is NOT a Renaissance value?
   (A) mastery of ancient languages
   (B) patronage of the arts
   (C) scholarly achievement
   (D) proficiency in the military arts
   (E) civic duty

3. Renaissance humanism
   (A) devalued mastery of ancient languages
   (B) urged the development of a single talent to perfection
   (C) valued ancient philosophers as the final authorities on all matters
   (D) denied the existence of God
   (E) valued scholarship for its own sake and for the glory it brought the city-state

4. The belief that by cultivating the finest qualities of their beings, human beings could commune with God was a conclusion of
   (A) guildsmen
   (B) neoplatonists
   (C) the lay piety movement
   (D) the Catholic Church in Renaissance Italy
   (E) the *doge*

5. Which of the following was NOT a factor that contributed to the Renaissance artistic achievement?
   (A) the patronage of the pope
   (B) the invasion of Italy by the French
   (C) the competitive spirit of competing elite groups
   (D) the apprentice system
   (E) the lack of separation between artistic and commercial aspects of the Renaissance art world

6. Which of the following did NOT enable the spread of the Renaissance?
   (A) the Treaty of Lodi
   (B) Milan's invitation to Charles VIII to bring troops to Italy
   (C) the printing press
   (D) students and teachers migrating in and out of the Italian peninsula
   (E) the lay piety movement

7. Renaissance art
   (A) was characterized by the severe specialization of its artists
   (B) was characterized by religious subject matter
   (C) abandoned painting in favor of sculpture
   (D) was characterized by its concern for the human form
   (E) did not require patrons

8. Northern humanism
   (A) was less secular than Italian humanism
   (B) linked scholarship and learning with religious piety
   (C) criticized the notion that priests were required to understand the Bible
   (D) contributed to the Reformation
   (E) all of the above

› Answers and Explanations

1. **C.** The religion of Renaissance Italy, which was Catholicism, was shared by many of the European kingdoms. Choice A is incorrect because the Italian peninsula's geographical location *was* a reason the Renaissance began there: As the gateway to Europe for Eastern trade coming in through the Mediterranean Sea, Italy was the first region to benefit from economic recovery and the influx of ancient texts. Choices B, D, and E are incorrect because the fact that the Italian peninsula was organized politically into independent city-states (choice B) that competed with each other commercially (choice E) meant that the traditional nobility was less powerful and that social status was less hierarchical and based on occupation (choice D). All these factors allowed for the development of the individual ambition and civic pride that characterized Renaissance values and ideals.

2. **D.** Proficiency in the military arts had been a traditional value of the nobility of medieval Europe, but it was downplayed in the Renaissance. The other choices are values particular to the Renaissance.

3. **E.** Renaissance humanism did indeed value scholarship. In contrast, choice A is incorrect because Renaissance humanism did not *devalue* the mastery of ancient languages; in contrast, it sought to *revive and encourage* such learning of Greek and Latin, for example. Choice B is incorrect because Renaissance humanism emphasized well-roundedness, *not* just the perfection of a single talent (think of today's use of the term "Renaissance man"). Choice C is incorrect because, although Renaissance humanists *respected* the ancient philosophers, they did not view them as the final authorities but instead believed they could enter into conversation with and eventually *surpass* them. Finally, choice D is incorrect because Renaissance humanists did not *deny the existence* of God at all: In contrast, they believed that all of man's abilities were *gifts from God* that should be developed to the fullest.

4. **B.** The belief that by cultivating the finest qualities of their beings, human beings could commune with God was a conclusion of the neoplatonists. Choice A is incorrect because the term *guildsmen* refers to members of the artisan class, not to a school of philosophy. Choice C is incorrect because the lay piety movement emphasized pious behavior and learning outside the Church bureaucracy, which obviously had nothing to do with communing with God. Choice D is incorrect because the Catholic Church in Italy maintained the traditional Christian view that pride in human achievement was a sin, a view at odds with aspiring to cultivate finer qualities in oneself. Finally, a *doge* was a military leader who wielded political power in some Italian city-states and had nothing to do with this (or any other) belief about communing with God.

5. **B.** The invasion of Italy by the French triggered the spread of the Renaissance to the rest of Europe, but it did not contribute to the Renaissance artistic achievement. Choice A is incorrect because the Renaissance popes *were* motivated by Renaissance ideals to patronize the arts, so they were a factor contributing to artistic achievement. Similarly, choice C is incorrect because the popes' elite counterparts in other city-states were also motivated to patronize the arts, so they were also a factor contributing to artistic achievement. Choice D is incorrect because the apprentice system helped increase the number of artists, which therefore led to more artistic works, increased ability to mix the techniques of various artistic media (e.g., painting and sculpting), and greater artistic achievement. Finally, choice E is incorrect because the commissioning of artistic works by specific business contracts meant that there was an unprecedented call for Renaissance artists.

6. **A.** The Treaty of Lodi, signed in the mid-fifteenth century, established a balance of power that helped keep other European powers out of the Italian peninsula, which therefore inhibited rather than enabled the spread of the Renaissance. Choice B is incorrect because Milan's invitation to Charles VIII to bring troops to Italy helped shatter that balance of power and isolation at the end of the fifteenth century, which then began a series of events that *did* lead to the

spread of the Renaissance. Choice C is incorrect because the invention of the printing press *helped* spread Renaissance ideas elsewhere in Europe. Choice D is incorrect because students and teachers who migrated in and out of the Italian peninsula also helped spread Renaissance ideas. Finally, choice E is incorrect because the lay piety movement associated learning with pious behavior, which also helped spread Renaissance ideas.

7. **D**. Renaissance art was characterized by its concern for the human form. Choice A is incorrect because Renaissance artists did *not* specialize; in contrast, they were trained in *all* media. Choice B is incorrect because this focus on the human form was a move away from religious subject matter, which characterized most art before the Renaissance (for example, think of all the Medieval Madonna-and-child paintings and depictions of other biblical scenes and Church icons). Choice C is incorrect for the same reason as choice A: Again, Renaissance artists did *not* abandon painting in favor of sculpture; instead, they were trained and worked in *all* media. Finally, choice E is incorrect because Renaissance art was, in fact, a business: Patrons commissioned and paid for all Renaissance art, so they were definitely required by artists during this time.

8. **E**. All of the answer choices are true: Choices A, B, and C are accurate and constitute the ways in which northern humanism helped to bring about the Reformation, thus choice D is also true.

CHAPTER 9

The Reformation, 1500–1600

IN THIS CHAPTER

Summary: In the sixteenth century, an attempt to reform the Christian Church developed into a Protestant movement that shattered the religious unity of Europe.

KEY IDEA

Key Ideas

✪ In the second decade of the sixteenth century, a German cleric, Martin Luther, created a rival theology based on the belief that salvation was achieved by faith alone.

✪ As Luther's theology spread, it was transformed into a Protestant movement with social and political dimensions.

✪ In England, Henry VIII used the Protestant movement as an excuse to break with the papacy in Rome and to create an English national church, known as the Church of England or the Anglican Church.

✪ The Catholic Church responded to the Protestant movement with both reforms and aggressive countermeasures.

Key Terms

Papal States	95 theses	predestination
indulgences	Peace of Augsburg	the elect
millenarianism	Huguenots	Anabaptists
salvation by faith alone	Edict of Nantes	Society of Jesus
scripture alone	Anglican Church	Council of Trent
priesthood of all believers	dissenters	the Inquisition

Introduction

The Reformation in sixteenth-century Europe began as an effort to reform the Christian Church, which many believed had become too concerned with worldly matters. Soon, however, the Church found itself facing a serious challenge from a brilliant German theologian, Martin Luther, and his followers. What began as a protest evolved into a revolution with social and political overtones. By the end of the century, a Europe that had been united by a single Church was deeply divided, as the Catholic and Protestant faiths vied for the minds and hearts of the people.

The Need for a Religious Reformation

By the onset of the sixteenth century, the Christian Church of Europe was facing a serious set of interconnected problems. Concern was growing that the Church had become too worldly and corrupt in its practices. The Church, and particularly the papacy in Rome, was widely seen to be more concerned with building and retaining worldly power and wealth than in guiding souls to salvation. The pope was not only the head of a powerful Church hierarchy but also the ruler of the *Papal States*, a kingdom that encompassed much of the central portion of the Italian peninsula. He collected taxes, kept an army, and used his religious power to influence politics in every kingdom in Europe.

The selling of *indulgences* (which allowed people to be absolved from their sins, sometimes even before they committed them, by making a monetary contribution to the Church) was just one way in which the Church seemed more concerned with amassing power and wealth than with guiding the faithful to salvation. To many common people who yearned for a powerful, personal, and emotional connection with God, the Church not only failed to provide it but worked actively to discourage it by:

- protecting the power of the priesthood
- saying the mass in Latin, a language understood by only the educated elite
- refusing to allow the printing of the Bible in the vernacular

The Lutheran Revolt

Martin Luther was an unlikely candidate to lead a revolt against the Church. The son of a mine manager in eastern Germany, Luther received a humanistic education, studying law before being drawn to the Church and being ordained as a priest in 1507. Continuing his education, Luther received a doctorate of theology from the University of Wittenberg and was appointed to the faculty there in 1512.

The revolutionary ideas that would come to define Lutheran theology were a product of Luther's personal search. Luther believed that he was living in the last days of the world and that God's final judgment would soon be upon the world. This view, now referred to as *millenarianism* and widespread in sixteenth-century Europe, led Luther to be obsessed with the question of how any human being could be good enough to deserve salvation. He found his answer through the rigorous study of scripture, and he formulated three interconnected theological assertions:

- *salvation by faith alone*, which stated that salvation came only to those who had true faith
- *scripture alone*, which stated that scripture was the only source of true knowledge of God's will

- *the priesthood of all believers*, which argued that all true believers received God's grace and were, therefore, priests in God's eyes

Each of Luther's assertions put him in direct opposition to the Church's orthodox theology:

- Salvation by faith alone contradicted the Church's assertion that salvation was gained both by having faith and by performing works of piety and charity.
- Scripture alone contradicted the Church's assertion that there were two sources of true knowledge of God: scripture and the traditions of the Church.
- The priesthood of all believers contradicted the Church's assertion that only ordained priests could read and correctly interpret scripture.

Creation and Spread of the Protestant Movement

In the autumn of 1517, Luther launched his protest by tacking *95 theses* or propositions that ran contrary to the theology and practice of the Church to the door of the Wittenberg castle church. His students quickly translated them from Latin into the German vernacular and distributed printed versions throughout the German-speaking kingdoms and provinces. With the aid of the printing press, Luther attracted many followers, but the survival of a Protestant movement was the result of the political climate.

Had the papacy moved quickly to excommunicate Luther and his followers, the movement may not have survived. However, Luther found a powerful protector in Frederick of Saxony, the prince of Luther's district. Frederick was one of seven electors, the princes who elected the Holy Roman Emperor, to whom the princes of the German districts owed their allegiance. Frederick's protection caused the pope to delay Luther's excommunication until 1520. By that time, it was too late: Luther and his followers had established throughout Germany congregations for the kind of Christian worship that, after 1529, would be known as Protestant.

Luther promoted his theology to both the nobility and common people. To the nobility, he wrote an "Address to the Christian Nobility of the German Nation" (1520), which appealed to the German princes' desire for both greater unity and power and to their desire to be out from under the thumb of an Italian Pope. To the common people, he addressed "The Freedom of the Christian Man" (1520), in which he encouraged common men to obey their Christian conscience and respect those in authority who seemed to possess true Christian principles. Through this strategy, Luther offered the noble princes of Germany an opportunity to break with the Roman Church and papacy without losing the obedience of the common people. It was an opportunity that was too good to pass up. By 1555, the German princes made it clear that they would no longer bow to Rome; they signed the *Peace of Augsburg*, which established the principle of "he who rules; his religion" and signaled to Rome that the German princes would not go to war with each other over religion.

Once it gained a foothold in northern Germany, Protestantism flourished in those areas where the local rulers were either unwilling or not strong enough to enforce orthodoxy and loyalty to Rome. Accordingly, the Protestant movement spread with success to the Netherlands, Scandinavia, Scotland, and England, but it encountered more difficulty and little or no success in southern and eastern Europe. The site of the most bloodshed was France, where Protestantism was declared both heretical and illegal in 1534. Initially French Protestants, known as *Huguenots*, were tolerated, but a civil war pitting Catholics against Protestants erupted in 1562. Peaceful coexistence was briefly restored by the *Edict of Nantes* in 1598, which established the principle of religious toleration in France, but the edict would be revoked in 1685.

The English Reformation

The English Reformation was unique. England had long traditions of dissent and anticlericalism that stemmed from a humanist tradition. In that context, Protestantism grew slowly, appealing especially to the middling classes, and by 1524, illegal English-language Bibles were circulating. But as the English monarch, Henry VIII, tried to consolidate his power and his legacy, he took the existence of a Protestant movement as an opportunity to break from Rome and create a national church, the Church of England, or *Anglican Church*.

Henry needed a divorce from his wife, Catherine of Aragon, because she could not provide him with a male heir to the throne. He also needed money and land with which to buy the loyalty of existing nobles and to create new ones that would owe their position to him. In 1534, he officially broke with the Church in Rome and had himself declared the head of the new Church of England. In 1536, he dissolved the English monasteries and seized Church lands and properties, awarding them to those loyal to him. It soon became apparent, however, that the church that Henry had created was Protestant only in the sense that it had broken from Rome. In terms of the characteristics opposed by most Protestant reformers—its episcopal or hierarchical nature, the existence of priests, and the retention of the sacraments and symbols of the traditional Roman church—the Church of England was hardly Protestant at all.

For the rest of the century, the unfinished Reformation left England plagued by religious turmoil. During the reign of Edward VI, the son of Henry and Jane Seymour, England was officially Anglican, but communities of those who refused to honor it and organized themselves along more Protestant lines grew to sufficient numbers for them to be known collectively as *Dissenters*. Upon the accession of Mary I (the daughter of Henry and his first wife, Catherine of Aragon), England was returned to Catholicism and Protestants were persecuted. Under the subsequent reign of Elizabeth I (the daughter of Henry and Anne Boleyn), England was again Anglican. While Catholics were initially persecuted under Elizabeth, there emerged during her long reign a kind of equilibrium in which a modicum of religious toleration was given to all.

Calvin and Calvinism

Once the break from the Roman Church was accomplished, Protestant leaders faced the task of creating new religious communities and systematizing a theology. The most influential of the second-generation Protestant theologians was John Calvin. Converting to Protestantism around 1534, Calvin was forced to leave his native France and flee to Switzerland, whose towns were governed by strong town councils who had historically competed with the Church bishops for local power. Calvin settled in Geneva where, in 1536, the adult male population had voted to become Protestant. For the next 40 years, Calvin worked in Geneva, articulating the theology and a structure for Protestant religious communities that would come to be known as Calvinism.

Calvinism accepted both Martin Luther's contentions that salvation is gained by faith alone and that scripture is the sole source of authoritative knowledge of God's will. But on the subject of salvation, Calvin went further, developing the doctrine of *predestination*, which asserted that God has predetermined which people will be saved and which will be damned. Those that are predestined to salvation were known as *the elect* and, although their earthly behavior could not affect the status of their salvation, Calvin taught that the elect would be known by both their righteous behavior and by their prosperity, as God would bless all their earthly enterprises.

In Calvinist communities, the structure and discipline of the congregation was integrated into that of the town. In place of the hierarchical structure of the Roman Church, Calvinist churches were organized by function:

- *Pastors* preached the gospel.
- *Doctors* studied scripture and wrote commentaries.
- *Deacons* saw to the social welfare of the community.
- *Elders* governed the church and the community in moral matters and enforced discipline.

Geneva soon became the inspirational center of the Protestant movement.

Social Dimensions and the Radical Reformation

The Protestantism of Martin Luther and John Calvin appealed to the industrious and prosperous commercial and merchant classes. At these higher rungs of the social hierarchy, people could read and react to criticism of both the doctrine and practice of the orthodox Roman Church. The strict discipline of the Calvinist communities mirrored the self-discipline their own professions demanded, and the promise that God would bless the worldly endeavors of the elect provided a self-satisfying justification for the wealth and prosperity that many were enjoying. Further down the social ladder, among the artisan and peasant classes, a more radical reformation was shaped.

The religious beliefs of the poorer and less educated classes were always less uniform than those of the elite. Their knowledge of Christian theology tended to be superficial and wedded to older folklore that deified the forces of nature. What they cared about was that the suffering they endured in this life would be rewarded in the next. Accordingly, leaders of Protestant movements among the artisan and peasant classes interpreted the doctrines of justification by faith alone and predestination to mean that God would never abandon the poor and simple people who suffered and that they could have direct knowledge of their salvation through an inner light that came to them directly from God. In some circles, this was combined with millenarian notions that the judgment day was near, to create a belief that the poor had a special mission to purge the world of evil and prepare it for the second coming of Christ.

The first and largest group of radical reformers was known as the *Anabaptists*. In 1534, proclaiming that judgment day was at hand, a group of them captured the German city of Münster, seized the property of nonbelievers, and burned all books except the Bible. To Protestant and Catholic elite alike, the Anabaptists represented a threat to the social order that could not be tolerated. Their rebellion was subsequently put down by an army led by the Lutheran Prince Philip of Hesse, and their movement was violently repressed and driven underground.

The Catholic Response

Although it was slow to believe that Protestantism could pose a threat to its power, the Roman Church—which was increasingly referred to as "catholic" (meaning one, true, and universal)—had begun to construct a response by the middle of the sixteenth century. Although sometimes referred to as the Counter-Reformation, the Catholic response actually had two dimensions: one aimed at reforming the Catholic Church and another aimed at exterminating the Protestant movement.

At the center of both dimensions was the *Society of Jesus*. Founded in 1534 by Ignatius Loyola, the Jesuits (as they came to be known) were a tightly organized order who saw themselves as soldiers in a war against Satan. Strategically, the Jesuits focused on education, building schools and universities throughout Europe. The Jesuits also served as missionaries, and they were often among the first Europeans to visit the new worlds that the age of exploration was opening up, thereby establishing a beachhead for Catholicism. Internally, they preached a new piety and pushed the Church to curb its worldly practices and to serve as a model for a selfless, holy life that could lead to salvation.

The Catholic reform movement reached its peak with the *Council of Trent*, which began its deliberations in 1545. Over many years, the Council passed reforms abolishing the worst of the abuses that had led to Protestant discontent. However, the Council of Trent also symbolized a defeat for Protestants who hoped for reconciliation, as the Council refused to compromise on any of the key theological issues and continued to insist that the Catholic Church was the final arbiter in all matters of faith.

At the heart of the Catholic Church's efforts to defeat Protestantism was the office known as the *Inquisition*. An old institution within the Church that investigated charges of heresy, its duties were revived and expanded to combat all perceived threats to orthodoxy and the Church's authority. Those who ran foul of the Inquisition ran the risk of imprisonment, torture, and execution. The Church's other main weapon in its aggressive response to the Reformation was censorship. Books that were considered unorthodox or at odds with the Church's teachings were placed on the *Index of Banned Books*.

› Rapid Review

By the sixteenth century, the Christian Church was faced with mounting criticism of its preoccupation with worldly matters and its failure to meet the emotional and spiritual needs of an increasingly literate population. In 1517, Martin Luther charged that the Church had abandoned scripture and strayed from its mission. He offered an alternative and simplified theology that asserted that salvation came by having faith alone and that scripture alone was the source of all knowledge about salvation. In the face of the Church's opposition and prevarication, a Protestant movement grew around Luther's theology, finding followers among both the German princes (who wished to break with Rome) and the poor (who felt oppressed).

In England, the powerful monarch Henry VIII used the existence of a Protestant movement to break with Rome in 1524 and to confiscate the lands the Church held in his kingdom. He created the Church of England, which retained the hierarchy and trappings of the Catholic Church, thereby creating within his own kingdom a group of Dissenters, who were Protestants for whom the Church of England was not reformed enough.

By mid-century, the Protestant movement had diversified and fragmented, as second-generation Protestant theologians faced the task of articulating the specific beliefs and structure of the new churches and communities they were building. Most influential among this second generation was John Calvin, who added the theological concept of predestination to Martin Luther's theology and oversaw the creation of Calvinist communities, whose center was Geneva.

Among the poorer classes, Protestantism became mixed with millenarianism and the desire for social reform. That fact, along with the propertied classes' opposition to such reform, was illustrated by the seizure of the German city of Münster by the Anabaptists in 1534, and by the ruthlessness with which the city was liberated by the Lutheran Prince Philip of Hesse.

The Catholic response to the Protestant movement was two-pronged. The Church, under the auspices of the Council of Trent, carried out many internal reforms that addressed the grievances of the faithful; it also put into motion a Counter-Reformation program, executed by the Society of Jesus and the Inquisition, which was aimed at stamping out Protestantism.

❯ Chapter Review Questions

1. Which of the following was NOT one of the problems facing the Christian Church in the sixteenth century?
   - (A) the pope's status as ruler of the Papal States
   - (B) its use of Latin in the mass and in the printed Bible
   - (C) an increasingly literate population
   - (D) its inability to tend to the physical needs of the poor
   - (E) its inability to tend to the emotional and spiritual needs of the population

2. Which of the following was part of Luther's theology?
   - (A) a belief in the need to create a Protestant Church
   - (B) the notion that nature could serve as a guide to salvation
   - (C) the idea that salvation came only through faith
   - (D) the assertion that charitable works were necessary to go to heaven
   - (E) the belief that the poor should be given more social and political power

3. Which of the following was NOT a reason that a Protestant movement emerged?
   - (A) the Society of Jesus took up Luther's cause
   - (B) Luther enjoyed the protection of some powerful Protestant princes
   - (C) Luther's students used the printing press to spread Luther's theology
   - (D) peasants saw Luther's theology as a justification for their dissatisfaction
   - (E) the Church was slow to excommunicate Luther and his followers

4. The Peace of Augsburg
   - (A) ended the war between the Church and the Protestant princes
   - (B) established Henry VIII's right to establish the Church of England
   - (C) established Geneva as the stronghold of Calvinism
   - (D) unified the German principalities under the Holy Roman Emperor
   - (E) established the principle of "he who rules; his religion"

5. The theology of Calvin differs from Luther's in which of the following ways?
   - (A) the belief that scripture alone is the guide to salvation
   - (B) the belief that salvation is earned by faith alone
   - (C) the belief that the church hierarchy is unwarranted and harmful
   - (D) the belief that some have been predestined for salvation
   - (E) the belief that the Bible should be printed in the vernacular

6. The uprising and subsequent repression of the Anabaptists illustrates all of the following EXCEPT
   - (A) the poorer classes understood the teachings of Protestantism to mean that the existing social hierarchy should be overthrown
   - (B) the Catholic Church still had the power to crush its opposition
   - (C) property-owning Protestant reformers were not looking to reform the social order
   - (D) the poorer classes linked Protestant theology with millenarianism
   - (E) Protestantism was a movement that encompassed many different, and sometimes opposing, views

7. The Council of Trent
   - (A) excommunicated Martin Luther
   - (B) established the Inquisition
   - (C) insisted that the Catholic Church was the final arbiter in all matters of faith
   - (D) reconciled Protestants and Catholics
   - (E) produced the Treaty of Augsburg

8. The term "Dissenters"
   - (A) refers to all Protestants who deny that good works can earn salvation
   - (B) refers to the Anabaptists
   - (C) refers to English Protestants
   - (D) refers to those who refused to sign the Peace of Augsburg
   - (E) refers to English Protestants who refused to join the Church of England

› Answers and Explanations

1. **D.** Choice D is the correct answer because the Church's network of poor relief was functioning as well as it ever had and was not, therefore, the problem. Choices A–C were all problems the Church faced. Choice A is not correct because the pope's status as ruler of the Papal States meant that the Church was constantly embroiled in the politics of the peninsula, thereby alienating Italians who lived in other city-states. Choice B is not correct because the Church's use of Latin, a language that only the elite could read, angered and alienated people. Similarly, choice C is incorrect because people were increasingly able to read the vernacular, but they still could not read Latin. Finally, choice E is incorrect because the Church *was* unable to tend to the emotional and spiritual needs of the population.

2. **C.** Luther's conclusion that salvation comes only through faith rather than through grace and good works as the Church argued, is the foundation of his theology. Choice A is incorrect because Luther's goal was to reform the Church, not to break with it. Choice B is incorrect because Luther believed that only scripture could give knowledge of how to achieve salvation. Choice D is incorrect because the Roman Church held that charitable works could help gain entrance into heaven; Luther disagreed. Choice E is incorrect because Luther did not advocate a change in the social or political order and denounced the peasant revolts.

3. **A.** The Society of Jesus was founded in order to *combat* the spread of Protestantism, not to promote it. Choice B is incorrect because the Protestant princes, sensing an opportunity to break with Rome, gave Luther the protection he needed. Choice C is incorrect because Lutheranism spread quickly thanks to the efforts of Luther's students and their use of the newly invented printing press. Choice D is incorrect because the peasants did see Luther's theology, or their own version of it, as a justification for their discontent. Choice E is incorrect because the Church did hesitate in excommunicating Luther, giving the movement valuable time to spread and gain strength.

4. **E.** The Peace of Augsburg was a treaty signed by the German princes that established the principle of "he who rules; his religion," thereby guaranteeing that they would not go to war with each other over the issue of religion. Choice A is incorrect because there was no war between the Church and the Protestant princes. Choice B is incorrect because the Peace of Augsburg was an agreement between the German princes and was not connected to the English Reformation. Choice C is incorrect because Geneva became the center of Calvinism because Calvin settled there and because the male population voted to become Protestant. Choice D is incorrect because, although the Holy Roman Emperor was elected by a group of the most powerful German princes, the process had no connection to the Peace of Augsburg.

5. **D.** The doctrine of predestination, which said that only a group known as the elect would enjoy God's salvation, was a theological conviction of Calvin and his followers; Luther taught that all who came to have true faith were saved. The other four answers are all theological beliefs that were shared by Luther and Calvin.

6. **B.** The Anabaptist movement was repressed by *Protestant* princes, not the Catholic Church. Choice A is incorrect because the fact that the Anabaptists seized the German city of Münster and the property of nonbelievers illustrates that the poorer classes understood the teachings of Protestantism to mean that the existing social hierarchy should be overthrown. Choice C is incorrect because the fact that the Protestant princes came to the aid of the property-owning classes demonstrates the fact that that property-owning Protestant reformers were not looking to reform the social order. Choice D is incorrect because the fact that the Anabaptists proclaimed that judgment day was at hand illustrates the link to millenarianism. Choice E is incorrect because the fact that the Anabaptist movement was crushed by Protestant princes illustrates the way in which Protestantism encompassed many different, and sometimes opposing, views.

7. **C.** Choice C is correct because, although the Council of Trent passed many reforms that pleased Protestants, it failed to reconcile Catholics and Protestants because it insisted that the Catholic Church was the final arbiter in all matters of faith. Choice A is incorrect because the Council of Trent did not excommunicate Luther. Choice B is incorrect because the Council of Trent did not establish the Inquisition; it was established by the pope. Choice D is incorrect because the Council of Trent *failed* to reconcile Protestants and Catholics. Choice E is incorrect because the Treaty of Augsburg was a secular treaty reached by the princes of Germany.

8. **E.** The term "Dissenters" refers to English Protestants who refused to join the Church of England. Choice A is incorrect because the term "Dissenter" implies a refusal to join the Church of England, not a reference to a specific theological stance. Choice B is incorrect because Anabaptists were just one of many groups in England to whom the term "Dissenters" was applied. Choice C is incorrect because the term "Dissenters" does not refer to all English Protestants, because members of the Church of England are Protestants. Choice D is incorrect because the Peace of Augsburg is unrelated to either "Dissenters" or English history.

CHAPTER 10

The Rise of Sovereignty, 1600–1715

IN THIS CHAPTER

Summary: From 1600 to 1715, social and economic change created new opportunities for monarchs to consolidate their power at the expense of the traditional, landed nobility.

KEY IDEA

Key Ideas

✪ A series of bad harvests and continual warfare pushed the overtaxed peasantry to the breaking point.

✪ European monarchs attempted to end the tax-exempt status of the nobility, town officials, and clergy.

✪ In those kingdoms in which the monarchs successfully allied themselves with a rising merchant middle class, they were able to curb the power of the nobility, town officials, and clergy and create a powerful centralized state.

✪ Russia was exceptional in that its monarchs were able to build a powerful centralized state by increasing the power of the nobility.

Key Terms

peasantry	*St. Therese in Ecstasy*	*Second Treatise of Civil Government*
nobility	*The Night Watch*	
monarchs	English Civil War	*intendent*
Divine Right of Kings	the Commonwealth	Versailles
tax revolts	Restoration	tsars
absolutism	the Glorious Revolution	Law Code of 1649
baroque	constitutional monarchy	

Introduction

In the period from 1600 to 1715, the traditional hierarchical structure of European society came under new pressures. As you recall, this structure was one in which a large class of poor agricultural laborers (the *peasantry*) supported a small and wealthy class of elite (the *nobility*). As the *monarchs* of Europe fought wars to expand their kingdoms and created larger state bureaucracies to manage them, the pressure to raise greater sums of money through taxes stretched the economies and social structures of European societies to the breaking point. Meanwhile, the continuous increase in trade and diversification of the economy was creating a new class of people: a middle class made up of merchants and professionals that did not fit comfortably into the traditional hierarchy. Changes in the social and political structure of the seventeenth century were mirrored in the evolution of artistic style.

Economic Stress and Change

A series of unusually harsh winters that characterized the "little ice age" of the 1600s led to a series of poor harvests, which, in turn, led to malnutrition and disease. In an effort to cope with increasing poverty, members of the besieged agricultural class opted to have smaller families. This combination of famine, poverty, and disease led to a significant decrease in the population during this period.

These "natural" problems that plagued the peasantry of Europe were exacerbated during this period by increasing demands from the nobility that ruled them. The endless warfare waged by the rival monarchs of Europe at this time further depleted the agricultural population by conscripting their sons into the army and taking them off to war. War also required money that the monarchs and their governments attempted to raise by increasing taxes. Because the nobility was largely exempt from taxes, the peasantry bore the brunt of this new economic burden. In many places, the peasantry resisted violently in a series of *tax revolts*, but temporary concessions won by them were quickly reversed.

Resistance to the monarchs' desire for increased power and wealth came from provincial nobles, town officials, and church leaders. The outcome of these power struggles varied from kingdom to kingdom.

Britain: The Triumph of Constitutionalism

In Britain, these tensions came to a head in the form of a struggle between the monarchs of the Stuart dynasty and the English Parliament. Already an old and important institution by 1600, the English Parliament was an assembly of the elite who advised the king. However, it differed from its counterparts in the other European kingdoms in several important ways:

- Its members were elected by the property-holding people of their county or district.
- Eligibility for election was based on property ownership, so its members included wealthy merchants and professional men as well as nobles.
- Members voted individually rather than as an order or class.

As a result, the English Parliament of the seventeenth century was an alliance of nobles and well-to-do members of a thriving merchant and professional class that saw itself as a voice of the "English people," and it soon clashed with the monarch it had invited to succeed the heirless Elizabeth I.

When James Stuart, the reigning king of Scotland (known there as James VI), agreed to take the throne of England as James I (1603–1625), he was determined to rule England in the manner described by the theory of *absolutism*. Under this theory, monarchs were viewed as appointed by God (an appointment known as the *Divine Right of Kings*). As such, they were entitled to rule with absolute authority over their subjects. Despite this tension, James I's reign was characterized by a contentious but peaceful coexistence with Parliament.

A religious element was added when James's son and successor, Charles I (1625–1649), married a sister of the Catholic king of France. That, together with his insistence on waging costly wars with Spain and France, led to a confrontation with Parliament. Having provoked the Scots into invading England by threatening their religious independence, Charles I was forced to call on the English Parliament for yet more funds. Parliament responded by making funds contingent on the curbing of monarchical power. This stalemate degenerated into the *English Civil War* (1642–1646). Forces loyal to the king fought to defend the power of the monarchy, the official Church of England, and the privileges and prerogatives of the nobility; forces supporting Parliament fought to uphold the rights of Parliament, to bring an end to the notion of an official state church, and for notions of individual liberty and the rule of law.

The victory of the Parliamentary forces led to the trial and execution of Charles I for treason and to the establishment of the *Commonwealth* (1649–1660). The Commonwealth deteriorated into a fundamentalist Protestant dictatorship under the rule of the Parliamentary army's leading general, Oliver Cromwell. Upon Cromwell's death in 1658, English Parliamentarians worked to establish a *Restoration* (1660–1688) of the English monarchy, inviting the son of the king they executed to take the throne as Charles II (1660–1685).

The relative peace of the Restoration period broke down when Charles's brother, a Catholic, ascended to the throne as James II (1685–1688). James was determined to establish religious freedom for Catholics, to avenge his father, and to restore absolute monarchy to Britain. To thwart James's plans, Parliament enlisted the aid of the king's eldest daughter, Mary, the Protestant wife of William of Orange of the Netherlands. The quick, nearly bloodless uprising that coordinated Parliament-led uprisings with the invasion of a Protestant fleet and army from the Netherlands, and which led to the quick expulsion of James II in 1688, is known as the *Glorious Revolution*. The reign of William and Mary marks the clear establishment of a *constitutional monarchy*, a system by which the monarch in Britain rules within the limits of the laws passed by a legislative body. The text written by the leading legal spokesman of the Parliamentary faction, John Locke's *Second Treatise of Civil Government* (1690), is still read today as the primary argument for the establishment of natural limits to governmental authority.

France: Absolutism

Several key differences allowed for a far different outcome in France. A series of religious and dynastic wars in the sixteenth century produced a kingdom in which the religious issue had been settled firmly in favor of the Catholic majority. The lack of religious turmoil in the seventeenth century allowed the French monarchy to cement an alliance with both the clergy and the middle class, and to use the great administrative expertise of both to build a powerful centralized government. Both Louis XIII (1610–1643) and Louis XIV (1643–1715) relied on well-connected Catholic cardinals to oversee the consolidation of royal power by transferring local authority from provincial nobility to a bureaucracy that was both efficient and trustworthy.

As chief minister to Louis XIII, Cardinal Richelieu used the royal army to disband the private armies of the great French aristocrats and to strip the autonomy granted to the few remaining Protestant towns. More significantly, he stripped provincial aristocrats and members of the elite of their administrative power by dividing France into some 30 administrative districts and putting each under the control of an *intendent*, an administrative bureaucrat, usually chosen from the middle class, who owed his position and, therefore, his loyalty directly to Richelieu.

These policies were continued by Richelieu's successor as chief minister, Cardinal Jules Mazarin, and perfected by Louis XIV when he took full control of the government upon Mazarin's death in 1661. To the intimidation tactics practiced by Richelieu and Mazarin, Louis added bribery. Building the great palace at *Versailles*, 11 miles outside of Paris, Louis presented the nobility of France with a choice: Oppose him and face destruction, or join him and be part of the most lavish court in Europe. In choosing to spend most of their time at Versailles, French nobles forfeited the advantages that made their English Parliamentary counterparts so powerful: control of both the wealth and loyalty of their local provinces and districts. As a result, Louis XIV became known as "the Sun King" because all French life seemed to revolve around him as the planets revolved around the sun.

Central and Eastern Europe: Compromise

Whereas the contests for power and sovereignty in Britain and France had clear winners and losers, similar contests in the European kingdoms farther to the east resulted in a series of compromises between monarchs and rival elite groups.

In general, kingdoms in central and eastern Europe, such as Brandenburg–Prussia, the independent German states, Austria, and Poland, were less economically developed than their western counterparts. The economies of Britain and France in the seventeenth century were based on an agricultural system run by a free and mobile peasantry and supplemented by an increasingly prosperous middle class consisting of artisans and merchants in thriving towns. In contrast, the land-holding nobility of the kingdoms in central and eastern Europe during this period managed to retain control of vast estates worked by serfs who were bound by the land. By doing so, they were able to avoid the erosion of wealth that weakened their counterparts in Britain and France.

In both Britain and France, the power struggle between the monarch and the elite was won by the side that managed to form an alliance with the wealthy merchant and professional class. In the European kingdoms farther east, however, these classes failed to gain in wealth and numbers as their counterparts in Britain and France had done. As a result, the stalemate between royal and aristocratic wealth and power remained more balanced, necessitating compromise.

Russia: Tsarist Absolutism

The seventeenth-century kingdom farthest to the east proved to be an exception to the rule, as its monarchs, the *Tsars*, managed to achieve a high degree of absolutism despite an agricultural economy based on serfdom and the lack of an alliance with a thriving middle class.

During the period beginning in 1613 and reaching its zenith with the reign of Peter the Great (1689–1725), the Romanov Tsars consolidated their power by buying the loyalty of the nobles. In return for their loyalty, the Romanov Tsars gave the nobility complete control over the classes of people below them. A prime example is the *Law Code of 1649*, which converted the legal status of groups as varied as peasants and slaves into that of a single class of serfs. Under the Romanov Tsars, the Russian nobility also enjoyed the fruit of new lands and wealth acquired by aggressive expansion of the Russian Empire eastward into Asia.

With the nobility firmly tied to the Tsar, opposition to the Tsar's power manifested itself only periodically in the form of revolts from coalitions of smaller landholders and peasants angered by the progressive loss of their wealth and rights. Such revolts, like the revolts of the Cossacks in the 1660s and early 1670s, were ruthlessly put down by the Tsar's increasingly modern military forces, and controlled thereafter by the creation of a state bureaucracy modeled on those in western Europe, and by encouraging the primacy and importance of the Russian Orthodox Church that taught that the traditional social hierarchy was mandated by God.

The Baroque Style

The dominant artistic style of the seventeenth century is known as baroque. In the most general sense, the baroque style was characterized by its emphasis on grandeur and drama. In response to the Reformation, the Catholic Church in Europe decreed that art should focus on religious themes and cultivate an environment of contemplation and holiness. The resulting artistic style, developed initially by artists of Rome, is sometimes known as Counter-Reformation Baroque. An excellent example in architecture is the Church of Sant'Andrea al Quirinale in Rome, designed by Gian Lorenzo Bernini. Bernini's *St. Theresa in Ecstasy* (1645–1652), which decorates the Cornaro Chapel in Rome, is an example of the Counter-Reformation Baroque style in sculpture, while Caravaggio's *Calling of St. Matthew* (c.1598) and *Conversion of St. Paul* (c.1602) exemplify the Counter-Reformation Baroque style in painting.

The grandeur of the baroque also appealed to the absolutist monarchs of the seventeenth century, and under their patronage the baroque evolved beyond religious subject matter. Louis XIV of France had his great Versailles Palace (1661–1668) built in the baroque style. The sculptor Bernini produced his famous portrait bust of Louis XIV in 1665. The painter Peter Paul Rubens created baroque masterpieces for many of the monarchs of Europe. Among the most renowned examples are his cycle of 21 large canvases for the walls of the Festival Gallery of Louis XIII's Luxembourg Palace, including *Henry IV Receiving the Portrait of Maria de Medici* (1622–1625).

The baroque style reached its pinnacle when it migrated away from the royal courts and flourished in the city of Amsterdam. There, Dutch masters adopted baroque style to depict the grandeur of that bustling center of trade and learning. Foremost among them was Rembrandt van Rijn (usually just known as Rembrandt), who captured the civic pride of the Dutch in such paintings as *The Night Watch* (1642) and who displayed his personal pride in his series of self-portraits.

› Rapid Review

During the period from 1600 to 1715, the dynamics of the traditional, hierarchical social structure of European kingdoms came under new pressures. As their economies underwent a transformation from a purely agricultural base to a more complex system that included expanding trade and the uneven growth of a middle class of merchants and professionals, European monarchs attempted to solidify their claims to sovereignty.

- In Britain, their attempts failed as a section of the traditional nobility (which was motivated by both self-interest and religious conviction) formed an alliance with like-minded members of the rising merchant and professional class within Parliament, creating a system of shared sovereignty known as constitutional monarchy.
- In France, the Bourbon monarchs managed to form alliances with both the French Catholic Church and the middle classes to establish a system of Royal absolutism.
- In central and eastern European kingdoms like Brandenburg–Prussia, the German States, Austria, and Poland, a less dynamic economy meant that the stalemate between monarchs and traditional nobility was harder to break, and a series of power-sharing arrangements was made.
- Farthest east, in Russia, the Romanov Tsars constructed an alliance with the grandest of the land-owning nobility at the expense of the classes below them and consolidated their power by expanding their empire and ruthlessly crushing opposition from below.
- Changes in the social and political structure were mirrored by the development of the baroque style in the arts.

› Chapter Review Questions

1. During the period from 1600 to 1715, the traditional social hierarchy of Europe came under pressure by all of the following EXCEPT
   (A) continuous warfare
   (B) climate change resulting in series of bad harvests
   (C) the rejection of religious practice by large numbers of people
   (D) increased trade and the diversification of the economy
   (E) the desire of monarchs to increase their power and authority

2. The English Parliament during the period from 1600 to 1715
   (A) was a relatively new institution
   (B) was exclusively an institution of the nobility
   (C) was an institution opposed to monarchy
   (D) was the institution in which nobles, merchants, and professionals formed an alliance to oppose the absolutist goals of the Stuart monarchs
   (E) was in favor of a one-man, one-vote system of democracy

3. In the period 1600–1715, the English had the greatest success in resisting the absolutist designs of their monarchs for all of the following reasons EXCEPT
   (A) the nobility forged an alliance with a wealthy and powerful merchant and professional class
   (B) the English nobility was the most powerful in all of Europe
   (C) the Parliament was an old and respected institution
   (D) the Stuart monarchs were perceived to have Catholic leanings and sympathies
   (E) the English economy was well-developed and diversified

4. Compared with the Romanov Tsars, the Bourbon monarchs of France in the period 1600–1715
   (A) made less use of the Church and its expertise and influence
   (B) were less reliant on the nobility for their power
   (C) were more absolutist in their style of government
   (D) sought to expand their empire to a larger extent
   (E) were more committed to the primacy of the privileges and prerogatives of the nobility

5. The single most important factor in explaining the need of central and eastern European monarchs and nobles to reach compromises on the issue of sovereignty during the period from 1600 to 1715 was
   (A) the lack of religiosity in the people
   (B) the lack of ambitious monarchs
   (C) the existence of strong peasant movements
   (D) the lack of strong armies
   (E) the lack of a well-developed middle class of merchants and professionals

6. The reign of Peter the Great of Russia (1682–1725) resulted in
   (A) the abolition of the Russian Orthodox Church
   (B) the territorial expansion of the Russian Empire
   (C) the weakening of serfdom
   (D) a decrease in the tax burden on poor peasants
   (E) the emergence of a wealthy middle class

7. Compared with their counterparts in Russia, the English peasantry of the early 1700s
   (A) bore a greater tax burden
   (B) enjoyed less freedom of movement
   (C) had a greater chance of improving their social and economic position
   (D) enjoyed less religious freedom
   (E) were more likely to live in towns

8. By the early eighteenth century, the kingdom whose political system afforded the greatest amount of self-rule to its subjects was
   (A) England
   (B) France
   (C) Brandenburg–Prussia
   (D) Austria
   (E) Russia

❯ Answers and Explanations

1. **C.** Nowhere in Europe during this period was there a large-scale rejection of religious practice; rather, the religious fervor that pitted Catholics against Protestants complicated the tensions created by the other four answers. Choice A is incorrect because continuous warfare put pressure on the traditional social hierarchy by disrupting the economy and increasing the demand for taxes. Choice B is incorrect because a series of bad harvests meant that there was less wealth in the economy at a time when monarchs were demanding more. Choice D is incorrect because increased trade and a more diversified economy gave birth to a class of economically powerful merchants who did not fit into the traditional social hierarchy. Choice E is incorrect because the desire of monarchs to increase their power and authority led them to wage wars of conquest, which put enormous stress on the economy.

2. **D.** The existence of Parliament as an institution that mixed traditional nobility with newly wealthy merchants and professionals allowed for an alliance between the two to form in opposition to Stuart absolutist designs. Choice A is incorrect because Parliament was, by 1600, an old and respected institution. Choice B is incorrect because Parliament's members were elected from local elite groups whose qualifications were based on property ownership, not noble birth. Choice C is incorrect because the Parliament was not opposed to monarchy as a form of government, but only to the notion that the monarch had absolute and unlimited power. Choice E is incorrect because Parliament's members did not, in this period, question the notion that only those who met certain property qualifications were entitled to vote.

3. **B.** The wealth and power of the English nobility as a class was in *decline* as the economy became more diversified and new forms of wealth created an economically strong middle class. Choice A is incorrect because the nobles inside Parliament did forge an alliance with a wealthy and powerful merchant and professional class to resist the absolutist designs of the Stuarts. Choice C is incorrect because the tradition of a powerful

Parliament gave the noble–merchant alliance credibility with the English people. Choice D is incorrect because the Stuart monarchs were perceived to have Catholic leanings and sympathies, which did not sit well with the English people. Choice E is incorrect because the advanced development of the English economy is what produced the merchant middle class with whom the nobles in Parliament allied.

4. **B.** The Bourbon monarchs of France built the power of their state at the expense of the nobility and, thus, did not rely on them in the way the Romanovs did. Choice A is incorrect because the Bourbons made extensive use of the clergy as they built their new administrative state. Choice C is incorrect because the Bourbons were every bit as absolutist as the Romanovs in their aims; they simply achieved the goal by different means. Choice D is incorrect because the Bourbons were *less* expansionist than the Romanovs. Choice E is incorrect because the Bourbons were, unlike the Romanovs, set on *curbing* the power and prerogatives of the nobility.

5. **E.** The key to successfully building or resisting a powerful centralized state in this period was the degree to which the monarchs or nobles could forge an alliance with and utilize the talents and wealth of a merchant middle class. Therefore, the lack of such a class forced compromise in the central and eastern kingdoms. Choice A is incorrect because all European peoples were equally religious during this period. Choice B is incorrect because the Monarchs of Europe were equally ambitious during this period. Choice C is incorrect because peasants in all the European kingdoms resisted encroachment on their rights and livelihood in the only way they could, through occasional tax and bread riots. Choice D is incorrect because all European monarchs were capable of raising sizable armies during this period.

6. **B.** The territorial holdings of the Russian Empire were greatly expanded under Peter the Great. Choice A is incorrect because the power of the Russian Orthodox Church was *strengthened* during the reign of Peter the Great. Choice C is

incorrect because the institution of serfdom was supported, not weakened, by Peter the Great. Choice D is incorrect because the tax burden on the Russian peasantry was *increased* under Peter the Great. Choice E is incorrect because no wealthy merchant class emerged in Russia during the reign of Peter the Great.

7. **C.** The English peasantry of the early 1700s had a greater chance of improving their social and economic position because the English economy was much more developed and diverse than that of Russia, and because the English Revolution of the seventeenth century had curbed the power of the monarchy and the nobility and established the rule of law. Choice A is incorrect because the English peasantry of the early 1700s bore a *lesser* tax burden than their Russian counterparts. Choice B is incorrect because the peasantry in England, where serfdom had long been abolished, enjoyed a greater freedom of movement than their Russian counterparts who still labored under a system of serfdom. Choice D is incorrect because the English peasantry enjoyed *greater* religious freedom than their Russian counterparts. Choice E is incorrect because "peasants" are agricultural laborers and, by definition, live in the countryside rather than in towns.

8. **A.** The constitutional monarchy and the rule of law that resulted from the English Revolution of the seventeenth century guaranteed its subjects the greatest amount of self-rule in Europe. Choice B is incorrect because the subjects of France lived under an absolutist regime constructed by the Bourbon monarchy. Choices C and D are incorrect because the subjects of Brandenburg–Prussia and of Austria enjoyed only a moderate amount of self-rule as the monarchs and nobility fought each other to a stand-off. Choice E is incorrect because Russians lived under an absolutist regime built through an alliance between the Tsar and the Russian nobility.

CHAPTER 11

The Scientific Revolution During the Seventeenth Century

IN THIS CHAPTER

Summary: In the seventeenth century, a small, interconnected society of thinkers created both a new way of knowing the natural world and a new model of the universe.

Key Ideas

✪ The traditional view of the cosmos was a combination of ancient Greek philosophy and Christian theology.

✪ In the seventeenth century, the development of new, more secular institutions created space for a new approach to investigating the natural world.

✪ In the early part of the seventeenth century, the mathematical philosopher Galileo championed a new view of the cosmos based on empirical and mathematical investigation.

✪ Near the end of the century, Isaac Newton created a new physics based on the concept of universal gravitation.

Key Terms

terrestrial realm
celestial realm
elements
qualities
geocentric
scholasticism

hermeticism
neoplatonism
heliocentric
Copernicanism
Kepler's laws
The Starry Messenger

Dialogue on the Two Chief Systems of the World
Discourse on Method
universal gravitation
Principia Mathematica

Introduction

The Scientific Revolution is the term given to a gradual development of a way of investigating and knowing the natural world. Although it has roots that stretch back earlier, the Scientific Revolution is considered by most historians to be a seventeenth-century phenomenon, beginning with Galileo's challenge to the old Aristotelian view of the cosmos and the authority of the Catholic Church in 1610, and culminating in the creation by Isaac Newton of the concept of a "universe" held together by the single force of universal gravitation in 1687.

The Traditional View of the Cosmos

The traditional view of the cosmos in European civilization was one that it had inherited from the ancient Greek philosopher Aristotle. The Aristotelian cosmos was based on observation and common sense. Because the Earth appeared, to all of one's senses, to stand still, Aristotle made the Earth the unmoving center point of the cosmos. The moon, the planets, and the stars were conceived of as "fixed" because they do not move relative to each other, and they were also understood to move in concentric circular orbits around the Earth because that is what they appeared to do.

The Aristotelian cosmos was divided into two realms:

- the *terrestrial realm*, which contained the Earth and all matter inside the orbit of the moon
- the *celestial realm*, or the realm of the heavens that existed beyond the orbit of the moon

In the Aristotelian cosmos, there were five basic *elements*, each of which was defined by its *qualities*:

1. earth, which was heavy and tended to sink toward the center of the cosmos
2. water, which was slightly lighter and accumulated on top of solid earth
3. air, which was lighter still
4. fire, which was the lightest of all and tended to try to rise above all the others
5. the ether, perfect matter that existed only in the celestial realm and which moved in a uniform circular motion

The qualities of the five types of matter served as the basis of Aristotelian physics. The motion of terrestrial matter was understood to be the result of its composition. For example, if you threw a rock, its motion described a parabola because the force of the throw gave its motion a horizontal component, while its heaviness gave it a vertical component toward the Earth. If you filled an airtight bag with air and submerged it in water, it would float to the top because the air was lighter than earth or water. The planets and stars of the celestial realm moved at a uniform rate in perfect circles around the Earth because they were composed purely of ether.

To the medieval church scholars who rediscovered and translated the writings of Aristotle, this Earth-centered, or *geocentric*, model of the cosmos not only made logical sense, but it confirmed the Christian theological doctrine that the perfect kingdom of God awaited in the heavens for those humans who could transcend the corruption of the world.

Alternative Traditions of Knowledge Before the Scientific Revolution

Although the dominant tradition of knowledge in European civilization prior to the Scientific Revolution was *scholasticism*, which derived its knowledge from ancient texts like those of Aristotle, there were other alternative traditions upon which the Scientific Revolution drew.

Hermeticism

One of these was the tradition of natural magic and alchemy, which understood the natural world to be alive with latent power, just waiting to be tapped by those who could learn its secrets. One strain of magical thought drew inspiration from a corpus of texts erroneously attributed to a supposed ancient Egyptian priest, Hermes Trismegistus. *Hermeticism* taught that the world was infused with a single spirit that could be explored through mathematics as well as through magic.

Neoplatonism

The most powerful and potent of the alternative traditions was developed by Renaissance humanists who rediscovered and revered the work of the ancient Greek philosopher Plato. *Neoplatonism* located reality in a changeless world of spirit, or forms, rather than in the physical world we experience. To the neoplatonists, mathematics was the language with which one could discover and describe the world of forms. Like the Hermetic tradition, neoplatonism taught that mathematics described the essential nature and the soul of the cosmos, a soul that was God itself.

The Platonic–Pythagorean Tradition

By the advent of the seventeenth century, these alternative traditions had fused into an approach to gaining knowledge of the natural world that has come to be known as the *Platonic–Pythagorean tradition* (after Plato and the ancient mathematically oriented school of Pythagoras), which had as its goal the identification of the fundamental mathematical laws of nature.

Development of New Institutions

Because the curricula of traditional universities were devoted to the teaching of Aristotle and other authorities in the scholastic tradition, new institutions were required for the alternative traditions to flourish. New institutions that emerged to fill that role included:

- royal courts, where kings, dukes, and other ruling nobles were determined to show off both their wealth and their virtue by patronizing not only great artists and musicians but also natural philosophers
- royal societies and academies, like the Royal Society of London and the Royal Academy of Sciences in Paris, both established in the 1660s, where organized groups of natural philosophers sought and received the patronage of the crown by emphasizing both the prestige and the practical applications of their discoveries
- smaller academies under the patronage of individual nobles, like the *Accademia dei Lincei*, which formed in 1657 under the patronage of Marquess of Monticelli in Italy
- new universities, particularly in Italy, that were funded by the civic-minded merchants in the Renaissance tradition and that were outside the control of the Church

The Rise of Copernicanism

The central challenge to the traditional view of the cosmos was made in the context of the Church's own effort to reform the calendar and, therefore, the science of astronomy.

The annual changes in the position of the Sun, the moon, and the planets with respect to the constellations of stars are the means by which human beings construct calendars that keep track of time and predict seasonal climate patterns. In keeping with the philosophy of scholasticism, European Church scholars constructed calendars based on ancient astronomical tables that dated back to the ancient Greek astronomer Claudius Ptolemy. Though amazingly accurate, the multiplication over thousands of years of small errors in the Ptolemaic astronomical tables led to a situation in the early sixteenth century where the calendars were dramatically out of sync with the actual seasons.

In 1515, a church council appointed to consider calendar reform summoned the Polish churchman and astronomer Nicolas Copernicus to remedy the situation. Educated in a neoplatonic academy and a proponent of the Platonic–Pythagorean tradition, Copernicus proposed to reconcile the calendar and the actual movements of the heavens by introducing a new Sun-centered, or *heliocentric*, astronomical model of the cosmos.

Copernicus's proposal alarmed Church authorities for several reasons:

- It questioned the authority of the Aristotelian tradition on which scholasticism relied.
- It contradicted the physical principles that served as the foundation of physics.
- It destroyed the theological coherence of the cosmos.
- It required the Church to admit it had been in error.

Shortly before Copernicus's death in 1543, the Church allowed his theory to be published in a work titled *De Revolutionibus Orbium Caelestum (On the Revolutions of the Heavenly Spheres)*, provided that it be accompanied by a preface that stated that the theory was only being presented as a useful hypothetical model, and not as a true account of the physical nature of the cosmos. Because Copernicus's great work was written in Latin (which was the language of educated scholars) and because it was a highly technical work, its publication created no great stir. But slowly, over the course of the next 70 years, *Copernicanism* (as the theory came to be known) spread in circles of men educated both within the Church and in newer academies and societies.

Kepler's Laws

By the seventeenth century, a loose network of Copernicans championed the new world view as part of a new empirical and mathematical approach to the study of the natural world. One was a German mathematician working in the hermetic and neoplatonic traditions, Johannes Kepler, who devoted his life to finding the mathematical harmonies of the cosmos. Between 1609 and 1619, he developed three laws of planetary motion that would come to be known as *Kepler's laws*.

1. The first law broke with the tradition of conceiving of the planets as moving in uniform circles, suggesting that the planetary orbits took the form of an ellipse, with the Sun as one of their foci.
2. The second law abandoned the notion that planetary motion was uniform and asserted that a planet's velocity varied according to its distance from the Sun, sweeping out equal areas in equal times.
3. The third law gave a mathematical description for the physical relationship between the planets and the Sun, asserting that the squares of the orbital period of a planet are in the same ratio as the cubes of their average distance from the Sun.

Galileo and the Value of Empirical Knowledge

Although Kepler worked in obscurity, Galileo Galilei was an ambitious self-promoter. Dubbing himself a "mathematical philosopher," Galileo championed an approach to knowing the natural world that emphasized the need to apply reason to observational and mathematical data. Also, following the English philosopher Francis Bacon, Galileo combined his approach with an appeal to the practical and pragmatic value of such knowledge.

Having dismantled and analyzed a spyglass he bought from Dutch merchants, Galileo drew up schematics for a larger, more powerful version. The result was the world's first telescope, and Galileo immediately turned his new invention on the heavens. In 1610, Galileo published his findings in a pamphlet titled *The Starry Messenger*. There, he announced several discoveries which, although they did not explicitly promote the Copernican theory, did implicitly call into question the veracity of the Aristotelian model. These discoveries included the following:

- the existence of countless stars previously unseen, suggesting that there was much about the cosmos that was not known
- the rugged, crater-filled surface of the moon, suggesting that it was not created of perfect celestial matter
- four moons orbiting the planet Jupiter, suggesting that it would not be so strange for the Earth to have a moon as well

Unfortunately, Galileo mistakenly believed that both his growing fame and his value to his powerful patron (the Grand Duke of Tuscany, Cosimo de Medici) would protect him from the wrath of the Catholic Church. Because of this mistaken belief, Galileo began to promote more boldly both the Copernican theory and his method of knowing nature through the application of reason to empirical observations. In 1615, he was summoned to Rome, where he narrowly escaped being branded a heretic only because he had a powerful friend, Cardinal Maffeo Barberini, who interceded on Galileo's behalf and managed to get the Church to brand the Copernican theory "erroneous" rather than "heretical." Galileo was set free with a stern warning. In 1623, Barberini became Pope Urban VIII. The following year, Galileo returned to Rome for a series of discussions with the Pope. He left having been given permission to teach Copernicanism as a theory, but not as a true account of the cosmos.

Over the next decade and a half, Galileo continued to promote his particular brand of natural philosophy. In 1632, chafing against the constrictions put upon him, Galileo effectively took his case to the public by abandoning the Latin prose of the scholarly elite for the vernacular Italian of the masses and publishing a thinly veiled attack on what he considered to be the absurdity of the Church's defense of the Aristotelian model. The book, *Dialogue on the Two Chief Systems of the World*, dismantled the arguments in favor of the traditional, Aristotelian view of the cosmos, and it presented the Copernican system as the only alternative for reasonable people. Early the following year, Galileo was summoned before the Inquisition and forced to recant. He was sentenced to spend the rest of his life under house arrest and forbidden to ever publish again. The long-term effect of Galileo's condemnation was to shift the locus of the Scientific Revolution to the Protestant countries of Europe.

Cartesian Skepticism and Deductive Reasoning

Although many of those who took the lead in the Scientific Revolution in the second half of the seventeenth century were born in Protestant countries, Rene Descartes had been a

Salons and Lodges

The development and spread of an intellectual movement required places for people to congregate and share ideas. While *philosophes* could be found in most major European cities, the culture of the *salons* flourished in Paris, making it the center of the Enlightenment. Originally, the term *salon* had referred to the room in aristocratic homes where the family and its guests gathered for leisure activities. During the Enlightenment, however, aristocratic and, eventually, upper-middle-class women transformed such rooms (and the term) by turning them into a place where both men and women gathered to educate themselves about and discuss the new ideas of the age in privacy and safety. In the more prestigious houses, the leading *philosophes* were often invited to give informal lectures and to lead discussions.

It was through the salons that women made their most direct contribution to the Enlightenment. As hostesses, they controlled the guest list and enforced the rules of polite conversation. They were, therefore, in control of what ideas were discussed in front of which influential men, and were somewhat able to affect the reception that those ideas were given. Additionally, they controlled an extensive international correspondence network, as they decided which letters from *philosophes* in other cities were to be read, discussed, and replied to.

Another eighteenth-century home of Enlightenment thought was the *Masonic Lodge*. The lodges were established and run by Freemasons whose origins dated back to the medieval guilds of the stonemasons. By the eighteenth century, the lodges were fraternities of aristocratic and middle-class men (and occasionally women), who gathered to discuss alternatives to traditional beliefs. Following the customs of the old guilds, the Masonic fraternities were run along democratic principles, the likes of which were new to continental Europe. Linked together by membership in the Grand Lodge, the lodges formed a network of communication for new ideas and ideals that rivaled that of the salons. Some of the most influential men of the eighteenth century were Masons, including the Duke of Montagu in England, Voltaire and Mozart in France, and Benjamin Franklin in America. In Berlin, Frederick the Great cultivated the Masonic Lodges as centers of learning.

Skepticism, Religion, and Social Criticism

Skepticism, or the habit of doubting what one has not learned for one's self, was also a key element in the Scientific Revolution that was developed more widely in the Enlightenment. A particular target of Enlightenment skeptics was religion. In his *Historical and Critical Dictionary* (1697), the French religious skeptic Pierre Bayle included entries for numerous religious beliefs, illustrating why they did not, in his opinion, stand the test of reason. More generally, Bayle argued that all dogma, including that based on scripture, should be considered false if it contradicted conclusions based on clear and natural reasoning.

The most prevalent form of religious belief among the *philosophes* was *deism*. The deists believed that the complexity, order, and natural laws exhibited by the universe were reasonable proofs that it had been created by a God. But reason also told them that once God had created the universe and the natural laws that govern it, there would no longer be any further role for him in the universe. A typical deist tract was John Toland's *Christianity Not Mysterious* (1696). There, Toland argued that the aspects of Christianity that were not compatible with reason should be discarded and that Christians should worship an intelligible God.

Some *philosophes* went further in their skepticism. The Scottish philosopher David Hume rejected Christianity, arguing that Christianity required a belief in miracles and that the notion of miracles was contradicted by human reason. Hume also attacked the deist position, arguing that the order we perceived in the universe was probably the product of our own minds and social conventions, concluding that all religion was based on "hope and fear." In the final analysis, Hume contended that reason must be the ultimate test and that belief should be in proportion to evidence.

The most famous skeptic of the Enlightenment wrote under the pen name of Voltaire. He raised satire to an art form and used it to criticize those institutions that promoted intolerance and bigotry. For his criticism of the French monarchy, aristocracy, and the church, he was briefly imprisoned in the Bastille. While in exile in England, he became an admirer of Newton and Locke. In *Letters Concerning the English Nation* (1733), he compared the constitutional monarchy, rationalism, and toleration that he found in England with the absolutism, superstition, and bigotry of his native France. Later, he produced a sprawling satire of European culture in *Candide* (1759). For a time he lived and worked with the most accomplished female *philosophe*, Madame du Châtelet, who made the only French translation of Newton's *Principia*.

Science in the Enlightenment

The physical sciences in the late seventeenth and early eighteenth centuries were dominated by two competing systems of natural philosophy, one building on the work of Isaac Newton and the other on the work of Rene Descartes.

The Newtonian approach was characterized by "analysis." Generally, analysis was understood to refer to the breaking down of complex phenomena into simple components, in the same way that Newton had used a prism to break light into its separate colored rays. In practice, eighteenth-century Newtonian analysis took two forms:

1. Setting up experiments and observations and drawing general conclusions from them
2. Resolving mathematical problems by reducing them to equations

An eighteenth-century example of the Newtonian approach was the calculation of the exact shape of the earth by the young Frenchman Pierre-Louis Moreau de Maupertuis based on observations of longitudinal measurement and the rates of pendulums at various points on the globe.

The Cartesian approach was characterized by "intelligibility." Followers of Descartes attempted to fashion intelligible explanations of natural phenomena. In practice, that usually meant the creation of some sort of physical or mechanical analogy to explain all natural phenomena. A good example of the Cartesian approach was the work of the Dutchman Christian Huygens, who explained the propagation of light by suggesting that it "flowed" like a fluid. The notion of "subtle fluids," substances that behaved like a fluid without mass, became very popular in the eighteenth century and was used to explain phenomena such as electricity and magnetism.

One of the greatest scientific achievements of the eighteenth century was the creation of the Linnaean system for the classification of living organisms. In *Systema Naturae* (1735), Carl Linnaeus, a Swedish botanist, physician, and zoologist, created a hierarchical system for the identification and classification of plants and animals. In Linnaeus's system, species of organisms were grouped by degree of physical similarity and difference into higher categories (genera), the genera into orders, orders into classes, and classes into kingdoms. Based on this system, Linnaeus created a simplified naming scheme by designating one Latin name to indicate the genus and one as a "shorthand" name for the species. An expanded and revised version of this system, which came to be called the binomial nomenclature, is still in use today.

The Arts in the Enlightenment

The dominant artistic style of the eighteenth century prior to the French Revolution is known as *rococo*. In the same way that the grandeur of the baroque reflected the grand designs of the seventeenth-century monarchs, rococo reflected the lighter touch of their eighteenth-century counterparts. The aesthetic preference was for subtlety and charm. The rococo style was first developed in the decorative arts and was often characterized by lighter design elements, especially the use of shell-like curves. Architectural examples of the rococo style include Sanssouci, the summer palace built for the Prussian monarch, Frederick the Great, in Potsdam, and the summer palace built for Catherine the Great of Russia in the town of Tsarskoye Selo, located just to the southeast of St. Petersburg. The rococo style as it influenced the visual arts is exemplified in such works as Antoine Watteau's *Music Party* (oil on canvas, c.1719) and by Jean Honoré Fragonard's *The Swing* (oil on canvas, 1766–1769).

The eighteenth century also saw the creation of new opportunities for artists, as the rise of a wealthy middle class broke the aristocratic monopoly on artistic patronage. The tastes of middle-class or bourgeois patrons were simpler than those of their aristocratic counterparts; the art produced for them was, consequently, less grand and less stylized. The middle class particularly patronized the visual arts, producing genre paintings that depicted more realistic scenes and themes from everyday life. The paintings of William Hogarth, such as the series titled *Marriage à la Mode* (c.1744), are examples of that genre.

The Radical Enlightenment

As the monarchs and ruling regimes of Europe showed the limits of enlightened despotism, the elements of Enlightenment thought came together in increasingly radical ways. The multivolume *Encyclopedia* (1751–1772) was produced by the tireless efforts of its coeditors Denis Diderot and Jean le Rond d'Alembert. Their stated goal was to overturn the barriers of superstition and bigotry and to contribute to the progress of human knowledge. The entries of the *Encyclopedia* championed a scientific approach to knowledge and labeled anything not based on reason as superstition. Its pages were strewn with Enlightenment thought and the rhetoric of natural rights that were egalitarian and democratic. King Louis XV of France declared that the *Encyclopedia* was causing "irreparable damage to morality and religion," and twice banned its publication.

Another more radical position was that of the German-born French *philosophe* the Baron d'Holbach, whose philosophy was openly atheist and materialist. In *System of Nature* (1770), d'Holbach offered the eighteenth-century reader a view of the world as a complex system of purely material substances, acting and developing according to laws of cause and effect that were purely mechanical rather than imposed by a rational God.

Perhaps the most influential radical voice emerged at midcentury, articulating a view of human nature that differed from Locke's *tabula rasa* and which suggested different political implications. In *Emile* (1762), Jean-Jacques Rousseau argued that humans were born essentially good and virtuous but were easily corrupted by society. Accordingly, Rousseau argued that the early years of a child's education should be spent developing the senses, sensibilities, and sentiments.

Politically, Rousseau agreed with his predecessors that men come together to form a civil society and give power to their government by their consent. But where Locke and Montesquieu were content with a constitutional monarchy, Rousseau's model was the ancient

Greek city-state where citizens participated directly in the political life of the state. He expressed his discontent with the political state of affairs in *The Social Contract* (1762), where he wrote: "Man is born free; and everywhere he is in chains." Accordingly, Rousseau believed that the virtuous citizen should be willing to subordinate his own self-interest to the general good of the community, and he argued that a lawful government must be continually responsible to the general will of the people. Toward the end of the century, as the ruling regimes of Continental Europe mobilized to protect their power and privilege, it would be Rousseau's version of the Enlightenment that resonated with an increasingly discontented population.

The Other Enlightenment

The Enlightenment of the *philosophes*, with their *salons* and lodges, was primarily a cultural movement experienced by aristocrats and upper-middle-class people. But further down the social hierarchy, a version of the Enlightenment reached an increasingly literate population through:

- excerpted versions of the *Encyclopedia*
- popular *almanacs*, which incorporated much of the new scientific and rational knowledge
- "*philosophical texts*," the underground book trade's code name for banned books that included some versions of philosophical treatises, and bawdy, popularized versions of the *philosophes*' critique of the Church and the ruling classes

In these texts the most radical of Enlightenment ideals—particularly those of Rousseau and d'Holbach—together with satirical lampooning of the clergy and the ruling class, reached a broad audience and helped to undermine respect for and the legitimacy of the ruling regimes.

❯ Rapid Review

In the eighteenth century, writers known as *philosophes* developed and popularized a vision of society based on reason. They wrote philosophical treatises, histories, novels, plays, pamphlets, and satires critical of the traditional social and political conventions and institutions like absolute monarchy and the Church. Initially, they hoped to reform society by educating the powerful monarchs of European kingdoms. When that strategy (known as enlightened despotism) faltered, the movement found new venues such as *salons* and Masonic Lodges, and the more egalitarian and democratic aspects of Enlightenment thought came to dominate, contributing to an atmosphere of political and social revolution that flourished in modern Europe at the end of the century. The eighteenth century was also the period in which the Newtonian approach in the physical sciences triumphed over its competitors, Linnaeus created a new system of taxonomy, and rococo became the dominant artistic style.

› Chapter Review Questions

1. Hobbes and Locke DISAGREED in their belief that
    (A) men are created equal
    (B) men tend to follow their own self-interest
    (C) the natural state of men is one of war
    (D) a government's power comes from the people
    (E) men are often ruled by their passions

2. Locke argued that the primary aim of government is
    (A) to guarantee peace by putting the fear of death into its subjects
    (B) to follow and enact the general will of the people
    (C) to provide and protect democracy
    (D) to ensure the right to property
    (E) to institute a constitutional monarchy

3. Which of the following is NOT true of the *philosophes*?
    (A) They used their positions as university professors to influence society.
    (B) They aimed to educate the public.
    (C) Their ultimate goal was a society governed by reason.
    (D) They wrote in many different genres.
    (E) They were often guests of and correspondents with the women who hosted *salons*.

4. The economic policy known as *laissez-faire*
    (A) advocates protectionist tariffs
    (B) is based on the notion that people have a right to do anything they want
    (C) is based on the notion that human self-interest produces natural laws that govern economic behavior
    (D) argues that the government should act as an "invisible hand" to regulate the economy
    (E) was instituted by enlightened despots

5. The religious belief of the majority of the *philosophes* was
    (A) Catholicism
    (B) Lutheranism
    (C) Calvinism
    (D) Deism
    (E) Atheism

6. The style of Enlightenment literature made famous by Voltaire was
    (A) the philosophical treatise
    (B) the satire
    (C) the play
    (D) the pamphlet
    (E) the novel

7. Which of the following presented the most radical challenge to the traditional ruling regimes of eighteenth-century Europe?
    (A) Locke's notion that humans are born *tabula rasa*
    (B) Hobbes's notion that human nature requires a ruler with absolute power
    (C) Beccaria's notion that the goal of a legal system should be the rehabilitation and reintegration of the criminal to society
    (D) the concept of religious toleration
    (E) Rousseau's notion that a lawful government must be continually responsible to the general will of the people

8. Which of the following is NOT part of Rousseau's thought?
    (A) Humans are born essentially good and virtuous but are easily corrupted by society.
    (B) The early years of a child's education should be spent developing the senses, sensibilities, and sentiments.
    (C) "Man is born free; and everywhere he is in chains."
    (D) All religion is based on "hope and fear."
    (E) The virtuous citizen should be willing to subordinate his own self-interest to the general good of the community.

〉Answers and Explanations

1. **C.** Locke believed that men could and did overcome their passions in civil society; Hobbes disagreed, believing that the fears and passions of men were so strong that their natural state was war and only a ruler with the power of life and death over his subjects could guarantee peace. Choices A and B are incorrect because both argued that men were created equal and tended to follow their own interest. Choice D is incorrect because both believed that a government's power came from the people. Choice E is incorrect because both believed that men were *often* ruled by their passions; they disagreed about whether those passions could be overcome.

2. **D.** Locke argued that the legitimate aim of government was the protection of individual liberty; that liberty was, for Locke, encapsulated in an individual's right to dispense with the fruits of his labor (property) freely. Choice A is incorrect because the notion that a government must be able to put the fear of death into its subjects belonged to Hobbes. Choice B is incorrect because the notion that a government has an obligation to follow and enact the general will of the people belonged to Rousseau. Choice E is incorrect because Locke, though part of a movement that instituted a constitutional monarchy in England, argued in the *Second Treatise of Government* that any form (monarchy, oligarchy, or democracy) of government could be legitimate, provided it ensured and protected the fundamental rights of its subject.

3. **A.** Universities in the eighteenth century were traditional institutions, mostly affiliated with the Church. Accordingly, very few *philosophes* held university posts. Choices B–E are incorrect because they all accurately describe the *philosophes*.

4. **C.** Adam Smith argued that human self-interest produces natural laws that govern economic behavior and, therefore, the government should refrain from legislation that tries to produce results that run counter to those laws. Choice A is incorrect because protectionist tariffs, taxes levied on foreign goods to protect the sales of domestic goods, are an example of the kind of

law that Smith argued would be either futile or harmful. Choice B is incorrect because the notion of *laissez-faire* applies only to economic behavior; it does not argue that people have a right to do anything they want. Choice D is incorrect because the "invisible hand" referred to the natural laws that Smith believed regulated the economy, not the government. Choice E is incorrect because *laissez-faire* was not popular with or instituted by enlightened despots.

5. **D.** Most *philosophes* were deists who believed that a rational God created the world and the laws by which it was governed, but took no further active role in the universe. Choices A–C are incorrect because, for the philosophes, Catholicism, Lutheranism, and Calvinism all failed the test of reason because they were based on received knowledge taken on faith. Choice E is incorrect because most *philosophes* were not atheists, who deny the existence of God, as they believed that a rational world governed by natural laws required a rational creator.

6. **B.** Voltaire is best known for his satire, as exemplified by both *Letters Concerning the English Nation* (1733) and *Candide* (1759). Choice A is incorrect because Voltaire wrote no philosophical treatises. Choices C–E are incorrect because they are not the styles for which Voltaire is best known.

7. **E.** Rousseau's notion that a lawful government must be continually responsible to the general will of the people explicitly challenged the right of the privileged classes to rule, a radical and dangerous idea in the eighteenth century. Choice A is incorrect because, although Locke's notion that humans are born *tabula rasa*, or like a blank slate, challenged the traditional Christian view of humans as depraved, it did not have the direct political implications of Rousseau's "general will." Choice B is incorrect because Hobbes's notion that human nature required a ruler with absolute power was a conservative one, and most compatible with the ideology of the ruling regimes in the eighteenth century. Choice C is incorrect because Beccaria's notion that the goal of a legal system should be the rehabilitation and

reintegration of the criminal to society was reformist in nature, while Rousseau was revolutionary. Choice D is incorrect because the concept of religious toleration was sometimes absorbed into the ideology of ruling regimes in the eighteenth century.

8. **D.** The proposition that all religion was based on "hope and fear" was articulated by Hume not Rousseau. Choices A, B, C, and E are all positions articulated by Rousseau.

CHAPTER 13

Social Transformation and Statebuilding in the Eighteenth Century

IN THIS CHAPTER

Summary: In the eighteenth century, new wealth from overseas trade transformed European society and created territorial rivalries between European states.

Key Ideas

✪ The development of a triangle of trade connecting Europe, the Americas, and Africa created large amounts of new wealth in the European economy.
✪ The development of market-oriented agriculture and cottage industries broke traditional limits on European population growth and economic productivity.
✪ The increased wealth led rulers of European states to attempt to expand their territorial holdings through war and diplomacy.

Key Terms

triangle of trade	cottage industry	the Pragmatic Sanction
the Middle Passage	putting-out system	War of the Austrian
manorial system	flying shuttle	Succession
cash crops	spinning jenny	Diplomatic Revolution
enclosure	cotton gin	Seven Years War

Introduction

In the eighteenth century, Great Britain and, to a lesser extent, France surpassed Spain, Portugal, and Holland as the dominant economic powers in Europe. They did so by controlling the majority of the increasingly lucrative triangle of trade that connected Europe to Africa and the Americas. The resulting wealth and prosperity set in motion a series of innovations that radically changed European agricultural and manufacturing production, which in turn produced changes in the social structure of Europe. Competition between Britain and France, and the desire of their eastern European rivals to catch up, led to innovations in diplomacy and war, the twin processes by which eighteenth-century European rulers built and expanded their states.

The Triangle of Trade

The phrase *triangle of trade* refers to a system of interconnected trade routes that quadrupled foreign trade in both Britain and France in the eighteenth century. Here are three characteristics of the triangle of trade:

- *Manufactured goods* (primarily guns and gin) were exported from Europe to Africa.
- *Slaves* were exported from Africa to serve as labor in European colonies in North America, South America, and the Caribbean.
- *Raw materials* (especially furs, timber, tobacco, rice, cotton, indigo dye, coffee, rum, and sugar) were exported from the colonies to Europe in exchange for the slaves and manufactured goods.

Prior to the eighteenth century, the primary destination of Africans taken into slavery by their rivals had been either the Mediterranean basin or Asia. The eighteenth-century expansion of the European colonies greatly increased the demand for African slaves and reoriented the slave trade to the west. The majority of slaves were destined for the West Indies and Brazil, with about 10 percent going to colonies in North America. The transportation of African slaves across the Atlantic on European trade ships was known as the *Middle Passage*. As many as 700 slaves per ship were transported, chained below deck in horrific conditions. It is estimated that somewhere between 50,000 and 100,000 Africans were transported each year during the height of the eighteenth-century slave trade.

Breaking the Traditional Cycle of Population and Productivity

The enormous wealth generated by the British and French colonies and the triangle of trade created pressure for social change that eventually affected the whole population. The effects were felt more strongly in Britain and led to changes that, taken together, constituted the first phase of an Industrial Revolution that began in Britain and then spread eastward throughout Europe, breaking the traditional cycle of population and productivity.

The traditional cycle worked like this:

- Population and productivity rose together, as an increase in the number of people working in an agricultural economy increased the agricultural yield.
- Eventually, the agricultural yield reached the maximum amount that could be produced given the land available and the methods in use.
- For a while, population would continue to rise but eventually, as the number of people far outstripped the agricultural yield, food would become scarce and expensive.

- Scarcity and high prices would eventually cause the population to decline.
- When the population was safely below the possible productivity, the cycle would begin again.

In the eighteenth century, several developments related to new wealth combined to break the cycle:

- Agriculture became market-oriented.
- Rural manufacturing spread capital throughout the population.
- Increased demand led to technical innovation.

The new market orientation of agriculture created a shift from farming for local consumption to a reliance on imported food sold at markets. The introduction of rural manufacturing put larger amounts of currency into the system and made the working population less dependent on land and agricultural cycles, thereby breaking the natural check on population growth.

Market-Oriented Agriculture

The rise in population created more mouths to feed. The existence of a vast colonial empire of trade created an increasingly wealthy merchant class who both bought land from and affected the behavior of the traditional land-holding elite. The result was the destruction of the traditional *manorial system* in which the landowning elite (lords of the manor) held vast estates divided into small plots of arable land farmed by peasants for local consumption and vast grounds known as commons where peasants grazed their livestock. That system was slowly replaced by a market-oriented approach in which *cash crops* were grown for sale and export.

The shift to cash crops created pressure that led to the reorganization of the social structure of the countryside. The traditional landowning elite abandoned their feudal obligations to the peasantry and adopted the attitude of the merchant class. Cash crops created a demand for larger fields. Landowners responded by instituting a process known as *enclosure* because of the hedges, fences, and walls that were built to deny the peasantry access to the commons, which were now converted to fields for cash crops. Later, the landowners extended enclosure into other arable lands, breaking traditional feudal agreements and gradually transforming much of the peasantry into wage labor. By the middle of the eighteenth century, three-quarters of the arable land in England had been enclosed informally or "by agreement" (though the peasantry had not, in fact, been given any choice); after 1750, the process continued more formally as land was enclosed via acts of Parliament.

Rural Manufacturing

The increase in population also created greater demand for the other necessities of life, particularly clothing. In the feudal system, all aspects of textile production had been under the control of guilds (which were organizations of skilled laborers, such as spinners and weavers), who enjoyed the protection of the town officials. Membership in a guild was gained only through a lengthy apprenticeship. In that way, the guilds kept competition to a minimum and controlled the supply of textiles, thereby guaranteeing that they could make a decent living. In the eighteenth century, merchants faced with an ever-expanding demand for textiles had to find a way around the guild system; the result was a system of rural manufacturing known variously as *cottage industry* or the *putting-out system*.

In the putting-out system, merchants went into the countryside and engaged the peasantry in small-scale textile production. Each month, the merchant provided raw material and rented equipment to peasant families. At the end of the month, he returned and paid the family for whatever thread or cloth they had produced. Initially, peasant families supplemented their agricultural income in this way; eventually, some of them gave up farming altogether and pooled their resources to create small textile mills in the countryside. As the system grew, the guilds of the town were unable to compete with the mills; cottage industry replaced the urban guilds as the center for textile production.

The new system of rural manufacturing went hand in hand with the shift to market-oriented agriculture; the destruction of the manorial system could not have been accomplished if some of the cash flowing into the economy had not found its way into the hands of the rural population. The creation of cottage industries provided the cash that enabled rural families to buy their food rather than grow it themselves.

However, the social change that accompanied the destruction of both the manorial system and the guilds also brought hardship and insecurity. The enclosure movement meant that thousands of small landholders, tenant farmers, and sharecroppers lost their land and their social status. Forced to work for wages, their lives and those of their families were now at the mercy of the marketplace. The destruction of the guilds produced similar trauma for the artisans and their families. For both the peasantry and the artisans, the economic and social changes of the eighteenth century meant the destruction of their traditional place and status in society: they were now faced with both new opportunities and great insecurity.

Technical Innovations in Agriculture and Manufacturing

It is important to remember that technical innovations are always responses to new challenges. The people of earlier centuries did not fail to innovate because they were less intelligent; they simply had no need for the innovations. The ever-growing population and demand for food and goods in the eighteenth century created a series of related demands that eventually led to technical innovations in both agriculture and manufacturing. Single innovations often created a need for further innovation in a different part of the process.

The key technical innovation in the agricultural sector in the eighteenth century was the replacement of the old three-field system (in which roughly one-third of the land was left fallow to allow the soil to replenish itself with the necessary nutrients) with new crops such as clover, turnips, and the potato, which replenished the soil while producing foodstuffs that could be used to feed livestock in winter. More and healthier livestock contributed products such as dairy and leather.

In the manufacturing sector, a number of interconnected technical innovations greatly increased the pace and output of the textile industry.

- In 1733, John Kay invented the *flying shuttle*, which doubled the speed at which cloth could be woven on a loom, creating a need to find a way to produce greater amounts of thread faster.
- In the 1760s, James Hargreaves invented the *spinning jenny*, which greatly increased the amount of thread a single spinner could produce from cotton, creating a need to speed up the harvesting of cotton.
- In 1793, the American Eli Whitney invented the *cotton gin*, which efficiently removed seed from raw cotton, thereby increasing the speed with which it could be processed and sent to the spinners.

These technical innovations greatly increased the pace and productivity of the textile industry. The need to supervise these larger, faster machines also contributed to the development of textile mills, which replaced the scattered putting-out system by the century's end.

Eastern Ambition

The prosperity and power of Britain and France caused their eastern European rivals to try to strengthen and modernize their kingdoms.

Prussia

In Prussia, Frederick William I built a strong centralized government in which the military, under the command of the nobles, played a dominant role. In 1740, his successor Frederick II (the Great) used that military to extend Prussia into lands controlled by the Hapsburgs. Challenging the right of Maria Theresa to ascend to the throne of Austria (which was a right guaranteed her by a document known as the *Pragmatic Sanction*), Frederick II marched troops into Silesia. In what came to be known as the *War of the Austrian Succession* (1740–1748), Maria Theresa was able to rally Austrian and Hungarian troops and fight Prussia and its allies, the French, Spanish, Saxons, and Bavarians, to a stand-off.

Russia

In Russia, the progress toward modernization and centralization made under Peter the Great had largely been undone in the first half of the eighteenth century. However, under the leadership of Catherine the Great, Russia defeated the Ottoman Turks in 1774, thereby extending Russia's borders as far as the Black Sea and the Balkan Peninsula. In 1775, Russia joined with Prussia and Austria to conquer Poland and divide its territories among the three of them.

War and Diplomacy

In eighteenth-century Europe, state-building was still primarily conducted through war and diplomacy. The competition between Britain and France in the triangle of trade meant that they would contend militarily for control of colonies in North America and the Caribbean, but the desire to weaken one another also led them to become entangled in land wars in Europe.

The expansionist aims of Frederick II of Prussia led to a shift in diplomatic alliances that is now referred to as the *Diplomatic Revolution*:

- Prussia, fearful of being isolated by its enemies, forged an alliance in 1756 with its former enemy Great Britain.
- Austria and France, previously antagonistic toward one another, were so alarmed by the alliance of Prussia and Great Britain that they forged an alliance of their own.

Colonial and continental rivalries combined to bring all of the great European powers into a conflict that came to be known as the *Seven Years War* (1756–1763). The conflict pitted France, Austrian, Russia, Saxony, Sweden, and (after 1762) Spain against Prussia, Great Britain, and the German state of Hanover. Land and sea battles were fought in North America (where it is sometimes known as the French and Indian War), Europe, and India. The European hostilities were concluded in 1763 by a peace agreement that essentially reestablished prewar boundaries. The North American conflict, and particularly the fall of Quebec in 1759, shifted the balance of power in North America to the British. The British had similar success in India.

As the eighteenth century progressed, the nature of European armies and wars changed in ways that would have profound implications for the ruling regimes. The standing army was different in several ways:

- The size of the standing army increased.
- The officer corps became full-time servants of the state.
- Troops consisted of conscripts, volunteers, mercenaries, and criminals who were pressed into service.
- Discipline and training became harsher and more extensive.

Weapons and tactics changed to accommodate the new armies:

- Muskets became more efficient and accurate.
- Cannons became more mobile.
- Wars were now decided not by a decisive battle, but by superior organization of resources.
- Naval battles were now often more crucial than land battles.

› Rapid Review

In the eighteenth century, Britain and France came to dominate the lucrative triangle of trade that imported valuable raw materials from North America and the Caribbean to Europe in exchange for slaves acquired from Africa. The influx of capital generated by the colonial trade served as a spur for unchecked population growth made possible by an agricultural revolution and the creation of a system of rural manufacturing. The changes in agricultural and manufacturing production destroyed the last vestiges of an economic system (manorialism) and a social system (feudalism) that dated back to the medieval period. In that process, both the traditional European peasantry and the guildsmen were converted to wage labor.

The intensifying rivalry between Britain and France, and the growing ambition of their eastern European counterparts, led to a series of midcentury wars, including the War of the Austrian Succession and the Seven Years War. Rivalries also led to a series of innovations in diplomacy and warfare.

› Chapter Review Questions

1. Which of the following was NOT part of the triangle of trade?
   (A) timber
   (B) tobacco
   (C) cotton
   (D) silk
   (E) slaves

2. Enclosure
   (A) changed the balance of military power
   (B) refers to the shackling of slaves below deck on the Middle Passage
   (C) denied peasants access to commons and farm land in England
   (D) made mills the center of textile production
   (E) destroyed the guilds

3. Which of the following did NOT contribute to the breaking of the traditional population cycle in Europe?
   (A) the shift of agriculture to a market orientation
   (B) the three-field system
   (C) rural manufacturing
   (D) the conversion to wage labor
   (E) technical innovation

4. Cottage industry
   (A) refers to the building of cottages in the countryside for the working population
   (B) helped to reinforce the traditional checks on population growth
   (C) refers to the establishment of large-scale, factory-based industrial production
   (D) is a component of the feudal system
   (E) refers to the engagement of the rural population in small-scale textile production

5. Which of the following was a key technical innovation in agricultural production in the eighteenth century?
   (A) new crops such as clover, turnips, and the potato
   (B) the flying shuttle
   (C) the spinning jenny
   (D) the cotton gin
   (E) the three-field system

6. The most significant impact of the introduction of rural manufacturing in the eighteenth century was
   (A) improved quality of clothing
   (B) a decrease in agricultural output
   (C) the spur to the economy provided by increased production and the spread of capital throughout the population
   (D) the creation of the triangle of trade
   (E) a shift in the population from towns to the countryside.

7. Which of the following is NOT true of the War of the Austrian Succession?
   (A) It began when Frederick the Great of Prussia challenged Maria Theresa's right to ascend to the throne of Austria.
   (B) It violated the terms of the Pragmatic Sanction.
   (C) Austria allied with Prussia to hold off French ambitions.
   (D) Maria Theresa was able to rally the Hungarians to her cause.
   (E) It was essentially fought to a standoff.

8. As a result of the Seven Years War,
   (A) the French monarchy fell
   (B) Maria Theresa ascended to the throne of Austria
   (C) Prussia was weakened
   (D) the Ottoman Turks were further weakened
   (E) Great Britain emerged as the dominant European power outside of the European continent

❯ Answers and Explanations

1. **D.** Although there was a silk trade between China and Europe, it was not part of the eighteenth-century triangle of trade. Choices A, B, and C are correct because tobacco, timber, and cotton were imported into Europe from the Americas. Choice E is correct because slaves were bought in Africa and sold in the Americas and West Indies.

2. **C.** Enclosure refers to the decision by English landowners to deny peasants access to both the commons and their traditional farming plots so that the lands could be converted to cash crops. Choice A is incorrect because the term *enclosure* does not refer to military organization. Choice B is incorrect because the term *enclosure* does not refer to the inhumane methods of transporting slaves. Choice D is incorrect because the term *enclosure* does not refer to textile production. Choice E is incorrect because it was the development of cottage industry, and not the enclosure movement, that destroyed the crafts guilds.

3. **B.** The three-field system, whereby one-third of the land was left fallow, was part of the traditional agricultural cycle which helped to *establish* limits on productivity and, therefore, on population increase. Choice A is incorrect because market-oriented agriculture meant a shift from farming for local consumption to a reliance on imported food sold at markets, thereby helping to break the natural limit on agricultural productivity which enforced a limit on population growth. Choice C is incorrect because the advent of rural manufacturing put cash into the pockets of the laboring class, enabling its members to buy food and, therefore, helping to remove the natural constraint on population growth. Choice D is incorrect because the conversion of the agricultural workforce to wage labor also furthered the spread of capital throughout the economy. Choice E is incorrect because technical innovation in agriculture ensured a healthy economy and increased the availability of food, thereby helping to remove natural constraints on population increase.

4. **E.** *Cottage industry* is the term that denotes the development of small-scale textile production in the countryside in the eighteenth century. Choice A is incorrect because *cottage industry* does not refer to the building of cottages. Choice B is incorrect because *cottage industry* refers to the engagement of the rural population in small-scale textile production that helped to *break* the traditional checks on population growth. Choice C is incorrect because *cottage industry* does not refer to the establishment of large-scale, factory-based industrial production, which was a nineteenth-century development. Choice D is incorrect because cottage industry helped to *destroy* the remaining vestiges of the feudal system.

5. **A.** The key technical innovation in the agricultural sector in the eighteenth century was the introduction of new crops such as clover, turnips, and the potato, which replenished the soil while producing foodstuffs that could be used to feed livestock in winter. Choices B and C are incorrect because the flying shuttle and the spinning jenny were technical innovations in the *textile industry*. Choice D is incorrect because, although cotton is an agricultural product, the cotton gin did not increase its production; it increased the speed with which it could be harvested, thereby increasing the speed with which it could be supplied to the textile producers. It is, therefore, properly understood as an innovation in the textile industry. Choice E is incorrect because the three-field system was *replaced* in the eighteenth century by new crops.

6. **C.** The most significant impact of the introduction of rural manufacturing in the eighteenth century was that it acted as a spur to the economy by increasing production and spreading capital throughout the population. Choice A is incorrect because the introduction of rural manufacturing had no significant effect on the quality of clothing, though it did increase the amount produced. Choice B is incorrect because the introduction of rural manufacturing had no negative effect on agricultural output. Choice D is incorrect because rural manufacturing played no role in the creation of the triangle of trade. Choice E is incorrect because, although the economies and social fabric of towns were damaged by the destruction of the guild system that resulted from the introduction of rural

manufacturing, there was no significant shift in the population from towns to the countryside.

7. **C.** The War of the Austrian Succession (1740–1748) was fought between Prussia and its allies, the French, Spanish, Saxons, and Bavarians, and the Austrian and Hungarian troops, who supported the right of the Hapsburg heir, Maria Theresa, to ascend to the throne; French aggression was not a factor. The other four choices are all accurate statements about the War of the Austrian Succession.

8. **E.** British victories in the Americas and in India allowed it to emerge from the Seven Years War as the dominant European power beyond the boundaries of the continent. Choice A is incorrect because the French monarchy did not fall as a result of the Seven Years War, though the financial strain put on the government was a contributing cause of the French Revolution. Choice B is incorrect because Prussia was Britain's continental ally in the Seven Years War and its power was not weakened by the outcome. Choice D is incorrect because the Ottoman Turks were not directly involved in the Seven Years War; their empire was further weakened by defeat in a conflict with Russia in 1774 that was unrelated to the Seven Years War.

CHAPTER > 14

The French Revolution and the Rise of Napoleon, 1789–1799

IN THIS CHAPTER

Summary: Between 1789 and 1799, the Kingdom of France experienced a revolution that challenged the social and political structure of Europe.

Key Ideas

- ✪ In 1789, the bourgeois leaders of the Third Estate attempted to force King Louis XVI to curb the power and privilege of the clergy and the nobility by withholding taxes and threatening violence.
- ✪ In 1791, the radicalized leadership of Paris's urban working class seized control of the revolution and attempted to create a more egalitarian society and a more equitable distribution of wealth.
- ✪ By 1794, the radicals had all been consumed by their own reign of terror, and the bourgeois moderates reasserted themselves.
- ✪ By 1799, the bourgeois moderates had come to rely so heavily on the military that they were powerless to stop a military coup.

Key Terms

Thermidor
bourgeoisie
Ancien Régime
Estates General
cahiers
National Assembly

Tennis Court Oath
Bastille
August Decrees
the Great Fear
Declaration of the Rights of Man and
    of the Citizen

March to Versailles
the Civil Constitution of the Clergy
sans-culottes
the flight to Varennes
Girondins
Jacobins

National Convention
Law of the Maximum
Committee of Public Safety
Reign of Terror
Directory
neoclassicism

Introduction

Between 1789 and 1799, the Kingdom of France underwent a political revolution that unfolded in three phases:

- a *moderate phase (1789–1791)*, in which the politically active portions of the *bourgeoisie*, or merchant class, attempted to curb the power and privilege of the monarchy, the aristocracy, and the clergy, and create a limited constitutional monarchy similar to that which existed in Britain
- a *radical phase (1791–1794)*, in which the politicized urban working class of Paris seized control and attempted to create a democratic republic and a more materially and socially egalitarian society
- an *end phase* known as *Thermidor (1794–1799)*, in which the moderate bourgeois faction reasserted itself and concentrated simply on restoring order

By 1799, the Thermidorian government, known as the Directory, was totally dependent on the military for its ability to govern. In November of that year, a military general, Napoleon Bonaparte staged a *coup d'état*, and embarked on an ambitious campaign to create a French Empire that spanned most of Europe. Upon his defeat in 1815 by a coalition of European powers, the French monarchy was restored and the kingdom of France was returned to its traditional boundaries.

The *Ancien Régime* in Crisis

The phrase *Ancien Régime*, or Old Regime, refers to the traditional social and political hierarchy of eighteenth-century France. It was composed of three "Estates":

1. the *First Estate*, made up of the clergy, which included all ordained members of the Catholic Church in France
2. the *Second Estate*, made up of the nobility, which included all titled aristocrats
3. the *Third Estate*, made up of the citizenry, which included everyone who was neither clergy nor nobility and whose membership accounted for 96 percent of the population of France

Together, the clergy and the nobility wielded enormous power and enjoyed tremendous privilege, while the various groups that made up the Third Estate bore the tax burden.

The Catholic Church in France functioned as a branch of the government bureaucracy. It registered births, marriages, and deaths; collected certain kinds of agricultural taxes; and oversaw both education and relief for the poor. The Church owned approximately 10 percent of land in France but paid no taxes to the government; instead, it made an annual gift to the crown in an amount of its own choosing. The clergy who populated the hierarchical structure of the Catholic Church in France ranged from poor, simple parish priests to the powerful cardinals who were connected to the pope in Rome, and who often served as chief advisers in the government of the French king.

The nobility were the traditional land-owning elite of France, though by this period they often supplemented their fortunes through banking and commerce. They owned somewhere between 25 and 33 percent of the land in France, but were exempt from most taxes, despite the fact that they still collected various types of manorial dues from peasant farmers. Members of the nobility held most of the high offices in the French government and army, and the Church.

The citizenry can be roughly divided into three social groups:

- the *bourgeoisie*, including merchants, manufacturers, bankers, lawyers, and master craftsmen
- the *peasantry*, including all agricultural laborers ranging from very prosperous land owners to poor sharecroppers and migrant workers
- *urban laborers*, including journeymen craftsmen, mill and other small-scale manufacturing workers, and all wage laborers that populated the cities and towns of France

By 1787, the government of King Louis XVI was in financial crisis. When he took the throne in 1774, Louis XVI had inherited a huge and ever-increasing national debt, most of it incurred by borrowing money to finance wars and to maintain an army. With interest on the debt mounting and bankers refusing to lend the government more money, Louis and his ministers attempted to reform the tax system of France and to pry some of the vast wealth out of the hands of the nobility. When the nobility resisted, he was forced to do something that had not been done since 1614; he called into session the *Estates General*. The Estates General was the closest thing to a legislative assembly that existed in eighteenth-century France. Members representing each of the three Estates met to hear the problems of the realm and to hear pleas for new taxes. In return, they were allowed to present a list of their own concerns and proposals, called *cahiers*, to the Crown. When the representatives arrived in Versailles, the palace of Louis XVI, in April of 1789, the representatives of the Third Estate presented a series of proposals that were revolutionary in nature.

The Moderate Phase of the French Revolution (1789–1791)

The representatives of the Third Estate, in reality all members of the bourgeoisie, demanded that the number of representatives for the Third Estate be doubled in order to equal the number of representatives in the other two orders combined and that representatives of all three Estates meet together and vote by head rather than by Estate. These demands were designed to give the Third Estate a chance to pass resolutions by persuading a single member of the nobility or clergy to side with it. The demands of the Third Estate posed a dilemma for Louis: granting the demands would give the Third Estate unprecedented power, but that power would come at the expense of the nobility and the clergy and could perhaps be used to get the tax reforms Louis and his ministers needed to solve France's financial crisis.

Demand for a New Constitution

While Louis considered his options, the representatives of the Third Estate grew bolder. Arguing that they were the voice of the nation, they declared themselves, on June 17, 1789, to be the *National Assembly* of France. When they were locked out of their meeting hall three days later, they pushed their way into Louis's indoor tennis court and vowed that they would not disband until a new constitution had been written for France. This proclamation became known as the *Tennis Court Oath*. On June 27 Louis decided in favor of the Third Estate, decreeing that all members should join the National Assembly.

Fear Causes Parisians to Storm the Bastille

While the bourgeois leaders of the new National Assembly worked on writing a constitution for France, the uncertainty of the situation created an atmosphere of fear and mistrust. Nervous nobles began to demand that Louis break up the new Assembly, which in turn demanded an explanation for the arrival of new regiments of mercenary troops in Versailles. By July of 1789, much of the urban population of Paris, which now looked to the Assembly as its champion, believed that the nobility and, perhaps, the king intended to remove the Assembly by force. Their fears focused on the infamous *Bastille*, a prison fortress in Paris which they wrongly believed housed the guns and ammunition that would be needed for the job.

On July 14, an angry crowd marched on the Bastille. The nervous governor of the Bastille ordered the crowd to disperse; when it refused, he had his guard fire into the crowd. The crowd responded by storming the Bastille. When it was over, 98 people had been killed and 73 wounded. The governor and his guard were killed, and their heads were paraded on pikes through the city. In the aftermath, Louis's advisors urged him to flee Versailles and raise an army to crush the Assembly and restore order to Paris. Louis decided to try to soothe the city instead, and he promised to withdraw the mercenary troops.

Rural Unrest Emboldens the Assembly

While order was restored in Paris, it was disintegrating in the countryside where peasants, aware that the nobility had been weakened and fearful that they would soon reassert their power with a vengeance, seized the opportunity and raided graneries to ensure that they had affordable bread and attacked the chateaus of the local nobility in order to burn debt records. In the context of that rural unrest, sometimes known as *the Great Fear*, the Assembly passed the *August Decrees* in which most of the traditional privileges of the nobility and the clergy were renounced and abolished. In an attempt to assure all citizens of France of their intention to bring about a new, more just society, the Assembly adopted, on August 27, 1789, the "*Declaration of the Rights of Man and of the Citizen*," a document that espoused individual rights and liberties for all citizens.

By the end of the summer of 1789, severe economic stress in the form of high bread prices and unemployment again prompted the people of Paris to take action on their own. Prompted by rumors that the nobility in Louis' court were plotting a coup and spurred on by an active tabloid press, the people of Paris rioted on October 5, 1789. The next day, a contingent of Parisian women organized an 11-mile march from Paris to the king's palace at Versailles. Along the way, they were joined by the Paris Guards, a citizen militia, and together they forced their way into the palace and insisted that Louis accompany them back to Paris. He did; and within two weeks the National Assembly itself had relocated from Versailles to Paris. The *March to Versailles*, as it came to be known, demonstrated two important things.

First, the crowds of Paris did not yet look upon Louis XVI as their enemy; they had marched to Versailles to *retrieve* him because they believed that, if he were with them in Paris, rather than isolated in Versailles where he was surrounded by his aristocratic advisers, he would side with them and support the Assembly's efforts.

Second, the crowd of Paris, and its willingness to do violence, had become a powerful political force.

The relocation of both the king and the National Assembly to Paris, within easy reach of the Parisian crowd, set the stage for the radical phase of the revolution.

The Radical Phase of the French Revolution (1791–1794)

The October Riot marked the beginning of a two-year period of relative calm. A gradual improvement in the economy eased the tension in Paris, and the Assembly's most determined aristocratic enemies either fled to the countryside or emigrated. The Assembly used the period of relative calm to complete the constitution and to draft and pass *the Civil Constitution of the Clergy*, a piece of legislation that turned clergymen into employees of the government and turned Church property into property of the state. The Assembly soon sold off the confiscated property to pay part of the national debt, but the attack on the clergy and the Church turned many faithful Catholics against the Assembly.

When Louis XVI signed the new constitution into law on September 15, 1791, the goals of the bourgeois leaders of the Assembly had been fulfilled: The power of the nobility and the Church had been broken, and France was now a constitutional monarchy. Four developments conspired to send the revolution into a more radical phase, each of which is reviewed in the sections that follow this list:

- the king's attempt to secretly flee Paris in June of 1791
- the outbreak of war with Austria and Prussia in April of 1792
- the division of the National Assembly into political factions
- the rise of a politicized laboring faction, known as the *sans-culottes* because of the long work pants they wore

The King's Attempt to Secretly Flee Paris

The king's attempt to flee Paris and head north to rally supporters, an event that came to be known as *the flight to Varennes*, was disastrous. He and the royal family were apprehended and forcibly returned to Paris. He was officially forgiven by the Assembly, but he had forever lost the trust of the people of Paris.

The Outbreak of War between France and Austria and Prussia

The war with Austria and Prussia came about partly because French aristocratic émigrés had been urging the Austrian and Prussian monarchies to come to the aid of the embattled Louis XVI. However, both Louis and the Assembly wanted the war, Louis because he believed that the country would have to turn to him to lead it in a time of war and the Assembly because its members believed it would unite Frenchmen in a common cause. When the combined forces of the Austrian and Prussian Armies invaded France, the French army collapsed and the country went into a panic.

The Division of the National Assembly into Political Factions

The development of political factions within the Assembly revealed the differing opinions about the goals and aims of the revolution that had always lurked under the surface of their united front against the nobility and the clergy. An attempt, in October of 1791, to diffuse factional rivalries by dissolving the National Assembly and electing a new Legislative Assembly failed to solve the problem.

The Rise of a Politicized Laboring Faction: The *Sans-Culottes*

From the beginning, the Parisian crowd and its willingness to do violence had been a factor in the revolution, but it had been a force with essentially traditional and conservative aims, insisting that the king pay attention to and take proper care of his people. By 1792, the crowd was different; the working people (bakers, shopkeepers, artisans, and manual laborers who were characterized by their long working pants—hence, *sans-culottes*, literally without short pants) now could be seen attending meetings of political clubs and discussing the reforms that were still needed, reforms that would bring about true equality.

Once the men and women of the *sans-culottes* began to assert themselves, political power belonged to whomever they would support. This fact became evident on August 10,

1792, when a crowd stormed first the royal palace and then the hall of the Assembly. Unable to resist the crowd, the leaders of the Assembly voted to depose and imprison the king and to immediately convene a new *National Convention* to deal with the crises facing the country.

The Vote to End the French Monarchy

The membership of the National Convention, elected by universal manhood suffrage, was more radical than its predecessors. In September of 1792, it voted to abolish the monarchy and to proclaim France a republic. It also managed to reorganize the French army and push the invading Austrian and Prussian forces back across the border. When the Convention proclaimed the war an extension of the revolution and vowed to carry it anywhere where people yearned for liberty and freedom, the monarchies of Europe responded by forming a coalition to crush the revolution.

In January of 1793, the convention put Louis XVI on trial for treason. The debate that followed his conviction revealed a split between two powerful factions with the Convention. The *Girondins*, whose membership tended to come from the wealthiest of the bourgeoisie, were mostly opposed to executing him; the *Jacobins*, whose members came from the lower strata of the bourgeoisie, were adamant that he must die. The vote was close, but the Jacobins prevailed, and Louis was sent to the guillotine on January 21, 1793.

A New Constitution and Robespierre's Reign of Terror

The execution of the king, combined with a decision to increase the number of men conscripted into the army, caused large anti-Convention uprisings throughout France. In Paris, the Jacobins used the revolt as an opportunity to purge the Girondins from the Convention. In June of 1793, a Jacobin-led mob occupied the Convention hall and refused to leave until the Girondins resigned. Those Girondins that refused to resign were arrested. The purged Convention then passed the *Law of the Maximum* to cap the price of bread and other essentials and drafted a new constitution that guaranteed universal manhood suffrage, universal education, and subsistence wages. In order to secure the egalitarian, democratic republic espoused by the new constitution, the Convention created a 12-man *Committee of Public Safety* and invested it with almost total power in order that it might secure the fragile Republic from its enemies. Within the Committee, a young lawyer from the provinces, Maximilien Robespierre gained control through his ability to persuade both his fellow Jacobins and the *sans-culottes* crowd to follow him.

Under Robespierre's leadership, the Committee instituted what has come to be known as the *Reign of Terror*. Arguing that, in times of revolution, terror was the necessary companion to virtue, Robespierre created tribunals in the major cities of France to try anyone suspected of being an enemy of the revolution. During the period of the Terror, between September of 1793 and July of 1794, between 200,000 and 400,000 people were sentenced to prison; between 25,000 and 50,000 of them are believed to have died, either in prison or on the guillotine.

Among the victims of the Terror were those who rivaled Robespierre for power. When, in April of 1794, Robespierre had the popular and influential Jacobin leader Georges-Jacques Danton arrested and executed for daring to suggest that it was time to reassess the Terror, he lost the support of both the Jacobins and the crowd. In July of 1794, Robespierre was arrested, tried, and executed by the same Terror machine that he had created. The execution of Robespierre marked the end of the radical phase of the revolution, as an exhausted Paris, devoid of its radical leaders, succumbed to a reassertion of power by the propertied bourgeoisie.

The Final Phase of the French Revolution: Thermidor and the Rise of Napoleon (1794–1799)

For several months following the execution of Robespierre, the revolutionary Terror was replaced by a terror of reaction as armed bands of men, hired by the wealthier bourgeois elite, roamed the cities hunting down and killing remaining Jacobins. In the Convention, the ascendant moderates wrote a new constitution that limited the right to vote for members of legislative bodies to wealthy property owners, and they removed price controls. The executive functions of the government were placed in the hands of a five-man board known as the *Directory*. Increasingly, the Directory relied on the military to keep order and to protect it from both the *sans-culottes*, who stormed the Convention in May of 1795, and from Royalists who attempted a coup five months later.

When the war against the European coalition began to go badly, conservative factions within the Convention conspired with the ambitious and popular army general Napoleon Bonaparte to overthrow the Directory. On November 9, 1799, the conspirators staged a successful coup, and Napoleon acquired the powers necessary to govern as "first consul." By 1804, Napoleon had rid himself of his co-conspirators and had France proclaimed an "Empire" and himself emperor. He governed France with a mixture of reform and traditionalism and oversaw the military expansion of the French Empire until his defeat at the hands of coalition forces at the Battle of Waterloo in 1815.

Neoclassicism and the French Revolution

The radical break tradition and convention ushered in by the French Revolution was also experienced in the world of art. Artists who sympathized with the democratic and nationalist philosophy of the revolution rejected the dominant rococo aesthetic in favor of a neoclassical style. The neoclassical style took its inspiration from the art of the ancient republics of Greece and Rome. *Neoclassicism* in the late eighteenth century became the dominant style of painters, who chose subjects that conveyed messages of social sacrifice and political courage. They rendered their characters in clean, strong lines that evoked ancient Greek and Roman sculpture, and they avoided decorative details or flourishes that might distract the viewer from the message of the painting. The greatest of the revolutionary era's neoclassical painters was Jacques Louis David. David's *Oath of the Horatii* (1784) is an example of the neoclassical rendering of a classic tale of the ancient world, while his *Death of Marat* (1793) illustrates the use of the neoclassical style to illustrate contemporary themes.

❯ Rapid Review

When Louis XVI was forced by financial difficulties to call the little-used Estates General into session in 1789, the bourgeois representatives of the Third Estate launched a revolution aimed at curbing the power and privilege of the nobility and the clergy, and they attempted to turn France into a constitutional monarchy. Supported by the Paris crowd, the leaders of the newly formed National Assembly nearly succeeded, but foreign intervention, persistent resistance from the nobility, the indecisiveness of Louis, and the development of factions within the Assembly allowed new, more radical leaders to win over the *sans-culottes* that now made up the Parisian crowd and set the revolution on a more radical course. Besieged by a coalition of the European powers and beset with factional strife, the radicals resorted to a Reign of Terror, which eventually consumed them. During the revolution, the radical break with tradition and convention was also experienced in the world of art. Artists who sympathized with the democratic and nationalist philosophy of the revolution rejected the dominant rococo aesthetic in favor of a neoclassical style.

By 1794, the propertied bourgeoisie had reasserted itself and concentrated on restoring order and repealing the gains of the radicals. In 1799, their executive organ known as the Directory was overthrown by a military general, Napoleon Bonaparte. He gradually assumed dictatorial powers and attempted to create a European-wide French Empire. Upon his defeat in 1815 by coalition forces, the French monarchy was restored, and the Kingdom of France was restored to its prerevolutionary boundaries.

› Chapter Review Questions

1. The main obstacle to solving France's financial problems was
   (A) the extravagant lifestyle of Louis XVI
   (B) the unwillingness of the Third Estate to pay more
   (C) the fact that both the nobility and clergy were exempt from most taxes
   (D) foreign wars
   (E) a bad economy

2. The significance of the storming of the Bastille was that
   (A) it put ammunition into the hands of the Paris crowd
   (B) it marked the beginning of a radical phase of the revolution
   (C) it freed important leaders from prison
   (D) it demonstrated that the crowd could be an important ally for the Assembly
   (E) it demonstrated that the crowd was tired of monarchy

3. The Great Fear of the summer of 1789
   (A) politicized the urban workers of Paris
   (B) catalyzed a European coalition against the French revolution
   (C) put greater pressure on the Assembly to enact more radical legislation
   (D) strengthened the position of the nobility
   (E) demonstrated the desperation of an over-taxed peasantry

4. The Civil Constitution of the Clergy
   (A) allied the clergy with the Assembly
   (B) curbed the power of the clergy but alienated many Catholics
   (C) brought the Assembly greater support among the Catholic population
   (D) reaffirmed the central place of the Church in the French government
   (E) made Catholicism illegal in France

5. All of the following precipitated the radical turn of the revolution EXCEPT
   (A) the rise of the *sans-culottes*
   (B) the flight of the king
   (C) the division of the Assembly into factions
   (D) the execution of the king
   (E) the outbreak of war with Austria and Prussia

6. The Reign of Terror
   (A) was necessary, according to Robespierre, to establish a democratic republic
   (B) was opposed by the Parisian crowd
   (C) was aimed only at the nobility
   (D) was anticlerical
   (E) was at its worst in the countryside

7. In Thermidor
   (A) the nobility reasserted its power
   (B) France was defeated by the European coalition
   (C) the French monarchy was restored
   (D) the *sans-culottes* chose to govern France directly
   (E) the moderate portion of the propertied bourgeoisie reasserted its power

8. The Directory turned to the military because
   (A) it lost the support of the *sans-culottes*
   (B) it lost the support of the nobility
   (C) it was threatened by both Jacobin and Royalist opposition
   (D) it feared it would lose the next election
   (E) it was overthrown by a general

› Answers and Explanations

1. **C.** It was the tax exempt status of the nobility and the clergy that prevented the government from gaining access to the majority of wealth in the French economy and, therefore, from solving its financial problems. Choice A is incorrect because, although Louis' lifestyle was a drain on government resources, there was sufficient wealth in France to cover its national debt. Choice B is incorrect because the various classes in the Third Estate were already taxed beyond what they could bear. Choice D is incorrect because, although Louis' foreign wars were a drain on France's finances, there was sufficient wealth in the economy to pay for them. Choice E is incorrect because there was sufficient wealth in the French economy to deal with all of France's financial difficulties.

2. **D.** The storming of the Bastille showed the members of the Assembly that the Parisian crowd could be used as a threat of further violence if its demands were not met. Choice A is incorrect because, despite its reputation, the Bastille did not contain much ammunition. Choice B is incorrect because, although the storming of the Bastille was surprisingly violent, it did not signal radical aims. Choice C is incorrect because, despite the Bastille's reputation, it did not contain many prisoners. Choice E is incorrect because the storming of the Bastille did not signify a loss of faith in the king.

3. **E.** The Great Fear was a traditional peasant uprising; the peasants protested high bread prices and burned records of taxes that they could not pay. Choice A is incorrect because the Great Fear was an uprising that took place in rural areas of France, not the urban areas. Choice B is incorrect because the Great Fear had no effect on France's foreign relations. Choice C is incorrect because, although the rural violence seems to have emboldened the Assembly, the pressure was applied to the king, Church, and nobility as the traditional sources of authority. Choice D is incorrect because the nobility's inability to deal with the financial crisis undermined its authority.

4. **B.** The Civil Constitution of the Clergy required clergymen to take an oath of loyalty to the state, something that their faith prohibited them from doing. The action alienated many French Catholics, who sided with their priests over the National Assembly. Choice A is incorrect because, although the Civil Constitution of the Clergy, in theory, made the clergy government employees and therefore subordinate to the Assembly, the conflict it caused further alienated the clergy. Choice C is incorrect because the Civil Constitution of the Clergy angered most Catholics and made them hostile to the Assembly. Choice D is incorrect because the Civil Constitution of the Clergy sought to subordinate the Church and make it less central in the government of France. Choice E is incorrect because Catholicism remained the dominant religion in France.

5. **D.** The execution of the king was an effect of the radicalization, not a precipitant or cause. Choice A is incorrect because the rise of the *sans-culottes* led to a shift to more radical aims because the *sans-culottes'* hopes of a more egalitarian and economically fair society were more radical than those of the bourgeois members of the Assembly. Choice B is incorrect because the flight of the king eroded the people's confidence in him and forced them to consider a more radical path. Choice C is incorrect because the development of factions within the Assembly meant that each faction had to compete for the support of the Paris crowd and, therefore, be more willing to listen to its radical demands. Choice E is incorrect because the war with Austria and Prussia created an air of crisis in which bolder action seemed required.

6. **A.** Robespierre justified the Terror by arguing that a virtuous, democratic republic could only be established and flourish once the tyrannical enemies of the revolution could be eliminated. Choice B is incorrect because the Reign of Terror was supported by the crowds in big cities such as Paris and Lyon. Choices C and D are incorrect because no one was safe from the accusation of being an "enemy of the revolution"; the Terror was not aimed at either the nobility or the clergy. Choice E is incorrect because the Terror was mostly an urban phenomenon.

7. **E.** In Thermidor, bourgeois moderates reasserted their power after the great leaders of the radical phase had been consumed by their own Terror

tribunals. Choice A is incorrect because the nobility were largely absent from Paris by the time of Thermidor, having had the resources to flee the Terror. Choice B is incorrect because France was not defeated by the coalition until 1815. Choice C is incorrect because the French monarchy was not restored until after the defeat of Napoleon in 1815. Choice D is incorrect because the *sans-culottes* had exhausted their energies by Thermidor and succumbed to the counter-terror of the bourgeois elite.

8. C. The Directory, being a government of bourgeois moderates, turned to the military to protect it from threats posed by both the more radical Jacobins and the more conservative Royalists. Choice A is incorrect because the Directory never had the support of the *sans-culottes*. Choice B is incorrect because the Directory never had the support of the nobility. Choice D is incorrect because the new constitution written by the moderates limited voting rights to the propertied classes who supported the Directory; thus they had no fear of elections. Choice E is incorrect because, although the Directory was eventually overthrown by a general, Bonaparte, it had by that time already been dependent on the military for several years.

UNIT 1 Summary: 1450 to the French Revolutionary and Napoleonic Era

Timeline

1337–1453	Hundred Years War between England and France
1350–1550	Renaissance begins on Italian Peninsula; spreads north throughout Western Europe
1453	Fall of Constantinople, Turkey
1455	Treaty of Lodi among Milan, Naples, and Florence
1455–1485	War of the Roses between Houses of York and Lancaster, England
1469	Marriage of Isabella and Ferdinand in Spain
1486	Pico's *Oration on the Dignity of Man* is published
1487	Portugal's Bartholomew Dias sails around the tip of Africa
1498	Portugal's Vasco da Gama reaches India
1504	Michelangelo's *David* sculpture completed
1513	Machiavelli's *The Prince* is published
1519–1522	Portugal's Magellan leads Spanish Expedition, circumnavigates the globe
1519–1521	Spain's Cortés conquers the Aztecs in Mexico
1534	Henry VIII is declared head of the Church of England
1534	Anabaptists capture the city of Münster, Germany
1536	Calvin's *Institutes of the Christian Religion* is published
1543	Copernicus's *On the Revolution of the Heavenly Spheres* is published
1545–1563	Catholic reform movement's Council of Trent is convened
1555	Peace of Augsburg—"whoever rules; his religion"—is signed by German princes
1598	Edict of Nantes is signed, establishing religious toleration in France
1610	Galileo's *Starry Messenger* is published
1632	Galileo's *Dialogue on the Two Chief Systems of the World* is published
1637	Descartes' *Discourse on Method* is published
1642–1646	English Civil War: Parliament tries to curb power of the monarchy, Church, nobility
1649–1660	The Commonwealth in England is established: King Charles I is executed
1651	Hobbes's *Leviathan* is published
1660–1688	The Restoration in England of the monarchy: Charles II becomes king
1685	Revocation of the Edict of Nantes in France
1687	Newton's *Principia Mathematica* is published
1688	The Glorious Revolution in England: King James II is expelled
1690	Locke's *Second Treatise of Civil Government* is published
1696	Toland's *Christianity Not Mysterious* is published
1733	Voltaire's *Letters Concerning the English Nation* are published
1733	Kay invents the flying shuttle
1740–1748	War of the Austrian Succession
1748	Montesquieu's *Spirit of the Laws* is published
1751–1772	Diderot and d'Alembert's *Encyclopedia* is published
1756–1763	Seven Years War among nine great European countries
1759	Voltaire's *Candide* is published
1762	Rousseau's *Emil* and *The Social Contract* are published
1764	Beccaria's *Crime and Punishment* is published

1770	d'Holbach's *System of Nature* is published
1776	Smith's *Wealth of Nations* is published
1789–1791	French Revolution, moderate phase
1791–1794	French Revolution, radical phase
1792	Wollstonecraft's *Vindication of the Rights of Women* is published
1793	Whitney invents the cotton gin
1794–1799	French Revolution, Thermidor, and the rise of Napoleon

Key Comparisons

1. Italian versus Northern European Renaissance values
2. Theology of Luther and Calvin
3. Nature and power of monarchies in England, France, Spain, Central Europe
4. Economic change in England versus Continental Europe
5. Enlightened despotism versus the radical Enlightenment
6. Moderate versus radical phases of the French Revolution

Thematic Change/Continuity

Economic changes
Development of triangle of trade
Creation of a Spanish Empire in the New World
Establishment of English and French colonies in North America
Shift to cash crops
Enclosure movement in England
Creation of cottage industry in Great Britain

Economic continuities
Agricultural economy with manufacturing and trade supplements

Social/cultural changes
Traditional population cycle broken
Creation and growth of a merchant class
Reformation fractures unity of the Christian Church
Creation of wage labor
Rise of scientific thinking and the Enlightenment

Social continuities
Patriarchal society
Privileges of the aristocracy
Dominance of the Catholic Church in France, Italy, and Spain
Serfdom in Russia

Political changes
Consolidation and centralization of power in the monarchy
Constitutionalism in England and Holland
Establishment of a republic in France

Political continuities
Monarchy as the normal form of government

UNIT 2

The Napoleonic Era to the Present

CHAPTER 15

Napoleonic Europe and the Post-Napoleonic Era, 1800–1848

IN THIS CHAPTER

Summary: Between 1800 and 1848, Europe was temporarily conquered and transformed by Napoleonic France before returning to the embattled rule of its traditional aristocratic houses.

Key Ideas

○ The Napoleonic Code, with its codification of egalitarianism and meritocracy, further eroded the traditional, feudal privileges of the aristocracy and the clergy and fostered a desire for further reform.

○ Resentment caused by Napoleon's rule, and particularly by the restrictions of the Continental System, led to the growth of a spirit of nationalism across Europe.

○ The aristocratic leaders of the coalition that defeated Napoleon constructed "the Concert of Europe" in an attempt to secure the domination of the traditional ruling houses of Europe and to restore the balance of power between them.

○ The conservative aims of the architects of the Concert of Europe ran counter to the growing desire for liberal, democratic reform and nationalist self-determination among the peoples of Europe; the result was a cycle of revolution and repression from 1820 to 1848.

Key Terms

the consulate	Continental System	Concert of Europe
Concordat of 1801	*The Third of May, 1808*	July Ordinances
Napoleonic Code	Grand Army	Frankfurt Assembly
Treaty of Tilsit	Battle of Waterloo	Arc de Triomphe
Battle of Trafalgar	Congress of Vienna	

Introduction

By 1802, Napoleon had crossed the Alps, knocked Austria out of the war, made peace with Russia, and persuaded Great Britain to sign what proved to be a temporary truce in the Peace of Amiens. But by 1805, further efforts to expand the Empire again put France at war with Great Britain and a new coalition. Napoleon would fight on for another 10 years, permanently transforming some aspects of the political and social landscape of Europe, before eventually overextending his reach and meeting defeat at Waterloo. Following Napoleon's defeat, the traditional aristocratic houses of Europe worked in concert to reestablish and defend their dominance over challenges from the forces of liberalism and nationalism.

Post-Revolutionary France and the Napoleonic Code

The French Revolution effectively came to an end with Napoleon's coup d'état in November of 1799 and the establishment of *the consulate*, a three-man executive body. In 1802, Napoleon was acknowledged as the sole executive officer and given the title "first consul for life." By the time Napoleon had himself declared Emperor in 1804, he was well on his way to completing the process, begun by the revolution, of creating a strong central government and administrative uniformity in France.

To solidify his position, Napoleon took the following measures:

- He suppressed royalists and republicans through the use of spies and surprise arrests.
- He censored and controlled the press.
- He regulated what was taught in schools.
- He reconciled France with the Roman Church by signing the *Concordat of 1801*, which stipulated that French clergy would be chosen and paid by the state but consecrated by the pope.

To provide a system of uniform law and administrative policy, Napoleon created the Civil Code of 1804, more widely known as the *Napoleonic Code*. It incorporated many principles that had been espoused during the revolution, some liberal and some conservative. In accordance with liberal principles, the Code:

- safeguarded all forms of property
- upheld equality before the law
- established the right to choose a profession
- guaranteed promotion on merit for employees of the state

In accordance with conservative principles, the Code:

- upheld the ban on working men's associations
- upheld the patriarchal nature of French society by granting men extensive rights over their wives and children

**KEY IDEA**

As Napoleon conquered Europe, he spread the Code across the continent. The overall effect of the Code on Europe was to erode the remnants of the old feudal system by further weakening the traditional power of the nobility and clergy.

Napoleon's Empire

Between 1805 and 1810, Napoleon's forces won a series of battles that allowed France to dominate all of Continental Europe except the Balkan Peninsula. The key victories included:

- the Battle of Austerlitz (December 1805), defeating Russo-Austrian forces
- the Battle of Jena (October 1806), defeating Prussian forces
- the Battle of Friedland (June 1807), defeating Russian forces

The resulting French Empire consisted of some states that were annexed directly into the French Empire, including:

- Belgium
- Germany to the Rhine
- the German coastal regions to the western Baltic
- west-central Italy, including Rome, Genoa, and Trieste

The Empire also included five satellite kingdoms ruled by Napoleon's relatives:

- Holland, ruled by his brother Louis
- Westphalia, ruled by his brother Jérôme
- Spain, ruled by his brother Joseph
- the kingdom of Italy, ruled by his stepson Eugène
- the Kingdom of Naples, ruled by his brother-in-law Joachim Murat

The remaining portions of the Empire consisted of a series of subservient states and confederations, which included:

- the Confederation of the Rhine, eventually consisting of 18 German states that had been part of the now-defunct Holy Roman Empire
- the 19 cantons of the Swiss Confederation
- the Duchy of Warsaw, carved out of Prussia's Polish lands

Those European states that remained independent from France were reluctant allies that simply had no choice but to bow to Napoleon's power. Such states included:

- Austria, where Francis II ruled a kingdom diminished by the disintegration of the Holy Roman Empire
- Prussia, now much smaller for losing its Polish lands and some areas to the Confederation
- Russia, which, following the defeat at Friedland, signed the *Treaty of Tilsit* on July 7, 1807, recognizing France's claims in Europe
- Sweden
- Denmark

The one European nation that still threatened Napoleon was Great Britain, whose superior naval power, as exemplified by its victory over the combined French and Spanish fleets at the *Battle of Trafalgar* on October 21, 1805, made it unconquerable. In order to weaken Britain, Napoleon established what came to be known as the *Continental System*, whereby the Continental European states and kingdoms under French control were forbidden to trade with Britain.

Belgium produced approximately 125,000 tons of steel. By 1913, they produced nearly 32 million tons.

New Sources of Power

Coal

Coal mines provided the most important fuel of the Industrial Revolution. Initially, coal was used to heat homes and to fuel the blast furnaces of the expanding iron and steel industry. Later, demand increased even further as steam engines devoured enormous quantities of coal for fuel. Wherever there were natural deposits of coal, huge mining industries grew around them; agricultural production in these areas was largely abandoned, and the peasants were drawn by the thousands to subterranean work in the mines.

Steam

The perfection of the *steam engine* increased both the scale and the pace of heavy industry by replacing human muscle and hydropower. The steam engine was first used in the early eighteenth century to pump water out of coal mines. It was perfected and made more efficient by Thomas Newcomen and James Watt. The improved version was used to drive machinery as diverse as the bellows of iron forges, looms for textile manufacture, and mills for grain. The shift to steam power allowed entrepreneurs to relocate their mills away from water sources. During the 1820s, entrepreneurs began to exploit the potential of the steam engine as a source of locomotive power. It was first used in the 1820s to power ships. In the 1830s, it was adapted to power railway locomotives.

Electricity

Towards the end of the nineteenth century, the Second Industrial Revolution received another boost from the widespread application of electrical power. More versatile and more easily transported than steam engines, electrical generators were used to power a wide variety of small- and large-scale factories and mills. By 1881, the first large-scale public power plant was constructed in Britain and, in the next two decades, plants were built and lines were run to illuminate houses across Europe.

Petroleum and the Internal Combustion Engine

In 1886, two German engineers, Gottlieb Daimler and Karl Benz, perfected the *internal combustion engine*, which burned petroleum as fuel, and mounted it on a carriage to create the automobile. The early German automobiles were luxury items, but in 1908 the American Henry Ford produced the "Model T," an automobile for the common man, and he mass produced it, creating yet another large factory-based industry. The internal combustion engine, along with its cousin the diesel engine, made transportation and travel cheaper and therefore more widely available.

The Railway Boom

In the 1820s, the British inventor George Stephenson developed a railway line with trains pulled by steam-powered locomotives. The Stockton and Darlington Line opened in 1825, and another major line went from Liverpool to Manchester by 1830. The speed and reliability of the new locomotives made them a huge success and began what would come to be known as the *railway boom* of the 1830s and 1840s, as Britain's competitors quickly developed their own systems. The development of railway systems further spurred the development of heavy industries, as railroads facilitated the speedy transportation of iron and steel while simultaneously consuming large quantities of both.

The Reciprocal Nature of Heavy Industry

The four major components of the Second Industrial Revolution—the iron and steel industry, the coal industry, steam power, and the railways—had a reciprocal effect on one another:

- The *iron and steel industry* required improvements in the steam engine to run its blast furnaces, greater amounts of coal to fuel the engines, and railways to transport both the coal and the smelted iron and steel.
- The *coal industry* required more and improved steam engines to pump water out of the mines and to power digging machinery; it also required railways to transport the coal.
- The *steam power industry* required iron and steel to forge the engines, coal to run them, and railways to transport them.
- The *railways* required huge amounts of steel and iron for the construction of the engines, cars, and tracks, steam engines to drive the locomotives, and coal to fuel the engines.

Working together, these four industries created an ever-increasing cycle of supply and demand that drove the Second Industrial Revolution of the nineteenth century.

The Spread of Industrialization

The process of industrialization varied greatly across Europe. The Second Industrial Revolution started in Great Britain and spread eastward across the continent of Europe.

Great Britain Industrializes First

Great Britain had several natural advantages that help to explain why it was first and why it held the lead for more than a century:

- It had a well-developed commercial economy that created a merchant class with capital to invest.
- Britain's extensive river system was ideal for transporting goods throughout the country.
- The country was rich in coal and iron deposits, two key components of the Second Industrial Revolution.
- Unlike much of Europe, Great Britain had no internal tariffs to inhibit trade.
- It had a uniform and stable monetary system and a national banking system.

Industrialization Spread Eastward from Britain

As the Industrial Revolution spread to the Continent, it moved eastward in a way that can be described by three generalizations:

- The farther east it went, the later the process began; for example, France industrialized later than Britain, Germany later than France, and Russia last.
- The farther east it went, the faster the process occurred (because innovations could be copied or purchased, rather than invented and developed); for example, France industrialized at a faster pace than Britain, Germany faster still, and Russia fastest of all.

- The farther east it went, the more the government was involved (because governments feared the political and military effects of falling behind their rivals, they invested heavily in industrialization); for example, there was no government involvement in the industrialization of Britain, some in France, more in Germany, and in Russia industrialization was almost totally government driven.

Russia Lags Behind

By 1850, large-scale industrialization had spread to northeastern France, Belgium, the northern German states, and northwestern Italy. The southern, central, and eastern areas of Europe—such as Italy, Poland, and Russia—lagged behind due to insufficient natural resources and the lack of a commercialized agricultural system to allow for a mobile workforce. These areas retained their rural character.

Russia lagged behind until two successive tsars—Alexander III (1881–1894) and Nicholas II (1894–1917)—determined that Russia should become an industrial power. In 1892, Alexander III appointed Serge Witte as finance minister. Under Witte's leadership, Russia became an iron- and steel-producing nation. By the end of the nineteenth century, factories had arisen in Moscow and St Petersburg. By 1904, the construction of a trans-Siberian railroad that linked the European portion of Russia with the East was nearly completed.

Social Effects

The Second Industrial Revolution transformed European society in significant ways:

- *Urbanization* increased rapidly, as the population moved into hastily built housing in cities in order to be nearer to the factories.
- *Families* were separated as the place of work shifted from the home to factories.
- *Work* lost its seasonal quality, as workers were required to follow a routine schedule.
- The *pace of work*, driven by machines, increased dramatically.
- The overall *health* of the workforce declined because of the harsh and unhealthy conditions of the factories.
- The *availability of work* became unpredictable as it rose and fell with the demand for goods.
- Gradually, *women* who had first been drawn into cities to work in the factories lost their manufacturing jobs as machines decreased the demand for labor; cut off from their families, many had no other option than prostitution.
- *Artisans* and *craftsmen* lost their livelihoods, unable to compete with the lower cost of mass-produced goods.
- The traditional impediment to *marriage*, which was the need for land, disappeared and people began to marry younger.
- A much greater portion of the population could afford *factory-made goods*.
- There was further *change in the class structure* as industrialization created both a class of newly wealthy industrialists and a precariously situated lower middle class of managers and clerks.
- Close working and living conditions produced a sense of *class consciousness* among the working class.

Artistic Movements in the Industrial Age

Artistic expression in the industrial age was dominated by three styles: *realism, impressionism,* and *postimpressionism.*

In the middle of the nineteenth century, young painters rejected both the romantic fantasies and the glorification of the past that had interested their predecessors. The realists sought instead to accurately and honestly render the life around them in meticulous detail. A primary example of the realist movement is the work of Gustav Courbet. In his *Burial at Ornans* (1849–1850), for example, Courbet depicted the members of a small village burying one of its community members without trying to convey any particular emotion or moral message.

By the late nineteenth century, realism gave way to the impressionist movement. The impressionists desired to render not the reality of the scene but the reality of the visual experience. The visual experience, the impressionists believed, consisted of the interaction between light, color, and human perception. Accordingly, they created images that evoked the visual experience by painting with visible brush strokes and heightened color. Édouard Manet's *Impressionisme soleil levant,* or *Impressionism, Sunrise* (1872), is often cited as the work that gave impressionism its name. Other influential impressionist painters of the period were Pierre Auguste Renoir, Edgar Degas, and Claude Monet.

After about a decade, a new generation of painters began to reject the limitations imposed by the impressionist movement. The result was a movement often known as postimpressionism, which combined the visible brush strokes, heightened color, and real-life subject matter of impressionism with an emphasis on geometric form and unnatural color to create a more emotionally expressive effect. Perhaps the most famous example of postimpressionist painting is Vincent van Gogh's *Starry Night* (1889). Other influential postimpressionist painters of the late nineteenth century include Georges Seurat, Mary Cassatt, Paul Gauguin, and Paul Cézanne.

Science in the Industrial Age

Advances in gas theory and a spirit of scientific realism dominated the physical sciences in the nineteenth century. Physicists in this period concentrated on providing a scientific understanding of the processes that drove the engines of the Industrial Revolution. In the middle of the nineteenth century, physicists such as the German Rudolph Clausius and the Scotsman James Maxwell developed the *kinetic theory of gases.* Their theory envisioned gas pressure and temperature as resulting from a certain volume of molecules in motion. Such an approach allowed them to analyze, and therefore to measure and predict, pressure and temperature statistically. Later in the century, physicists such as Robert Mayer, Hermann von Helmholtz, and William Thompson pursued this kind of statistical analysis to articulate the laws of thermodynamics.

The success of the "matter in motion" models in physics created a wider philosophical movement that argued that all natural phenomena could and should be understood as the result of matter and motion. The movement, known as *materialism,* was first articulated by a trinity of German natural philosophers: Karl Vogt, Jakob Moleschott, and Ludwig Büchner. By the end of the nineteenth century, materialism had become a foundational assumption of the scientific view of the world.

The natural sciences in the nineteenth century were dominated by Charles Darwin's theory of evolution by natural selection. As a young man, Darwin had sailed around the globe as the naturalist for the H.M.S. *Beagle*. During the *Beagle*'s five-year voyage, commencing December 27, 1831, and ending October 2, 1836, Darwin collected specimens for shipment home to England and made observations on the flora and fauna of the many continents he explored. Twenty-three years later, he published a book titled *On the Origin of Species by Means of Natural Selection or the Preservation of Favoured Races in the Struggle for Life*. In *Origin,* Darwin offered an explanation of the two questions at the heart of nineteenth-century natural science: why was there so much diversity among living organisms, and why did organisms seem to "fit" into the environments in which they lived? Darwin's answer, unlike earlier answers that referred to God's will and a process of creation, was materialist in nature. He argued that both the wide range of diversity and the environmental "fit" of living organisms to their environment were due to a process that he termed "natural selection." The fact that many more organisms were born than could survive led, Darwin explained, to a constant "struggle for existence" between individual living organisms. Only those individuals that survived the struggle passed their physical characteristics on to their offspring. Over millions of years, that simple process had caused populations of organisms to evolve in ways that produced both the amazing diversity and the environmental "fit."

Origin went through six editions, and Darwin's theory became the central organizing principle of the science of biology, which developed in the late nineteenth and early twentieth centuries. In 1871 Darwin published *The Descent of Man*, which explained Darwin's views on how human beings had come into existence through the process of natural selection.

❯ Rapid Review

Between 1820 and 1900, the demand for goods on the part of a steadily increasing population was met by entrepreneurs who created the factory system. The new system standardized and increased industrial production. As the century went on, the development of four interrelated heavy industries—iron and steel, coal mining, steam power, and railroads—combined to drive Europe's economy to unprecedented heights, constituting a Second Industrial Revolution. The urbanization, standardization of work, and effects of the class system wrought by the Second Industrial Revolution significantly transformed social life in Europe.

The changes wrought by the Industrial Revolution provoked new developments in both the arts and sciences. In the arts, the three related styles of realism, impressionism, and postimpressionism developed. Progress in the physical sciences manifested itself in the development of the kinetic theory of gases, while the natural sciences were dominated by Charles Darwin's innovative theory of evolution by natural selection.

› Chapter Review Questions

1. Which of the following was NOT an effect of the division of labor?
   (A) It increased the supply of labor available to manufacturers.
   (B) It raised wages for manufacturing workers.
   (C) It increased the volume that manufacturers could produce.
   (D) It allowed manufacturers to sell their products more cheaply.
   (E) It allowed manufacturers to increase their profits.

2. The invention of new forms of power such as steam and electricity
   (A) led to the creation of the factory system
   (B) facilitated the invention of the automobile
   (C) decreased demand for coal
   (D) allowed manufacturers to relocate their mills away from water sources
   (E) doomed the shipping industry

3. In general, the Second Industrial Revolution in Europe
   (A) began on the Continent and spread in all directions
   (B) took place in Great Britain
   (C) took place more slowly in Eastern Europe
   (D) was stimulated by government investment in Western Europe
   (E) took place later but more rapidly in Eastern Europe

4. The railway boom of the 1830s and 1840s
   (A) increased demand for steel but decreased demand for coal
   (B) did not affect the demand for steel
   (C) increased demand for both steel and coal
   (D) increased demand for coal but decreased demand for steel
   (E) did not affect the demand for coal

5. Which of the following was an advantage enjoyed by Great Britain that helps to explain why the Second Industrial Revolution originated there?
   (A) an extensive river system
   (B) the lack of internal trade tariffs
   (C) a well-developed commercial economy
   (D) natural resources
   (E) all of the above

6. In Russia
   (A) industrialization occurred rapidly under the direction of the government
   (B) industrialization was a gradual process
   (C) textile production was crucial to the industrialization process
   (D) railway construction was deemed unnecessary for industrialization
   (E) industrialization occurred early and rapidly due to trade with the East

7. One of the ways in which the Second Industrial Revolution affected the social structure of Europe was to produce
   (A) a more even distribution of wealth
   (B) a lower middle class of managers and clerks
   (C) poor people
   (D) a merchant class
   (E) gender equity

8. As a result of the Second Industrial Revolution, the majority of skilled artisans and craftsmen
   (A) prospered
   (B) became managers in factories
   (C) lost their livelihoods
   (D) moved to towns and cities
   (E) were women

> Answers and Explanations

1. **B.** The division of labor increased the supply of labor available, thereby causing wages for manufacturing workers to fall, not increase. Choice A is incorrect because the division of labor *did* increase the supply of labor available to manufacturers by making all jobs unskilled jobs. Choice C is incorrect because the division of labor increased volume by speeding up the manufacturing process. Choices D and E are incorrect because the combination of increased productivity and cheaper labor allowed manufacturers to sell their products more cheaply and still increase their profits through increased volume.

2. **D.** The shift to steam and electrical power and away from hydropower allowed manufacturers to move away from water sources and move to more convenient locations. Choice A is incorrect because the factory system is a way of organizing labor; it is not dependent on a particular source of power. Choice B is incorrect because the invention of the automobile was facilitated by the invention of the internal combustion engine, not steam and electricity. Choice C is incorrect because both steam engines and electrical generators relied on coal for fuel, thereby *increasing* demand for it. Choice E is incorrect because, although the invention of the steam locomotive led to a railway boom, the application of it to ships allowed the shipping industry to prosper as well.

3. **E.** The Second Industrial Revolution originated in Britain and took place later but more rapidly in Eastern Europe, which was able to copy and purchase key industrial innovations. Choice A is incorrect because the Second Industrial Revolution originated in Great Britain and spread *eastward* across Europe, not in all directions. Choice B is incorrect because the Second Industrial Revolution was not unique to or contained in Britain. Choice C is incorrect because the Second Industrial Revolution occurred *later* but more rapidly in Eastern Europe. Choice D is incorrect because there was more government investment involved in *Eastern* Europe where governments feared falling economically and technologically behind their Western rivals.

4. **C.** The railway boom increased demand for steel because steel was required for the manufacture of railway engines, cars, and rails; it also increased demand for coal because coal was the fuel for steam locomotives. Choices A and D are incorrect because the railway boom increased demand for *both* steel and coal. Choice B is incorrect because the railway boom did affect the demand for steel: It increased demand. Similarly, choice E is incorrect because the railway boom did affect the demand for coal: it increased demand.

5. **E.** All of the choices are correct. Britain's extensive river system (choice A) allowed it to move raw materials and manufactured goods with relative ease. The lack of internal trade tariffs (choice B) allowed manufacturers to buy and transport materials without tariffs eating into their profit. Britain's well-developed commercial economy (choice C) provided both a merchant class and capital for investment. Finally, Britain's rich deposits of iron and coal (choice D: Britain's natural resources) provided the necessary raw materials.

6. **A.** Industrialization occurred rapidly in Russia under the direction of finance minister Serge Witte. Choice B is incorrect because Russia industrialized *later* than its European rivals but *very rapidly*, with most of the process taking place between 1892 and 1904. Choice C is incorrect because Russian industrialization was driven by its railway construction and steel production, not by its textile industry. Choice D is incorrect because the construction of the trans-Siberian railway was *very* necessary—indeed, a crucial part of Russian industrialization. Choice E is incorrect because again, Russia did *not* industrialize early; it industrialized *later* than its European counterparts.

7. **B.** The factory system that was characteristic of the Second Industrial Revolution required and produced a class of managers and clerks whose pay and status located them precariously at the lower end of the middle class. Choice A is incorrect because the Second Industrial Revolution did nothing to distribute wealth *more evenly*

throughout the population; instead, it made a *relatively small number* of industrialists and entrepreneurs fabulously wealthy and made some workers better off than before. Choice C is incorrect because the poor had existed before the Second Industrial Revolution. Similarly, choice D is incorrect because a merchant class existed in Europe prior to the Second Industrial Revolution. Choice E is incorrect because, although many women initially found work in the factories of the Second Industrial Revolution, they were not paid equally and were the first to be let go when increasing mechanization decreased the demand for labor.

8. **C.** Because factory-produced goods could be made in greater quantity and sold more cheaply, most skilled artisans and craftsmen were unable to compete and lost their livelihoods. Choice A is incorrect because the skilled artisans and craftsmen did *not* prosper; instead, they faced either unemployment or factory work at wages much lower than the profits they had made in their shops. Choice B is incorrect because a factory manager was a new breed whose job was to keep the factory running at peak efficiency and whose skills were unrelated to those of the old artisans and craftsmen. Choice D is incorrect because, unlike their agricultural counterparts, artisans and craftsmen had *always* located themselves in towns and cities. Choice E is incorrect because neither men nor women were being drawn into these professions during the Second Industrial Revolution.

CHAPTER 17

The Rise of New Ideologies in the Nineteenth Century

IN THIS CHAPTER

Summary: Nineteenth-century European intellectuals coped with the changes and challenges wrought by the French and Industrial Revolutions by fashioning various ideologies, which were consistent sets of beliefs that prescribed specific social and political actions.

Key Ideas

- ✪ *Conservatism* held that tradition was the only trustworthy guide to social and political action.
- ✪ *Liberalism* asserted that the task of government was to promote individual liberty.
- ✪ *Romanticism* urged the cultivation of sentiment and emotion by reconnecting with nature and with the past.
- ✪ *Nationalism* asserted that a nation was a natural, organic entity whose people shared a cultural identity and a historical destiny.
- ✪ *Anarchism* saw the modern state and its institutions as the enemy of individual freedom.
- ✪ *Socialism* sought to reorder society in ways that would end or minimize competition, foster cooperation, and allow the working classes to share in the wealth being produced by industrialization.
- ✪ *Communism* was dedicated to the creation of a class-free society through the abolition of private property.
- ✪ *Social Darwinism* asserted that competition was natural and necessary for the evolutionary progress of a society.

Key Terms

conservatism	utopian socialism	means of production
liberalism	technocratic socialism	bourgeoisie
laissez-faire	psychological socialism	proletariat
iron law of wages	industrial socialism	social Darwinism
nationalism	scientific socialism	eugenics
Romanticism	communism	anarchism

Introduction

The French Revolution had challenged Europeans' beliefs in and assumptions about society; the Second Industrial Revolution seemed to be transforming society at a dizzying pace. In order to cope with these changes, and to answer the questions posed by them, nineteenth-century European intellectuals created, or elaborated on, a variety of ideologies, each claiming to hold the key to creating the best society possible.

Conservatism

In the nineteenth century, *conservatism* was the ideology that asserted that tradition is the only trustworthy guide to social and political action. Conservatives argued that traditions were time-tested, organic solutions to social and political problems. Accordingly, nineteenth-century conservatives supported monarchy, the hierarchical class system dominated by the aristocracy, and the Church. They opposed innovation and reform, arguing that the French Revolution had demonstrated that they led directly to revolution and chaos. Supporters of the conservative position originally came from the traditional elites of Europe, the landed aristocracy.

The British writer and statesman Edmund Burke is often considered "the father of conservatism," as his *Reflections the Revolutions in France* (1790) seemed to predict the bloodshed and chaos that characterized the radical phase of the revolution. The French writer Joseph de Maistre's *Essay on the General Principle of Political Constitutions* (1814) is a prime nineteenth-century example of conservatism's opposition to constitutionalism and reform.

Liberalism

Nineteenth-century *liberalism* was the ideology that asserted that the task of government was to promote individual liberty. Liberals viewed many traditions as impediments to that freedom and, therefore, campaigned for reform. Pointing to the accomplishments of the Scientific Revolution, nineteenth-century liberals asserted that there were God-given, natural rights and laws that men could discern through the use of reason. Accordingly, they supported innovation and reform (in contrast to conservatives), arguing that many traditions were simply superstitions. They promoted constitutional monarchy over absolutism, and they campaigned for an end to the traditional privileges of the aristocracy and the Church in favor of a *meritocracy* and middle-class participation in government. Supporters of liberalism originally came from the middle class.

Two British philosophers, John Locke and Adam Smith, are usually thought of as the forefathers of liberalism. In *The Second Treatise of Government* (1690), Locke made the argument for the existence of God-given natural rights and asserted that the proper goal of government was to protect and promote individual liberty. In *Wealth of Nations* (1776), Smith made the case for the existence of economic laws which guided human behavior like an "invisible hand." Smith also promoted the notion of *laissez-faire*, which stated that governments should not try to interfere with the natural workings of an economy, a notion that became one of the basic tenets of liberalism in the nineteenth century.

Late-eighteenth- and early-nineteenth-century thinkers extended and hardened Smith's ideas. In *An Essay on the Principle of Population* (1798), Thomas Malthus asserted that free and constant competition would always be the norm in human societies because the human species would always reproduce at a greater rate than the food supply. By midcentury, liberal economic thinkers alleged that there was an *iron law of wages*, which argued that competition between workers for jobs would always, in the long run, force wages to sink to subsistence levels. The "law" is sometimes attributed to the English economist David Ricardo, but was promoted most prominently by the German sociologist Ferdinand LaSalle.

As the nineteenth century progressed, liberalism evolved. The followers of the English philosopher Jeremy Bentham espoused *utilitarianism*, which argued that all human laws and institutions ought to be judged by their usefulness in promoting "the greatest good for the greatest number" of people. Accordingly, they supported reforms to sweep away traditional institutions that failed the test and to create new institutions that would pass it. Utilitarians tended to be more supportive of government intervention than other liberals. For example, they drafted and supported new legislation to limit the hours that women and children could work in factories and to regulate the sanitary conditions of factories and mines.

Early-nineteenth-century liberals had been leery of democracy, arguing that the masses had to be educated before they could usefully contribute to the political life of a country. But by midcentury, liberals began advocating democracy, reasoning that the best way to identify the greatest good for the greatest number was to maximize the number of people voting. The best example of midcentury utilitarian thought is John Stuart Mill's *On Liberty* (1859), which argued for freedom of thought and democracy but also warned against the tyranny of the majority. Together, Mill and his companion Harriet Taylor led the liberal campaign for women's rights, Taylor publishing *The Enfranchisement of Women* (anonymously in 1851) and Mill publishing *The Subjection of Women* (1869).

Romanticism

Romanticism was a reaction to the Enlightenment and industrialization. The nineteenth-century Romantics rebelled against the Enlightenment's emphasis on reason and urged the cultivation of sentiment and emotion. Fittingly, Romantics mostly avoided political tracts and expressed themselves mostly through art and literature. Their favorite subject was nature.

The roots of Romanticism are often traced back to the works of Jean Jacques Rousseau because in *Emil* (1762), he had argued that humans were born essentially good and virtuous but were easily corrupted by society, and that the early years of a child's education should be spent developing the senses, sensibilities, and sentiments. Another source of Romanticism was the German *Sturm und Drang* (Storm and Stress) movement of the late eighteenth century, exemplified by Johann Wolfgang von Goethe's *The Sorrows of Young Werther* (1774), which glorified the "inner experience" of the sensitive individual.

In response to the rationalism of the Enlightenment (and to some degree, of liberalism) the Romantics offered the solace of nature. Good examples of this vein of nineteenth-century Romanticism are the works of the English poets William Wordsworth and Samuel Taylor Coleridge, who extolled the almost mystical qualities of the Lake District of northwest England.

Romantic painters like John Constable in England and Karl Friedrich Schinkel in Germany offered inspiring landscapes and images of a romanticized past. Beethoven, Chopin, and Wagner expressed the imaginative, intuitive spirit of Romanticism in music.

Nationalism

Nationalism, in the nineteenth century, was the ideology that asserted that a nation was a natural, organic entity whose people were bound together by shared language, customs, and history. Nationalists argued that each nation had natural boundaries, shared cultural traits, and a historical destiny to fulfill. Accordingly, nineteenth-century nationalists in existing nation states like Britain and France argued for strong, expansionist foreign policies. Nationalists in areas like Germany and Italy argued for national unification and the expulsion of foreign rulers.

In the early nineteenth century, nationalism was allied with liberalism. Both shared a spirit of optimism, believing that their goals represented the inevitable, historical progress of humankind. In the nonunified lands of Germany and Italy, occupation by Napoleonic France had helped to foster a spirit of nationalism. Under Napoleon's rule, Germans and Italians came to think of their own disunity as a weakness. The best early examples of this kind of nationalism are the German writers Johann Gottlieb Fichte, whose *Addresses to German Nation* (1808) urged the German people to unite in order to fulfill their historical role in bringing about the ultimate progress of humanity, and Georg Wilhelm Friedrich Hegel, who argued that every nation had a historical role to play in the unfolding of the universe and that Germany's time to take center stage in that drama had arrived.

Like the Romantics, early nineteenth-century nationalists emphasized the role that environment played in shaping the character of a nation, and sentimentalized the past. A good example of Romantic nationalism is the work of Ernst Moritz Arndt, who urged Germans to unify through a shared heritage and through love of all things German. Strains of Romanticism can also be seen in the work of the great Italian nationalist of the early nineteenth century, Giuseppe Mazzini, whose nationalist movement, Young Italy, made appeals to unity based on natural affinities and a shared soul.

Anarchism

Anarchism was the nineteenth-century ideology that saw the state and its governing institutions as the ultimate enemy of individual freedom. Early anarchists drew inspiration from the writings of Pierre Joseph Proudhon, who argued that man's freedom had been progressively curtailed by industrialization and larger, more centralized governments. Anarchy had the greatest appeal in those areas of Europe where governments were most oppressive; in the nineteenth century, that meant Russia. There, Mikhail Bakunin, the son of a Russian noble, organized secret societies whose goal was to destroy the Russian state forever. Throughout Europe, nineteenth-century anarchists engaged in acts of political terrorism, particularly attempts to assassinate high-ranking government officials.

Utopian Socialism

Nineteenth-century socialism was the ideology that emphasized the collective over the individual and challenged the liberal's notion that competition was natural. Socialists sought to reorder society in ways that would end or minimize competition, foster cooperation, and allow the working classes to share in the wealth being produced by industrialization.

The earliest forms of socialism have come to be called *utopian socialism* for the way in which they envisioned, and sometimes tried to set up, ideal communities (or utopias) where work and its fruit were shared equitably. In the nineteenth century, there were three distinct forms of utopian socialism, described in the following sections.

Technocratic Socialism

This type of socialism envisioned a society run by technical experts who managed resources efficiently and in a way that was best for all. The most prominent nineteenth-century advocate of technocratic socialism was a French aristocrat, Henri Comte de Saint-Simon, who renounced his title during the French Revolution and spent his life championing the progress of technology and his vision of a society organized and run by scientifically trained managers or "technocrats."

Psychological Socialism

This type of socialism saw a conflict between the structure of society and the natural needs and tendencies of human beings. Its leading nineteenth-century advocate was Charles Fourier, who argued that the ideal society was one organized on a smaller, more human scale. He advocated the creation of self-sufficient communities, called *phalansteries*, of no more than 1,600 people, in which the inhabitants did work that suited them best.

Industrial Socialism

This type of socialism argued that it was possible to have a productive, profitable industrial enterprise without exploiting workers. Its leading advocate was a Scottish textile manufacturer, Robert Owen. Owen set out to prove his thesis by setting up industrial communities like the New Lanark cotton mill in Scotland and, later, a larger manufacturing community in New Harmony, Indiana, that paid higher wages and provided food, shelter, and clothing at reasonable prices.

Scientific Socialism and Communism

By the middle of the nineteenth century, the exploitation of European workers had grown more evident and the dreams of the utopian socialists seemed less plausible. In their place arose a form of socialism based on what its adherents claimed was a scientific analysis of society's workings. The most famous and influential of the self-proclaimed scientific socialists was the German revolutionary Karl Marx. In *The Communist Manifesto* (1848), a slim pamphlet distributed to workers throughout Europe, Marx and his collaborator Freidrich Engels argued that "all history is the history of class struggle." In the *Manifesto*, and later in the much larger *Capital* (vol. 1, 1867), Marx argued that a human being's relationship to the *means of production* gave him a social identity. In the industrial age of the nineteenth century, Marx argued, only two classes existed: the *bourgeoisie*, who controlled the means of production; and the *proletariat*, who sold their labor for wages. The key point in Marx's analysis was that the bourgeoisie exploited the proletariat because competition demanded it; if a factory owner chose to treat his workers more generously, then he would have to charge more for his goods and his competitors would drive him out of business.

Marx's analysis led him to adopt a position that came to be known as *communism*, which declared that the only way to end social exploitation was to abolish private property. If no one could claim to own the means of production, then there could be no distinction between owner and worker; all class distinctions would disappear, and the workers would be free to distribute the benefits of production more equally.

Social Darwinism

The socialist notion that competition was unnatural was countered by yet another nineteenth-century ideology that came to be known as *social Darwinism*. In 1859, the British naturalist Charles Darwin published *The Origin of Species*, which argued that all living things had descended from a few simple forms. In *Origin*, Darwin described a complex process in which biological inheritance, environment, and competition for resources combined over millions of years to produce the amazing diversity in living forms that exists in the world.

The social philosopher Herbert Spencer argued that Darwin's theory proved that competition was not only natural, but necessary for the progress of a society. Spencer coined the phrase "survival of the fittest" (a phrase adopted by Darwin in the sixth and final edition of *Origin*) and argued along liberal lines that government intervention in social issues interfered with natural selection and, therefore, with progress. By the last decades of the nineteenth century, social Darwinism was being used to argue that imperialism, the competition between nations for control of the globe, was a natural and necessary step in the evolution of the human species. *Eugenics*, the notion that a progressive, scientific nation should plan and manage the biological reproduction of its population as carefully as it planned and managed its economy, also flourished in the last decades of the nineteenth century.

❯ Rapid Review

In the nineteenth century, intellectuals articulated numerous ideologies in order to make sense of a rapidly changing world. By the end of the century, a thinking person could choose from or create combinations from a spectrum of ideologies that included and can be summarized as follows:

- conservatism—championing tradition
- liberalism—urging reform
- Romanticism—encouraging the cultivation of sentiment and emotion
- nationalism—preaching cultural unity
- anarchism—scheming to bring down the state
- socialism—trying to design a more equitable society
- communism—working to abolish private property
- social Darwinism—advocating the benefits of unfettered competition

› Chapter Review Questions

1. In the nineteenth century, conservatives
   - (A) argued that governments should not interfere with the natural tendencies of the economy
   - (B) emphasized the development of sentiment and emotion
   - (C) favored constitutional monarchy
   - (D) supported the privileges of the aristocracy and clergy
   - (E) espoused utilitarianism

2. Nineteenth-century Romanticism can be understood as a reaction against
   - (A) conservatism
   - (B) changes wrought by the Enlightenment and industrialization
   - (C) nationalism
   - (D) social Darwinism
   - (E) scientific socialism

3. Which of the following is NOT true of nineteenth-century liberalism?
   - (A) It asserted that the task of government was to promote individual liberty.
   - (B) It opposed government intervention in the economy.
   - (C) It supported the privileges of the clergy.
   - (D) It believed in the existence of natural laws that governed human behavior.
   - (E) It drew its support primarily from the middle classes.

4. Goethe's *The Sorrows of Young Werther* is an example of
   - (A) the anarchist movement
   - (B) socialism
   - (C) early liberalism
   - (D) nationalism
   - (E) the *Sturm und Drang* movement

5. Utilitarians differed from other liberals by
   - (A) supporting government regulation of working conditions in factories
   - (B) calling for the abolition of many traditional institutions
   - (C) believing in the existence of natural laws that govern human behavior
   - (D) calling for the abolition of private property
   - (E) regarding many religious practices as mere superstitions

6. Nineteenth-century anarchists were most active in
   - (A) Britain
   - (B) France
   - (C) Russia
   - (D) Italy
   - (E) Germany

7. Industrial socialism
   - (A) advocated the abolition of private property
   - (B) sought to create a profitable industrial enterprise without exploiting workers
   - (C) called for the creation of *phalansteries*
   - (D) advocated a return to small-scale production by skilled artisans
   - (E) advocated government regulation of working conditions

8. The idea that competition was natural and necessary for social progress was promoted by
   - (A) Karl Marx
   - (B) Charles Darwin
   - (C) Charles Fourier
   - (D) Herbert Spencer
   - (E) Robert Owen

› Answers and Explanations

1. **D.** The conservatives' belief in traditions as time-tested and organic solutions to social and political problems led them to support the traditional privileges of the aristocracy and the clergy. Choice A is incorrect because the position that government should not interfere with the natural tendencies of the economy was a *liberal* position, not a conservative one, in the nineteenth century. Choice B is incorrect because it was the *Romantics* who emphasized the development of sentiment and emotion. Choice C is incorrect because conservatives' belief in the importance of tradition led them to *oppose* constitutionalism. Choice E is incorrect because utilitarianism was espoused by mid-to-late-nineteenth-century *liberals*.

2. **B.** The emphasis on sentiment and emotion by nineteenth-century Romantics can be understood as a reaction against the Enlightenment's emphasis on reason; their glorification of nature can be understood as a reaction to industrialization. Choice A is incorrect because the conservatives' belief in the importance of traditional forms of life often put them in line with, not against, the Romantics. Choice C is incorrect because early nineteenth-century nationalists *had* Romantic tendencies, as they emphasized the role that environment played in shaping the character of a nation, and often sentimentalized the past. Choices D and E are incorrect because both social Darwinism and scientific socialism developed *after* Romanticism.

3. **C.** Nineteenth-century liberalism *opposed* the traditional privileges of the clergy as an anachronism that stood in the way of individual liberty. The other four answers are true of nineteenth-century liberalism, which believed that the task of government was to promote individual liberty (choice A), and in the existence of natural laws that governed human behavior (choice D). They opposed government intervention in the economy (choice B) because they thought it only got in the way of the operation of those natural laws. Because of their agenda for revoking the traditional privileges of the aristocracy and the clergy, liberals drew their support primarily from the middle classes (choice E) to whom such privileges were denied.

4. **E.** Johann Wolfgang von Goethe's *The Sorrows of Young Werther* (1774) is an example of the German *Sturm und Drang* (storm and stress) movement of the late eighteenth century. Its glorification of the "inner experience" of the sensitive individual was a forerunner of nineteenth-century Romanticism. Choice A is incorrect because, although both Goethe's *Sorrows* and anarchism share a romanticized view of preindustrial society, the anarchist movement was dedicated to the eradication of the modern nation state, a theme that is not present in *Sorrows*. Choice B is incorrect because socialists were more concerned with designing a harmonious and equitable society than with inner life and sentimentality. Choice C is incorrect because the early liberals emphasized the reform of society based on reason, not sentiment and emotion. Choice D is incorrect because, although *Sorrows* emphasized the power of environment to shape the individual, it did not emphasize the shared cultural identity of nations.

5. **A.** The utilitarians' belief that usefulness (i.e., the creation of the greatest good for the greatest number) ought to be the test for all laws and institutions led them to depart from the standard liberal opposition to government intervention in economic matters and to advocate the regulation of working conditions. Choice B is incorrect because utilitarians *joined with* all liberals in calling for the abolition of many traditional institutions on the basis that they inhibited social progress. Similarly, choice C is incorrect because utilitarians *shared* the liberal belief in the existence of natural laws that governed human behavior and assumed that natural laws were causing some laws and institutions to be useful and others to be useless. Choice D is incorrect because *liberals* did not call for the abolition of private property; that was a *communist* position. Choice E is incorrect because the utilitarians were *in line with* other liberals in believing that many specific religious practices were mere superstitions and that society should be

organized in harmony with natural laws based on reason.

6. **C.** Because they believed that the modern nation state and its powerful government institutions were the enemies of individual freedom, anarchists dedicated themselves to carrying out terror campaigns designed to disrupt and, if possible, bring down governments. There was, therefore, a correlation between the repressive nature of government and the activity of anarchists. Because nineteenth-century Russia had the most repressive regime, it had the most active anarchist movement.

7. **B.** Industrial socialists like Robert Owen sought to create manufacturing communities that paid *higher wages* and provided a *good quality of life* for its workers while still making a profit. Choice A is incorrect because the abolition of private property was advocated only by *communists*, not by socialists. Choice C is incorrect because the creation of *phalansteries* (which were communities of no more than 1,600 people in which the inhabitants did work that suited them best) was advocated by Charles Fourier, a *psychological* socialist, rather than an *industrial* socialist.

Choice D is incorrect because industrial socialism sought to end the *exploitation* of workers, not the abandonment of industrial modes of *production*. Choice E is incorrect because industrial socialists saw the *factory owner*, not the *government*, as the proper agent of reform.

8. **D.** The idea that competition was natural and necessary for social progress was promoted by social Darwinists, whose leading advocate was Herbert Spencer. Choice A is incorrect because Karl Marx was the founder of communism, which argued against competition because the control of the means of production was the root of class conflict. Choice B is incorrect because Charles Darwin confined his speculations to the role that competition for natural resources played in creating *biological diversity* and remained skeptical about the claims of the so-called social Darwinists. Choice C is incorrect because Charles Fourier was a psychological socialist who believed that human nature was essentially *cooperative*, not competitive. Similarly, choice E is incorrect because Robert Owen was an industrial socialist who sought to build industrial communities where people labored in a spirit of *cooperation*.

CHAPTER 18

Nationalism and Statebuilding, 1848–1900

IN THIS CHAPTER

Summary: In the second half of the nineteenth century, nationalism became a tool of conservative state-builders, and Italy and Germany became unified nation states.

Key Ideas

○ In the second half of the nineteenth century, the Romantic and conservative tendencies of nationalism came to the fore.
○ Between 1855 and 1866, Italy was unified by the actions of the conservative statesman Count Camillo Cavour and the Romantic nationalist Giuseppe Garibaldi.
○ The conservative Prussian aristocrat Otto von Bismarck used diplomacy and war to unify Germany under the rule of the Hohenzollern dynasty of Prussia.
○ Nationalism was a key component in the destruction of the anachronistic Austrian-dominated Hapsburg Empire.

Key Terms

Carbonari
Risorgimento
Crimean War
Treaty of Villafranca

Junkers
Realpolitik
Schleswig–Holstein
  Affair

Austro-Prussian War
Ems telegram
Compromise of 1867

Introduction

In the second half of the nineteenth century, nationalism triumphed over all the other competing ideologies. In areas where people lived under foreign domination, nationalism was used by conservative statesmen to bring about the unification of Italy and Germany. In the Hapsburg Empire, the nationalist aspirations of ethnic minorities worked to undermine Austrian domination. In France and Russia, the force of nationalism was used to end the remaining dreams of liberals and to strengthen the hold of autocratic rulers.

The End of Liberal Nationalism

In the first half of the nineteenth century, liberals and nationalists tended to ally themselves against the forces of conservatism. Both believed that political sovereignty resided in the *people*, and they shared an optimistic belief that progress toward their goals was inevitable. Campaigns for liberal reform (which attempted to break the conservative aristocracy's grip on political power and to promote individual rights) tended to merge with the struggle for national rights or self-determination. Accordingly, most liberals supported in principle the idea of a free and unified nation state in Germany and Italy, the rebirth of Poland, and Greek independence; most conservatives opposed these ideas.

However, both partial victory and eventual defeat drove a wedge between liberals and nationalists. When liberals won temporary victories over conservative aristocrats between 1830 and 1838, fundamental differences between the agendas of liberal reformers and nationalists began to emerge. The emphasis on individual liberty and limited government did not mesh well with the nationalist emphasis on the collective national tribe or with the desire of nationalists to have a strong national government. In short, liberals believed in promoting the rights of *all peoples*; nationalists cared only about their *own rights*.

When, in 1848, the more radical liberal agenda of democratic reform emerged, the conservative tendencies of nationalism came to the fore. Nationalists not only shared the conservatives' belief in the value of historical traditions but also tended to mythologize the past and dream of the return of an era of national glory. Ultimately, however, what drove a wedge between liberals and nationalists was the failure of liberals to hold the power they had temporarily seized. As the conservative reaction in the second half of 1848 smashed liberal movements everywhere in Europe, nationalists dreaming of a strong unified country free from foreign rule increasingly turned to conservative leaders.

The Unification of Italy

The Forces against Unity in Italy

The settlement after the defeat of Napoleon in 1815 had greatly disappointed those hoping for an Italian nation state. The Italian peninsula consisted of separate states controlled by powerful enemies of Italian nationalism:

- The *Hapsburg Dynasty of Austria* controlled, either directly or through its vassals, Lombardy and Venetia in the north, and the duchies of Tuscany, Parma, and Modena.
- The *pope* governed an area known as the Papal States in central Italy.
- A branch of the *Bourbon dynasty* (which ruled France) controlled the Kingdom of the Two Sicilies in the south.

- An *Italian dynasty, the House of Savoy*, controlled both the Island of Sardinia in the south and Piedmont in the northwest.

In addition to political divisions and foreign interests, the Italian peninsula was also divided by economic and cultural differences:

- The northern areas of the peninsula were well developed economically and more sophisticated culturally than the still largely rural and agricultural areas of the south.
- Culturally, the people of the more developed northern region felt little connection to the poor peasants in the south, who often spoke an entirely different dialect.
- Socially and politically, the middle-class merchants and manufacturers, located mostly in the north, wanted a greater degree of unity for easier trade and tended to support liberal reforms; they were opposed by the staunchly conservative, traditional landed elite.

Italian Nationalism to 1850

Italian nationalism had been forged in opposition to Napoleon's rule. After 1815, dreams of a unified Italy were kept alive in secret societies like the *Carbonari*, secret clubs whose members came mostly from middle-class families and from the army. In 1820, the Carbonari briefly succeeded in organizing an uprising that forced King Ferdinand I of the Kingdom of the Two Sicilies to grant a constitution and a new Parliament. But Austrian troops, with the blessing of the Concert of Europe, crushed the revolt. The Austrians put down a similar revolt by Carbonari in Piedmont in 1831–1832.

In the 1840s, Giuseppe Mazzini's Young Italy had carried the banner of Italian nationalism. Both a Romantic and a liberal, Mazzini fought for the establishment of an Italian republic that would serve, as he believed ancient Rome had, as a beacon for the rest of humanity. By midcentury, Mazzini had forged a movement known as the *Risorgimento*, which was composed mostly of intellectuals and university students who shared his idealism. From 1834 to 1848, the *Risorgimento* attempted a series of popular insurrections, briefly establishing a Roman Republic in 1848 until it was crushed (like its liberal counterparts throughout Europe) by the forces of reaction. In defeat, it was evident that the *Risorgimento* had failed to win the support of the masses.

Cavour and Victory over Austria

At midcentury, a new leader of Italian nationalist hopes emerged in the person of Count Camillo Benso di Cavour, the chief minister of King Victor Emmanuel II of the Kingdom of Piedmont-Sardinia. Cavour differed from Mazzini and other previous leaders of the Italian nationalist movement in several significant ways:

- Cavour was a *conservative aristocrat* with ties to the most powerful Italian ruler on the peninsula, rather than a *middle-class intellectual*.
- Cavour advocated a *constitutional monarchy* under Victor Emmanuel II, rather than a republic.
- Cavour was a cautious and *practical* statesman, rather than an *idealist*.

Cavour's strategy was that of an opportunist: he sought to increase the amount of territory under the control of Piedmont whenever possible and to weaken the opponents of Italian unification by playing them against each other. Between 1855 and 1860, Cavour took advantage of several such opportunities and managed to unite all of northern Italy under Piedmont:

- In 1855, Cavour brought Piedmont and its army into the *Crimean War* on the side of England and France, who were fighting Russia. This resulted in no immediate gains, but the peace conference afforded Cavour an opportunity to denounce Austrian occupation of Italian lands.

- In 1858, Cavour reached a secret agreement with Napoleon III of France gaining a promise of French support should Austria attack Piedmont.
- In 1859, Cavour goaded the Austrians into attacking Piedmont by mobilizing forces and refusing an ultimatum to disarm. French and Piedmontese troops defeated the Austrians at the battles of Magenta and Solferino, driving the Austrians out of Lombardy. Further gains by Piedmont were thwarted by Napoleon III's abrupt signing of the *Treaty of Villafranca* with the Austrians.
- By 1860, inspired by the Piedmontese victory over Austria, the majority of the northern and north-central duchies shook off their Austrian rulers and voluntarily united with Piedmont.

Garibaldi and Victory in the South

The success of northern Italians in throwing off Austrian domination inspired their southern counterparts. A series of peasant revolts, tinged with anti-Bourbon sentiment, arose in the south.

Southern Italian nationalists found a different kind of leader in Giuseppe Garibaldi and, in 1860, launched a series of popular uprisings that put all of southern Italy under his control. The southern nationalist movement differed from its northern counterpart in several significant ways:

- Garibaldi was a Romantic nationalist who had been an early supporter of Mazzini.
- The southern movement was a genuine revolt of the masses rather than the political maneuverings of a single kingdom.
- Garibaldi hoped to establish an Italian republic that would respect the rights of individuals and improve the lot of the peasants and workers.

In May of 1860, Garibaldi raised an army of 1,000 red-shirted Italian patriots and landed in Sicily to aid a peasant revolt underway there. In a few short months, Garibaldi and his red-shirts provided leadership to a nationalist revolt that took control of most of southern Italy and set its sights on Rome.

The Kingdom of Italy and the Completion of Italian Unification

Cavour had publicly condemned Garibaldi's conquests but secretly aided them. When Garibaldi's troops began to threaten Rome, Cavour persuaded Napoleon III, who had sworn to protect the pope, to allow the Piedmontese army to invade the Papal States in order to head off Garibaldi. By September of 1860, Piedmont controlled the Papal States and set up a ring around Rome.

When Piedmontese forces, led by King Victor Emmanuel II himself, met Garibaldi and his forces outside Rome in September of 1860, Garibaldi submitted and presented all of southern Italy to Victor Emmanuel; in the end, Garibaldi's dream of a unified Italy was stronger than his commitment to the idea of a republic. In March of 1861, the Kingdom of Italy was formally proclaimed. It was a constitutional monarchy under Victor Emmanuel II and a parliament elected by limited suffrage. It contained all of the Italian peninsula except the city of Rome (which was still ruled by the pope and protected by French troops) and Venetia (which was still occupied by Austrian troops). The unification of Italy was completed when Venetia came into the Kingdom of Italy during the Austro-Prussian War of 1866, and Rome (with the exception of the Vatican City) followed during the Franco-Prussian War of 1870.

The Unification of Germany

Forces Against Unity in Germany

Unlike Italy, Germany in the middle of the nineteenth century was free of direct foreign domination. It existed as a loose confederation of independent states. Within that loose confederation, several forces worked against national unity:

- cultural differences between the rural, conservative, Protestant north and the urban, liberal, Catholic south
- a long history of proud independence on the part of the individual German states
- the powerful influence of Hapsburg Austria, which controlled or influenced a large portion of the German Confederation

Prussian Leadership

With the failure of the liberal Frankfort Assembly in 1848, leadership in the German nationalist movement passed to Prussia. Prussia was a strong northern kingdom ruled by the Hohenzollern dynasty and supported by a powerful class of landed aristocrats known as *Junkers*. Prussia also had the strongest military in Germany and led the way in establishing the *Zollverein*, a large free-trade zone. This combination of military and economic power led many Germans to look to Prussia for leadership.

Bismarck and War with Denmark and Austria

In 1861, Prussia's new monarch, William I, wanted to reorganize and further strengthen the military, but the liberal legislature resisted, and a power struggle between the monarch and the legislature ensued. William turned to the conservative Junker Otto von Bismarck to be his prime minister. Bismarck forced a showdown, and it quickly became apparent that the support of the Prussian people was with the king, the army, and Bismarck. With the power of the army and the government fully established, Bismarck set out on a policy to unify Germany under the Prussian crown that has come to be known as *Realpolitik*, which asserted that the aim of Prussian policy would be to increase its power by whatever means and strategies were necessary and useful. Bismarck asserted that the unification of Germany would be accomplished by a combination of "blood and iron."

Bismarck quickly concluded that a war with Austria was inevitable, and he engineered one in an episode that has come to be known as the *Schleswig–Holstein Affair*. He began by enlisting Austria as an ally in a war with Denmark over two duchies, Schleswig and Holstein, that had a large German-speaking population. Once Denmark was forced to cede the two duchies, Bismarck provoked an argument with Austria over control of them. Bismarck's next moves were a perfect illustration of *Realpolitik* in action:

- First, Bismarck obtained Italian support for a war with Austria by promising Italy the province of Venetia.
- Next, he ensured Russian neutrality by supporting Russia's actions against its rebellious Polish subjects.
- Then, he met secretly with Napoleon III of France and persuaded him that a weakening of Austrian power was in the best interests of France.
- Finally, and only after those preparations were in place, he carried out a series of diplomatic and military maneuvers that provoked Austria into declaring war.

In the resulting *Austro-Prussian War* of 1866, Prussian troops surprised and overwhelmed a larger Austrian force, winning victory in only seven weeks. The result was that Austria was expelled from the old German Confederation and a new North German Confederation was created, which was completely under the control of Prussia.

War with France

All that remained was to draw the south German states into the new Confederation. But the south (which was predominantly Catholic and liberal) feared being absorbed by the Protestant and authoritarian Prussians. Bismarck concluded that only one thing would compel the south Germans to accept Prussian leadership: a war with a powerful foreign enemy. So he set about engineering one.

The opportunity came when both France and Prussia got involved in a dispute over the vacant throne in Spain. Bismarck, with the support of the Prussian military leadership, edited a communication between Napoleon III and William I (a communication that is now known as the *Ems telegram*) to make it seem as though they had insulted one another, and Bismarck released this telegram to the press. Tempers flared, and France declared war. The south German states rallied to aid Prussia. Combined German forces quickly routed the French troops, capturing Napoleon III, and taking Paris in January of 1871.

The Second Reich

On January 18, 1871, the unification of Germany was completed. The heads of all the German states gathered in the Hall of Mirrors in the palace of Versailles outside Paris and proclaimed William I Kaiser (emperor) of the German Empire (formally the Second Reich, honoring the old Holy Roman Empire as the first Reich). The new empire took the provinces of Alsace and Lorraine from France and billed the French 5 billion francs as a war indemnity.

Nationalism in the Hapsburg Empire

In an age of nation-building, the Hapsburg Empire, with its Austrian minority dominating an Empire consisting of Hungarians (also known as Magyars), Czechs, Serbs, Romanians, and other ethnic groups, was an anachronism. The forces of nationalism, therefore, worked to tear it apart. After Austria's defeat by Prussia in 1866, the Austrian Emperor Franz Joseph attempted to deal with what has come to be called "the nationalities problem." By agreeing to the *Compromise of 1867*, he set up the dual monarchy of Austria–Hungary, where Franz Joseph served as the ruler of both Austria and Hungary, each of which had its own parliament. This arrangement essentially set up an alliance between the Austrians and the Hungarians against the other ethnic groups in the empire.

Nationalism in France

Louis-Napoleon Bonaparte had originally been elected president of the Second Republic in 1848. When the National Assembly refused to amend the constitution to allow him to run for a second term, he staged a coup d'état on December 2, 1851. The public overwhelmingly sided with Louis-Napoleon, who granted them universal manhood suffrage. They responded, in two plebiscites, by voting to establish a Second Empire and to make Louis-Napoleon hereditary emperor.

Like his namesake, Louis-Napoleon attempted to increase his popularity by expanding the empire, but soon his foreign adventures began to erode his popularity. By 1870, the liberal parliament had begun to reassert itself. The humiliating defeat in the Franco-Prussian War brought down both Louis-Napoleon and the Second Empire; it also set in motion a battle between monarchists and the people of Paris who, having defended Paris from the Germans while the aristocrats fled, now considered themselves to represent the nation of France.

Nationalism in Russia

At midcentury, Russia's government was the most conservative and autocratic in Europe. The peasants of Russia were still bound to the land by serfdom. The Crimean War (1853–1856), in which Russia essentially battled Britain and France for control of parts of the crumbling Ottoman Empire, damaged the reputation of both the tsar and the military. Alexander II, who ascended to the throne in 1855, was determined to strengthen Russia by reforming and modernizing it. He abolished serfdom, made the judiciary more independent, and created local political assemblies.

However, Russia was plagued by its own nationalities problem. Alexander attempted to deal with it by relaxing restrictions on the Polish population within the Russian Empire, but this fanned the flames of nationalism and led to an attempted Polish Revolution in 1863. Alexander responded with increased repression of Poles and other ethnic minorities within the Russian Empire. And after an attempt on his life in 1866, Alexander gave up all notions of liberal reform and proceeded to turn Russia into a police state.

› Rapid Review

The failure of the revolutions of 1848 broke the fragile alliance between liberalism and nationalism. The unification of northern Italy under Victor Emmanuel II was accomplished through the statesmanship of the conservative Count Camillo Cavour. The Romantic nationalist Giuseppe Garibaldi led a massive popular uprising and took control of southern Italy, then presented it to Victor Emmanuel in the name of Italian unity to create the Kingdom of Italy in 1861. The remaining two areas, Venetia and Rome, came into Italy in 1866 and 1870, respectively.

Germany was unified under William I of Prussia through the machinations of the conservative Prussian statesman Otto von Bismarck. A unified German empire, called the Second Reich, was proclaimed, following a Prussian victory in the Franco-Prussian War in 1871. The Hapsburg Empire was plagued by a nationalities problem and became Austria–Hungary in 1867. France's defeat led to the fall of the Second Empire, while Alexander II turned Russia into a police state.

› Chapter Review Questions

1. The strongest conservative element in nineteenth-century nationalism was
   - (A) the desire for a republican form of government
   - (B) its emphasis on the concept of natural borders
   - (C) its desire to resist the rule of traditional aristocratic dynasties
   - (D) its belief in the value of historical traditions
   - (E) its belief that political sovereignty rested with the people

2. Cavour was able to unite northern Italy under the Kingdom of Piedmont through a combination of
   - (A) war and diplomacy
   - (B) diplomacy and bribery
   - (C) peasant revolts and military action
   - (D) war and secret dealings with the pope
   - (E) diplomacy and royal marriage

3. Garibaldi's capitulation to King Victor Emmanuel II illustrates
   - (A) the failure of nationalism in Italy
   - (B) the triumph of liberal nationalism
   - (C) the degree to which the nationalist desire for unity had triumphed over the liberal desire for individual rights
   - (D) the power of the Hapsburg dynasty in Italy
   - (E) the power of the Bourbon dynasty in Italy

4. The Schleswig–Holstein Affair is an example of
   - (A) the *Risorgimento*
   - (B) Russian conservatism
   - (C) German liberalism
   - (D) French imperialism
   - (E) *Realpolitik*

5. Which of the following was the factor that brought south Germans into Bismarck's new German Confederation?
   - (A) their Catholicism in the face of war with France
   - (B) their liberalism in the face of war with Austria
   - (C) their nationalism in the face of war with a foreign enemy
   - (D) their desire for a strong, authoritarian central government
   - (E) the existence of a dominant aristocratic class of Junkers in south Germany

6. By agreeing to the Compromise of 1867, the Hapsburg emperor Franz Joseph was
   - (A) acknowledging the rights of all ethnic groups within the Hapsburg Empire
   - (B) enlisting the Hungarians in an alliance against the other ethnic minorities within the Empire
   - (C) acknowledging Prussian supremacy in the German Confederation
   - (D) ending serfdom in Russia
   - (E) ending the Crimean War

7. In France, the Second Empire was brought to an end by
   - (A) France's defeat in the Franco-Prussian War
   - (B) Louis-Napoleon Bonaparte's coup d'état on December 2, 1851
   - (C) two plebiscites
   - (D) the Crimean War
   - (E) the unification of Italy

8. In Russia, Tsar Alexander II's attempts to liberalize Russia were brought to an end by
   - (A) the abolition of serfdom
   - (B) the Crimean War
   - (C) the unification of Germany
   - (D) the Russian Revolution
   - (E) the Polish Revolution of 1863 and an attempt on his life in 1866

› Answers and Explanations

1. **D.** The belief in the value of historical traditions was the strongest conservative element in nationalism, which tended to use a mythologized version of history as a way to create a unified national identity. Choice A is incorrect because nationalism tended to put concerns for the *strength and unity of the nation* ahead of concerns for a particular form of government. Choice B is incorrect because the emphasis on the concept of natural borders was *shared* by liberal and conservative nationalists alike. Choices C and E are incorrect because the desire to resist the rule of traditional aristocratic dynasties like the Hapsburgs and the Bourbons and the belief that political sovereignty rested with the people were *liberal* tendencies of nationalism, not *conservative* elements.

2. **A.** Cavour's successful strategy for uniting northern Italy under Piedmont worked through a combination of secret diplomatic arrangements with France and successful war with Austria. Choice B is incorrect because the smaller Kingdom of Piedmont was in no position to *bribe* the wealthier French Bourbons and Austrian Hapsburgs. Choice C is incorrect because peasant revolts were important in the unification of *southern* Italy, not northern. Choice D is incorrect because Cavour's secret dealings were with Napoleon III of France, not the pope. Choice E is incorrect because *no* royal marriages were concluded in the unification of northern Italy.

3. **C.** Garibaldi had pledged to establish an Italian republic that protected the rights of all individuals; his willingness to hand over the southern portion of the peninsula to an aristocratic monarch, therefore, illustrates the degree to which the nationalist desire for unity had triumphed over the liberal desire for individual rights. Choice A is incorrect because Garibaldi's willingness to hand the south over to King Victor Emmanuel and Piedmont guaranteed that a unified Kingdom of Italy would come into being and, therefore, illustrates the *triumph* (not the *failure*) of Italian nationalism. Choice B is incorrect because Garibaldi's willingness to forgo his dream of a republic illustrates the *death* of liberal nationalism (not the *triumph*). Choice D is incorrect because the fact that the fate of Italy was being decided by two Italians demonstrates the degree to which Austrian Hapsburg's power in Italy had *declined*. Choice E is similarly incorrect because the meeting between Garibaldi and Victor Emmanuel II illustrates the *limited* ability of the French Bourbon dynasty to dictate events in Italy.

4. **E.** Bismarck's use of the Schleswig–Holstein Affair to manufacture a war with Austria is an example of his policy of *Realpolitik*, which increased Prussian territory and power by any means available. Choice A is incorrect because the *Risorgimento* refers to the mid-nineteenth-century Italian nationalist movement. Choice B is incorrect because *Russia* was only tangentially involved in the Schleswig–Holstein Affair. Choice C is incorrect because Bismarck's disregard for the rights of individuals and groups of people is the *antithesis* of liberalism. Choice D is incorrect because France had only a *minor* role in the Schleswig–Holstein Affair and did not stand to increase the size of its empire as a result.

5. **C.** Bismarck used the strong nationalist feelings of south Germans who were aroused by war with France to convince them to join his new confederation and accept Prussian dominance. Choices A and B are incorrect because both the Catholicism and the liberalism of south Germans caused them to *fear* being dominated by the Protestant and conservative Prussians. Choice D is incorrect because the liberal south Germans had *no* desire for the strong, authoritarian central government favored by Prussians. Choice E is incorrect because the Junkers were the dominant aristocratic class in *Prussia*, not south Germany.

6. **B.** The Compromise of 1867 set up the dual monarchy of Austria–Hungary with two parliaments, each under Emperor Franz Joseph; it was done as a concession to the Hungarians in order to enlist them in an alliance against the other ethnic groups in the empire. Choice A is incorrect because the Compromise did nothing for *any*

ethnic group other than the Hungarians. Choice C is incorrect because the Compromise did *not* acknowledge Prussian supremacy in the confederation: The Austrians had been expelled from the confederation by the victorious Prussians following the Austro-Prussian war of 1866. Choice D is incorrect because the compromise did *not* concern Russia; serfdom in Russia was ended by royal decree. Choice E is incorrect because the compromise had *nothing* to do with the Crimean War, which ended in 1856.

7. **A.** The Second Empire was brought to an end by France's defeat in the Franco-Prussian War; Napoleon III was captured, and the victorious Germans proclaimed the Second Empire to be dissolved. Choices B and C are incorrect because it was the Second French *Republic* (not the Second Empire) that was brought to an end by a combination of Napoleon Bonaparte's coup d'état on December 2, 1851, and two plebiscites that declared France to be an empire and Napoleon III to be its hereditary emperor. Choice D is incorrect because, although France's involvement in the Crimean War hurt Napoleon III's popularity, it did *not* jeopardize the Second Empire. Choice E is incorrect because the unification of Italy had *no* direct bearing on the fall of the Second Empire in France.

8. **E.** Alexander II's attempts to liberalize Russia were brought to an end by the combination of the Polish Revolution of 1863 (which was sparked by his granting Polish subjects more autonomy) and an attempt on his life in 1866 (which spurred him to crack down on his enemies and to build a police state). Choice A is incorrect because the abolition of serfdom was *part* of his attempts to liberalize Russia. Similarly, choice B is incorrect because the poor performance of the Russian military in the Crimean War was *part* of his motivation for modernizing and liberalizing Russia. Choice C is incorrect because Alexander II's liberal phase was over *before* German unification in 1871. Similarly, choice D is incorrect because Alexander II's liberal phase was over *before* the Russian Revolution, which did not occur until 1917.

CHAPTER 19

Mass Politics in Europe and Imperialism in Africa and Asia, 1860–1914

IN THIS CHAPTER

Summary: Between 1860 and 1914, the development of mass politics helped to fuel an expansion of European influence and dominance across the globe that came to be called the New Imperialism.

Key Ideas

○ The New Imperialism of the last decades of the nineteenth century was characterized by a shift to active conquest and direct political control of foreign lands by the European powers.

○ The phrase "mass politics" refers to the participation of increasingly larger portions of the population in the political process in European nations in the second half of the nineteenth century.

○ The British seizure of the Suez Canal in Egypt and Belgium's aggressive expansion into the Congo set off a "scramble for Africa."

○ European imperialism in Asia was exerted through the control of the local elite rather than by direct conquest.

Key Terms

Chartism	Midlothian Campaign	*Kulturkampf*
Reform Bill of 1867	Paris Commune	Russianization
Reform Bill of 1884	Boulanger Affair	Suez Canal

Berlin Conference of 1885   Opium War   Boxer Rebellion
Sepoy Rebellion of 1857   Treaty of Nanking   Meiji Restoration
Indian National Congress   Taiping Rebellion   Russo-Japanese War

Introduction

In the last decades of the nineteenth century, the European powers shifted from indirect commercial influence to active conquest and the establishment of direct political control of foreign lands around the globe, particularly in Africa and Asia. This imperial expansion of European influence and control is known as the New Imperialism.

Causes of the New Imperialism

The causes of the New Imperialism are a matter of debate among historians, but all explanations contain the following elements to some degree:

- the need for *new raw materials* in the expanding industrial economy of Europe
- the need for *new markets* to sell European manufactured goods and to invest newly created capital
- the *technological innovations in weaponry and transportation* that encouraged European military adventurism
- the *rampant nationalism* of the nineteenth century that unified European nations and gave them a sense of historical destiny
- the traditional identity of the European political elite who competed for *fame and glory through conquest*
- the need for competing the European political elite to win the *support of the newly politicized and enfranchised masses*

The Development of Mass Politics

Mass politics was the participation, in increasingly aggressive yet unstable ways, of the masses in the governing of European nations. The development of mass politics took different forms in different nations, as described in the following sections.

Mass Politics in Great Britain

By 1860, Britain had already experienced mass politics. The threat of violence from the masses had provided the pressure that enabled the Liberals to force through the Great Reform Bill of 1832, enfranchising most of the adult, male middle class. But in the decades that followed, the Liberals seemed satisfied with limited reform. The rise of *Chartism* (1837–1842) demonstrated the degree to which the lower-middle and working classes desired further reform. Chartists organized massive demonstrations in favor of the People's Charter, a petition that called for:

- universal manhood suffrage
- annual Parliaments
- voting by secret ballot
- equal electoral districts
- abolition of property qualifications for members of Parliament
- payment of members of Parliament

If enacted into law, the People's Charter would have had the effect of creating a completely democratic House of Commons, but Parliament rejected the Charter on numerous occasions.

In 1867, the new leader of the Conservative (or Tory) Party, Benjamin Disraeli, convinced his party that further reform was inevitable and engineered the passage of the *Reform Bill of 1867*. The bill doubled the number of people eligible to vote and extended the vote to the lower middle class for the first time. Additionally, the Conservatives passed a number of laws regulating working hours and conditions, and the sanitary conditions of working-class housing.

In 1884, the Liberals under William Gladstone again took the lead, engineering the passage of the *Reform Bill of 1884*. This bill included the following reforms:

- It extended the right to vote further down the social ladder, thereby enfranchising two-thirds of all adult males.
- It made primary education available to all.
- It made military and civil service more democratic.

The result of this move toward mass politics was competition between the Liberals and Conservatives for the newly created votes. In 1879, Gladstone embarked on the first modern political campaign, which came to be known as the *Midlothian Campaign*, riding the railway to small towns throughout his district to give speeches and win votes. Disraeli and the Conservatives countered with a three-pronged platform of "Church, Monarchy, and Empire."

Mass Politics in France

Napoleon III had granted his subjects universal manhood suffrage, but the masses did not often recognize the results of democratic elections in the period between 1870 and 1914. France's defeat in the Franco-Prussian war brought an end to Napoleon III's Second Empire. When subsequent elections resulted in a victory for the monarchists, the people of Paris refused to accept the results and set up their own democratic government that came to be known as the *Paris Commune*. The Commune ruled the city of Paris in February and March of 1871, before being crushed by the French army.

Monarchists initially controlled the government of the new Third Republic, but they remained divided between factions. By the end of the 1870s, France was ruled by a liberal government elected by universal manhood suffrage. However, in the late 1880s, conservative nationalists supported an attempted coup by General George Boulanger. The attempt—which has come to be known as the *Boulanger Affair*—failed, but it underscored the fragility of French democracy and the volatility of mass politics in France.

Mass Politics in Germany

In the newly united Germany, the constitution of the Second Reich called for universal manhood suffrage. But the masses supported the kaiser and his chancellor, Otto von Bismarck. In the 1870s, Bismarck appealed to the masses' strong sense of nationalism in an attack on the nation's Catholics. In what has come to be called the *Kulturkampf* (or war for civilization), Bismarck passed a number of laws restricting the religious freedom of Catholics in Germany. The ultimate result, however, was to revive and strengthen the Catholic political party, known as the Roman Catholic Center Party.

In 1878, Bismarck conceded defeat and repealed much of the anti-Catholic legislation in order to garner Catholic support for his war against socialist parties in Germany. When he was unable to stamp out the socialist parties, he tried to undermine their working-class political base by passing, between 1883 and 1889, a comprehensive system of social insurance. Ultimately, however, the socialist parties remained strong and the aging Bismarck was dismissed by the new monarch, Kaiser William II, in 1890.

Mass Politics in Austria–Hungary

In the dual monarchy of Austria–Hungary, mass politics continued to mean the competition between nationalities for greater autonomy and relative supremacy within the empire. The introduction of universal manhood suffrage in 1907 made Austria–Hungary so difficult to govern that the emperor and his advisers began bypassing the parliament and ruling by decree.

Mass Politics in Russia

In the autocratic police state built by Alexander II of Russia, mass politics took the form of terrorism. Radical groups like The People's Will carried out systematic acts of violent opposition, including the assassination of Alexander II with a bomb in 1881. His successor, Alexander III, countered by waging war on liberalism and democracy. Initiating a program of *Russianization*, he attempted to standardize language and religion throughout the Russian empire.

The Scramble for Africa

KEY IDEA

Two developments spurred an unprecedented "scramble" on the part of the European powers to lay claim to vast areas of the African continent: the British takeover of the Suez Canal in Egypt and Belgium's aggressive expansion into the Congo.

The *Suez Canal*, connecting the Mediterranean Sea through Egypt to the Red Sea and the Indian Ocean, was built by a French company and opened in 1869. In 1875, Great Britain took advantage of the Egyptian ruler's financial distress and purchased a controlling interest in the canal. By the early 1880s, anti-British and French sentiment was building in the Egyptian army. In the summer of 1882, the British launched a preemptive strike, landing troops in Egypt, defeating Egyptian forces, and setting up a virtual occupation of Egypt. Supposedly temporary, the occupation lasted 32 years. Britain's control of Egypt led to further European expansion in Africa in two ways:

- In order to provide greater security for Egypt, Britain expanded farther south.
- In return for France's acceptance of British occupation of Egypt, Britain supported French expansion into northwest Africa.

A new competition for imperial control of sub-Saharan Africa was initiated by the expansion of Belgian interests in the Congo. In 1876, King Leopold II of Belgium formed a private company and sent the explorer Henry Stanley to the Congo River Basin to establish trading outposts and sign treaties with local chiefs. Alarmed by the rate at which the Belgians were claiming land in central Africa, the French expanded their claims in western Africa and Bismarck responded with a flurry of claims for Germany in eastern Africa. This sudden burst of activity led to the *Berlin Conference of 1885*. There, representatives of the European powers established free-trade zones in the Congo River Basin and set up guidelines for the partitioning of Africa. The guidelines essentially set up two principles:

- A European nation needed to establish enough physical presence to control and develop a territory before it could claim it.
- Claimants must treat the African population humanely.

After the conference, European nations completed the scramble for Africa until nearly the entire continent was, nominally at least, under European control. Unfortunately, the principle of humane treatment of Africans was rarely followed.

Dominance in Asia

In the era of the New Imperialism, European powers also exerted control over Asia. Here, however, the general method was to rule through the local elite.

India: Ruled by Great Britain

In India, the British dominated, initially through the British East India Company, a private trading company that used its economic and military power to influence local politics. Following the *Sepoy Rebellion of 1857* (sometimes known as the Sepoy Mutiny), an organized, anti-British uprising led by military units of Indians who formerly served the British, the British government took direct control and restructured the Indian economy to produce and consume products that aided the British economy.

A sense of Indian nationalism began to develop as a response to the more intrusive British influence, resulting in the establishment of the *Indian National Congress* in 1885. The Congress, though really an organization of the Hindu elite, promoted the notion of a free and independent India.

Southeast Asia: Dominated by France

In Southeast Asia, the French emulated the British strategy of ruling through the local elite and fostering economic dependence. During the 1880s and early 1890s, France established the Union of Indochina, effectively dominating in the areas that would become Vietnam, Laos, and Cambodia.

China: Increasing European Control

China had been infiltrated by British traders in the 1830s. The British traded opium grown in India to Chinese dealers in exchange for tea, silk, and other goods that were highly prized in Britain. When the Chinese government attempted to end the trade, Britain waged and won the *Opium War* (1839–1842) and forced the Chinese to sign the *Treaty of Nanking*. The treaty ceded Hong Kong to Britain, established several tariff-free zones for foreign trade, and exempted foreigners from Chinese law.

The humiliation of the Manchu rulers and the undermining of the Chinese economy that resulted from foreign interference led to the *Taiping Rebellion* (1850–1864). To maintain control, the Manchus became even more dependent on Western support. Chinese nationalism and resistance to foreign influence again manifested itself in the *Boxer Rebellion* (1899–1900). The combined forces of the European powers were able to suppress the rebellion, but in 1911, a revolution led by Sun Yat-sen succeeded in overthrowing the Manchu dynasty and proclaimed a Chinese republic.

Japan: Westernization

Japan had been forcibly opened to Western trade by an American fleet commanded by Commodore Matthew J. Perry in 1853. The Japanese government signed a number of treaties granting the Western powers effective control of foreign trade. The result was civil war and revolution which culminated in the *Meiji Restoration*, in which modernizers, determined to preserve Japanese independence, restored power to the emperor and reorganized Japanese society along Western lines. By 1900, Japan was an industrial and military power. In 1904, the Japanese quarreled with Russia over influence in China and stunned the world with their victory in the *Russo-Japanese War*.

› Rapid Review

The New Imperialism was the result of a complex set of impulses that included economic needs created by industrialization; the traditional desire of European nations to compete with one another; and the need for those political elite to find ways to win the support of a new political force, the masses. Mass politics, the participation of increasingly larger portions of the population in the political process, developed unevenly in Europe, with Britain leading the way and Russia resisting the trend. The New Imperialism resulted in the scramble for Africa, in which the European powers laid claim to the entire continent in the last two decades of the nineteenth century. In Asia, the New Imperialism took the form of indirect European control exerted through the local elite.

› Chapter Review Questions

1. Which of the following was NOT a possible cause of the New Imperialism?
   (A) the need for new markets to sell European manufactured goods and to invest newly created capital
   (B) the rampant nationalism of the nineteenth century that unified European nations and gave them a sense of historical destiny
   (C) the ability of the European political elite to act without worrying about public opinion
   (D) the technological innovations in weaponry and transportation that encouraged European military adventurism
   (E) the need for competing the European political elite to win the support of the newly politicized and enfranchised masses

2. In Britain, the call for a completely democratic House of Commons was put forward in
   (A) the Great Reform Bill of 1832
   (B) the Reform Bill of 1867
   (C) the Reform Bill of 1884
   (D) the People's Charter
   (E) the Midlothian Campaign

3. The nation in which the development of mass politics was vigorously resisted by the political elite was
   (A) Britain
   (B) Russia
   (C) Austria–Hungary
   (D) France
   (E) Germany

4. The term *Kulturkampf* describes
   (A) Gladstone's political campaign of 1879
   (B) the attempt by a French general to overthrow the Third Republic of France
   (C) Bismarck's campaign against Catholicism in Germany
   (D) the restoration of the Japanese emperor and modernization of Japan
   (E) the war between France and Prussia in 1871

5. The Suez Canal is significant in the history of the New Imperialism because
   (A) it connected the Mediterranean Sea through Egypt to the Red Sea and the Indian Ocean, making control of it vital to European trade
   (B) the need to control it led the British to occupy Egypt in the summer of 1882
   (C) the need to protect British interests in it led Britain to expand its African holdings south of Egypt
   (D) the need for French acceptance of its control of the canal in Egypt led Britain to support French expansion in northwest Africa
   (E) all of the above

6. The most direct cause of the Berlin Conference of 1885 was
   (A) the unification of Germany following the Franco-Prussian War
   (B) the occupation of Egypt by British troops
   (C) the setting up of criteria for European claims on African territory
   (D) the establishment of the principle that European powers claiming African territory must treat the African population humanely
   (E) the rapid expansion of Belgian interests in the Congo

7. The long-term result of Western imperialism in China was
   (A) the fall of the Manchu dynasty
   (B) the Opium War
   (C) the Treaty of Nanking
   (D) the Taiping Rebellion
   (E) the Boxer Rebellion

8. The event that caused the British government to take direct control of India was
   (A) the Indian National Congress
   (B) the Sepoy Rebellion
   (C) the Berlin Conference of 1885
   (D) the passage of the Reform Bill of 1884
   (E) the Boxer Rebellion

› Answers and Explanations

1. **C.** The New Imperialism occurred simultaneously with the full flowering of mass politics in Europe; public opinion, therefore, was of *great concern* to the political elite in Europe and a possible cause of the New Imperialism. Choice A is incorrect because industrialization did create a need for new markets to sell European manufactured goods to and to invest newly created capital and was, therefore, a possible cause of the New Imperialism. Choice B is incorrect because the rampant nationalism of the nineteenth century that unified European nations and gave them a sense of historical destiny seemed to justify and require imperial expansion. Choice D is incorrect because the technological innovations in weaponry and transportation made the New Imperialism seem almost inevitable. Choice E is incorrect because the New Imperialism was one way in which the European political elite appealed to the newly enfranchised masses for support.

2. **D.** The creation of a completely democratic House of Commons required Members of Parliament to be chosen from an open field by universal suffrage. Only the People's Charter came close to making those demands (and even it lacked a provision for women's suffrage). Choice A is incorrect because the Great Reform Bill of 1832 extended voting rights only to the adult, male middle class. Choice B is incorrect because the Reform Bill of 1867 extended the vote to the lower middle class but still excluded the working class. Choice C is incorrect because the Reform Bill of 1884 enfranchised only two-thirds of the adult male population. Choice E is incorrect because the Midlothian Campaign, the first modern political campaign, contained no call for reforms that would have democratized the House of Commons.

3. **B.** In Russia, Alexander II resisted calls for liberalization and democratization by establishing a police state. In response, proponents of mass politics turned to terrorism, assassinating Alexander II in 1881. His successor, Alexander III, intensified royal opposition to reform through a policy of Russianization. Choice A is incorrect because Britain *led the way* with reforms that introduced mass politics in the Reform Bills of 1832, 1867, and 1884. Choice C is incorrect because the Hapsburg emperor made *numerous* reforms culminating in the introduction of universal manhood suffrage in 1907. Choices D and E are incorrect because both France and Germany had *mixed* records with regards to mass politics. In France, Napoleon III supported it, while the conservative elite resisted it. In Germany, Bismarck ushered in reforms when doing so coincided with his ultimate goals of consolidating power in the Prussian monarchy.

4. **C.** The *Kulturkampf*, or war for civilization, is a term that describes Bismarck's largely unsuccessful attempt to curtail the influence and rights of Catholics in Germany in the 1870s. Choice A is incorrect because Gladstone's political campaign of 1879 is known as the Midlothian Campaign, for the region in which it was conducted. Choice B is incorrect because the attempt by the French General George Boulanger to overthrow the Third Republic in the late 1880s is known as the Boulanger Affair. Choice D is incorrect because the restoration of the Japanese emperor and the modernization of Japan in response to Western intervention is known as the Meiji Restoration. Choice E is incorrect because the war between France and Prussia in 1871 is known as the Franco-Prussian War.

5. **E.** All of the choices are correct. The connection between the Mediterranean Sea through Egypt to the Red Sea and the Indian Ocean was vital to European trade with the East because of the time saved. Without access to the canal, goods had to be hauled overland or shipped around Africa. Anti-Western sentiment growing in the Egyptian military in the summer of 1882 caused the British to fear a loss of access to the canal and prompted them to stage a military occupation of Egypt. Subsequently, concerns about the security of Egypt and the canal led the British to expand southward into the Sudan. In order to gain French acceptance of the British occupation of Egypt, the British supported the expansion of French interests in northwest Africa.

The Interwar Years and World War II, 1918–1945

IN THIS CHAPTER

Summary: The two decades following World War I were characterized by an economic depression and social and cultural insecurity, which led to the rise of fascism and World War II.

Key Ideas

✪ The interwar years, the 1920s and 1930s, were years of economic, social, and cultural uncertainty.

✪ In 1928, Joseph Stalin instituted the first of a series of five-year plans that transformed the Soviet Union into an industrial economy and created a culture of conformity.

✪ In 1929, the New York Stock Exchange crash crippled an already fragile European economy, triggering the Great Depression.

✪ Fascism—an ideology of the downtrodden which pandered to nationalism, racism, and fantasies of military glory—flourished in Europe.

✪ In 1938 and 1939, Germany's Adolf Hitler repudiated the Treaty of Versailles with a series of aggressive actions that triggered, on 1 September 1939, World War II.

Key Terms

Metropolis	*Freikorps*	socialism in one country
The Wasteland	New Economic Plan	five-year plans
Weimar Republic	Soviet Constitution	collectivization of
Spartacists	of 1923	agriculture

purges	*Guernica*	Nazi–Soviet
gulags	*Cartel des*	Non-Aggression Pact
Great Depression	*Gauches*	Maginot Line
Blackshirts	*Anschluss*	Grand Alliance
National Socialist German	appeasement	Atlantic Charter
Workers' Party	Munich Agreement	V-2 rockets

Introduction

The 1920s were a period of deep uncertainty, as the population of Europe grappled with the experiences and consequences of World War I. In the 1930s, the politics of the extreme flourished, as fascism emerged as an ideology that appealed to the downtrodden. By 1939, Adolf Hitler and his Nazi party controlled Germany, and his systematic repudiation of the Versailles Treaty led to World War II, which raged from 1939 to 1945.

The Interwar Years

The men who survived the Great War, as World War I was called in the 1920s and 1930s, came home to a world of economic, social, and cultural uncertainty.

Problems and Challenges after World War I

Governments had borrowed heavily to finance their war efforts, and now interest payments were coming due. The need to pay out enormous sums in veteran and war widow benefits and unemployment benefits further burdened economies. The inability of economies to meet the reviving demand for goods added inflation to an already grim economic mix. Across Europe, for the first 10 years following the war, Europe experienced a roller-coaster economy, as recessions followed brief periods of prosperity.

Socially, conditions were equally uncertain. Class deference was a casualty of World War I; lingering notions that the wealthier classes were somehow superior to working people were eroded by their experience of working and fighting side by side. Traditional views on gender had also been challenged by the wartime need to suspend restrictions on where and how women worked. In rapid succession, women across Europe gained the right to vote and fought to hold onto the greater freedom they had enjoyed during the war years.

Politically, the uncertainty fuelled continued radicalization. In France, ultraconservative and socialist parties vied for power. In Britain, the wartime coalition government led by David Lloyd George stayed intact and won another term in office, but the Labour Party made great gains at the expense of the Liberals. The various subjects of the British Empire, who had supported Britain in the war effort, now began to demand that their loyalty and sacrifice be rewarded, and independence movements coalesced in Ireland and India. In the newly created or reconstituted nations of East-Central Europe—Hungary, Poland, and Yugoslavia—liberal democracy failed to take root, and right-wing authoritarian regimes came to power.

The cultural developments of the interwar years also reflected the deep uncertainty of the period. The 1920s have often been referred to as "the Roaring Twenties." The cabaret culture, where men and women mixed easily, seemed to reflect a loosening of social conventions and a pursuit of pleasure after the sacrifices of the war years. But cultural historians have increasingly pointed out that the culture of the interwar years seemed to reflect a deep anxiety for the future. An excellent example is Fritz Lang's film *Metropolis* (1925). Filmmaking became a popular art form in the interwar years, and film stars became celebrities whose lifestyle seemed to epitomize the Roaring Twenties, but Lang's *Metropolis* depicts a world in which humans are dwarfed by an impersonal world of their own creation. Similarly, T. S. Eliot's epic poem *The Wasteland* (1922) depicts a world devoid of purpose or meaning.

The Weimar Republic in Germany

The problems and uncertainties of the interwar years were felt most keenly in Germany. The new government, known as the *Weimar Republic*, was a liberal democracy led by a moderate Social Democrat, Friedrich Ebert. It was a government doomed to failure because of several factors:

- Liberal democracy was a form of government largely alien to the German people, whose allegiance had been to the Kaiser.
- It was a government that was perceived to have been *imposed* on Germany by its vengeful war enemies.
- It was wrongly blamed for the *humiliating* nature of the Treaty of Versailles.
- It was faced with insurmountable *economic problems*, as the general economic difficulties of interwar Europe were compounded by Germany's need to pay the huge war reparations imposed on it.

Almost immediately, the government of the Weimar Republic was challenged by Marxist revolutionaries, known as *Spartacists*, led by Rosa Luxemburg and Karl Leibknecht, who were dedicated to bringing a socialist revolution to Germany. In order to defeat them, Ebert turned to the old imperial army officers, who formed regiments of war veterans known as the *Freikorps* (or Free Corps). Once the right-wing forces gained the upper hand, they too tried to overthrow the Weimar government in a coup attempt in 1920 that has come to be known as the Kapp Putsch. The government was saved, ironically, by the workers of Germany, who forced the right-wing insurgents to step down by staging a general strike. Just as the Weimar government began to stabilize, it found itself unable to pay the reparations demanded of it. When the French occupied the Ruhr Valley in retaliation, Germans again went on strike. The overwhelming uncertainty caused by the situation triggered hyperinflation that made German currency essentially worthless.

The Soviet Union in Economic Ruins

By the onset of the 1920s, the bloody civil war between the monarchist "Whites" and the Bolshevik-led "Reds" was finally over, and Lenin held uncontested leadership of Russia. But it was a country in ruins, whose people could find neither jobs nor food. In order to deal with the crisis, Lenin launched the *New Economic Plan* (NEP), which allowed rural peasants and small-business operators to manage their own land and businesses and to sell their products. This temporary compromise with capitalism worked well enough to get the Russian economy functioning again.

In July of 1923, Lenin constructed *The Soviet Constitution of 1923*. On paper it created a Federal State, renamed the Union of Soviet Socialist Republics but, in practice, power continued to emanate from Lenin and the city that he named the capital in 1918, Moscow. Lenin died unexpectedly from a series of strokes in 1924. The man who won the power struggle to succeed him was the Communist Party secretary, Joseph Stalin. From 1924 to 1929, Stalin used a divide-and-conquer strategy combined with his control of the party bureaucracy to gain full control of the party and, thereby, of the Soviet Union. In the autumn of 1924, Stalin announced, in a doctrine that came to be known as *socialism in one country*, that the Soviet Union would abandon the notion of a worldwide socialist revolution and concentrate on making the Soviet Union a successful socialist state.

In 1928, Stalin ended the NEP and initiated the first of a series of *five-year plans*, which rejected all notions of private enterprise and initiated the building of state-owned factories and power stations. As an extension of the plan, Stalin pursued the *collectivization of agriculture*, destroying the culture of the peasant village and replacing it with one organized around huge collective farms. The peasants resisted and were killed, starved, or driven into Siberia in numbers that can only be estimated but which may have been as high as eight million.

Between 1935 and 1939, Stalin set out to eliminate all centers of independent thought and action within the party and the government. In a series of *purges*, somewhere between seven and eight million Soviet citizens were arrested. At least a million of those were executed, while the rest were sent to work camps known as *gulags*. The end result was a system that demanded and rewarded complete conformity to the vision of the Communist Party as dictated by Stalin.

The Great Depression

The post–World War I European economy was built on a fragile combination of international loans (mostly from the United States), reparations payments, and foreign trade. In October of 1929, the New York stock market crashed, with stocks losing almost two-thirds of their value. Unable to obtain further credit, trade dried up. The result was an economic collapse that has come to be known as the *Great Depression*. Attempts to deal with the problem in traditional ways—by cutting government expenditure, tightening the supply of money, and raising tariffs on imported goods—only made things worse. By 1932, the economies of Europe were performing at levels that were only half those of 1929. Jobs became scarce as the economy contracted and large segments of the population fell into poverty.

The British economist John Maynard Keynes argued that governments needed to increase their expenditures and run temporary deficits in order to "jump start" the stagnant economy, but his ideas were only slowly accepted. Europe's economies recovered very slowly, and, in the interim, parts of Europe succumbed to a new ideology of the desperate and downtrodden—fascism.

The Rise of Fascism in Italy and Germany

Historians struggle with definitions of fascism because it has no coherent ideology and its form varied from nation to nation. But all fascism was a mixture, to one degree or another, of the following ingredients:

- an intense form of nationalism
- a professed belief in the virtues of struggle and youth
- a fanatical obedience to a charismatic leader
- an expressed hatred of socialism and liberalism

Mussolini and Italian Fascism

The birthplace of fascism was Italy, which became the first country in Europe to have a fascist government. Italy, though a member of the Triple Alliance with Germany and Austria–Hungary, had originally chosen to remain neutral in World War I. In 1915, Italy entered the war on the side of the Entente in hopes of gaining lands from Austria–Hungary. Italian war veterans returned home doubly disillusioned, as the war experience turned out to be a nightmare and Italy gained nothing in the peace settlement. One such veteran, a former socialist named Benito Mussolini, founded the National Fascist Party in 1919. The new party began to field candidates for the Italian legislature and to establish itself as the party that could save Italy from the threat of socialism. By 1922, squads of fascist *Blackshirts* (*squadristi*), largely recruited from disgruntled war veterans, were doing battle with bands of socialist "Redshirts," and the Italian government was increasingly unable to keep order. In October of 1922, Mussolini organized 20,000 fascist supporters and announced his intention to march on Rome. King Victor Emmanuel III responded by naming Mussolini prime minister of the Italian government.

Mussolini quickly moved to consolidate his power by pushing through a number of constitutional changes. A showdown between Mussolini and what parliamentary forces still existed in Italy came in the summer of 1924, when fascists were implicated in the murder of the socialist member of the Italian parliament, Giacomo Matteotti. The masses supported Mussolini, and by early 1926 all opposition parties had been dissolved and declared illegal, making Mussolini the effective dictator of Italy.

Hitler and German Nazism

Understanding the rise of Adolf Hitler and the Nazi Party in Germany requires an understanding of the post–World War I context. Wartime propaganda had led the German public to believe that the war was going well. As a result, Germany's surrender came as an inexplicable shock. The peace settlement seemed unfair and unduly harsh, and there was a growing sense among the German people that Germany must have been betrayed. In that context, the Nazis became popular by telling the German people several things they desperately wanted to hear:

- The Nazis appealed to displaced veterans and young people by telling them that they would build a Germany that had a place for them.
- They promised to get rid of the hated war reparations and to return Germany to military greatness.
- They provided the Germans with someone to blame for defeat by claiming that the Jews had betrayed Germany.
- They appealed to frightened business interests and the Church in Germany by promising to protect them from the socialists.

The so-called *National Socialist German Workers' Party* (NSDAP), or the Nazi Party, began as a small right-wing group and one of the more than 70 extremist paramilitary organizations that sprang up in postwar Germany. It was neither socialist nor did it attract many workers; it was a party initially made up of war veterans and misfits. The man responsible for its rise to power in Germany was Adolf Hitler, a failed Austrian art student and war veteran.

Hitler incorporated military attitudes and techniques, as well as expert propaganda, to turn the NSDAP into a tightly knit organization with mass appeal. Hitler and the Nazis made their first bid for power in November of 1923 in the "Beer Hall putsch," when they tried to stage a coup to topple the Bavarian government in Munich. It failed, but Hitler gained national attention in the subsequent trial where he publicly decried the terms of the Treaty of Versailles and espoused his views of racial nationalism. Years of reorganization and building of grass-roots support produced significant electoral gains in the elections of 1930.

In the elections of 1932, the Nazis won over 35 percent of the vote. Hitler refused to take part in a coalition government and the German president, the aging military hero Paul von Hindenburg, made the crucial decision to appoint Hitler chancellor of Germany (the equivalent of prime minister). Early in 1933, the German parliament building, the Reichstag, burned down. Hitler declared a state of emergency and assumed dictatorial powers. He then used them to eliminate socialist opposition to Nazi rule. In the elections of 1933, Nazis won 288 seats out of 647. With the support of 52 deputies of the nationalist party, and in the absence of communist deputies who were under arrest, the Nazis were able to rule with a majority. By bullying the Reichstag into passing the Enabling Act of March 1933, Hitler was essentially free to rule as a dictator.

Dictatorship in Spain and Portugal: Franco and Salazar

In both countries, Western-style parliamentary governments faced opposition from the Church, the army, and large landowners. In 1926, army officers overthrew the Portuguese republic that had been created in 1910, and gradually Antonio de Oliveira Salazar, an economics professor, became dictator.

In Spain, antimonarchist parties won the election of 1931, and King Alphonso XIII fled as the new Spanish Republic was set up. When a socialist cartel won the election of 1936, General Francisco Franco led a revolt against the Republic from Spanish Morocco, plunging Spain into a bloody civil war. Franco received support from the Spanish monarchy and Church, while Germany and Italy sent money and equipment. The Republic was defended by brigades of volunteers from around the world (famous writers George Orwell and Ernest Hemingway were among them), and eventually received aid from the Soviet Union. The technological might provided by the Germans allowed Franco's forces to overwhelm the defenders of the Republic. Pablo Picasso's 25-foot-long mural *Guernica* (1937), depicting the bombing of the town of Guernica by German planes in 1937, poignantly illustrated the nature of the mismatch. By 1939, Franco ruled Spain as a dictator.

Fascism in France

During the war, France had essentially been administered by the military. At the war's conclusion, the Parliament rushed to reassert its dominance, and France was governed by moderate coalitions. But the elections of 1924 swept the *Cartel des Gauches*, a coalition of socialist parties, to power, causing a reaction in the form of a flurry of fascist organizations, with names like Action Francaise, The Legion, and the Jeunesses Patriots. These organizations remained on the political fringe, but they provided extremist opposition and a source of anti-Semitism, which became prominent in the collaboration of the Vichy regime during the German occupation of France in World War II.

Fascism in Britain

In Great Britain, small right-wing extremist groups were united in the 1930s under the leadership of Sir George Oswald Mosley, who created the British Union of Fascists. Members were united by their hatred of socialism and their anti-Semitism. Although never politically significant in Britain, the BUF did mount a serious public disturbance in October of 1934 when it battled with socialists and Jewish groups in an incident that has come to be known as the "Battle of Cable Street." More importantly, the existence of the BUF and the initial reluctance of the British government to ban it, demonstrate the existence of some sympathy for its authoritarian and anti-Semitic views among powerful people in Britain. Once the war broke out, the BUF was banned, and Mosley was jailed.

The Road to World War II

Hitler had come to power by promising to repudiate the Treaty of Versailles. In March of 1936, he took his first big step by moving his revitalized armed forces into the Rhineland, the area on the west bank of the Rhine River that the treaty had deemed a demilitarized zone. When that move provoked no substantive response from France or Britain, Hitler embarked on a series of moves to the east that eventually triggered World War II:

- In March 1938, Germany annexed Austria without opposition (an event sometimes referred to as the *Anschluss*).
- Hitler then claimed the Sudetenland, a region of Czechoslovakia that was home to 3.5 million German speakers.

- Britain reacted with what has been called a policy of *appeasement*, agreeing in the *Munich Agreement* of September of 1938 to allow Hitler to take the Sudentenland over Czech objections in exchange for his promise that there would be no further aggression.
- In March 1939, Hitler broke the Munich Agreement by invading Czechoslovakia.
- As Hitler threatened Poland, the hope of Soviet intervention was dashed by the surprise announcement, on August 23, 1939, of a *Nazi–Soviet Non-Aggression Pact*, guaranteeing Soviet neutrality in return for part of Poland.
- On September 1, 1939, Germany invaded Poland.
- On September 3, 1939, both France and Britain declared war on Germany.

In order to understand why Britain followed a policy of appeasement and was slow to recognize the pattern of aggressive expansion in Hitler's actions in 1938 and 1939, one has to take into account the following:

- Britain and its allies, unlike Hitler's Germany, had not begun any kind of military buildup and were in no position to back up any ultimatums they might give to Hitler.
- Unlike the Germans, many of whom thought things could get no worse and were eager to avenge the humiliation of defeat in World War I, the British public hoped that they had fought and won the "war to end all wars," and wanted no part of renewed hostilities.
- Many of the British leaders privately agreed with the Germans that the Versailles Treaty had been unprecedented and unwarranted.
- Given British public opinion, a decision to pursue a military response to Hitler's actions would have been political suicide for British leaders.

The Course of the War

Blitzkrieg and "the Phony War" (1939–1940)

As Germany invaded Poland, Britain and France were not yet in a military position to offer much help. The Poles fought bravely but were easily overrun by the German *blitzkrieg*, or lightning war, which combined air strikes and the rapid deployment of tanks and highly mobile units. Poland fell to Germany in a month.

Meanwhile, Britain sent divisions to France, and the British and French general staffs coordinated strategy. But the strategy was a purely defensive one of awaiting a German assault behind the *Maginot Line*, a vast complex of tank traps, fixed artillery sites, subterranean railways, and living quarters, which paralleled the Franco-German border but failed to protect the border between France and Belgium. Over the winter of 1939 and 1940, war was going on at sea, but on land and in the air there was a virtual standstill that has come to be termed "the phony war." During the lull, however, the Soviet Union acted on its agreement with Hitler, annexing territories in Poland and Eastern Europe, including Estonia, Latvia, and Lithuania, and invading Finland.

The Battles of France and Britain (1940)

In April of 1940, the phony war came to an abrupt end as the German *blitzkrieg* moved into Norway and Denmark to prevent Allied intervention in Scandinavia and to secure Germany's access to vital iron ore supplies, and then into Luxembourg, Belgium, and the Netherlands in preparation for an all-out attack on France.

By early June 1940, the German army was well inside France. The Maginot Line proved useless against the mobility of the German tanks, which skirted the line by going north through the Ardennes Forest. On June 14, 1940, German troops entered Paris. Two days later the aging General Marshal Pétain assumed control of France and signed an armistice with

Germany according to which the German army, at French expense, occupied the northern half of France, including the entire Atlantic coast, while Pétain himself governed the rest from the city of Vichy. Not all of France was happy with the deal. General Charles de Gaulle escaped to Britain and declared himself head of a free French government. In France, many joined a Free-French movement that provided active resistance to German occupation throughout the remainder of the war.

In Britain, Prime Minister Neville Chamberlain, who had been the architect of Britain's appeasement policy, resigned. King George VI turned to the 65-year-old Winston Churchill, who had been nearly the lone critic of the appeasement policy. Churchill used his oratory skill throughout the war to bolster moral and strengthen the Allies' resolve. The German *blitzkrieg* now drove to the English Channel, trapping the Allied Army at the small seaport of Dunkirk. In an episode that has come to be known as "the Miracle of Dunkirk," more than 338,000 Allied troops (224,000 of them British) surrounded on all sides by advancing German units, were rescued by a motley flotilla of naval vessels, private yachts, trawlers, and motorboats. The episode buoyed British spirits, but Churchill was somber, pointing out that "wars are not won by evacuations."

Hitler, and many neutral observers, expected Britain to seek peace negations, but Churchill stood defiant. The German high command prepared for the invasion of Britain, but the invasion never came. Instead, in one of the most significant moments in the war, Hitler changed his mind and turned on the Soviet Union. Several components make up the explanation for this fateful decision:

- Hitler's racialist view of the world made him wary of the British, whom he considered to be the closest related race to the Germans.
- Members of Hitler's staff were handicapped by both the lack of time given to them and by their relative lack of experience in mounting amphibious operations.
- A successful invasion of England required air superiority over the English Channel; a combination of daring air fighting by the Royal Air Force and a coordinated effort of civilian defense operations all along the coast foiled German attempts to gain it.

A frustrated Hitler responded by ordering a nightly bombing of London in a two-month attempt to disrupt industrial production and to break the will of the British people. In the end, neither was achieved. In mid-October, Hitler decided to postpone the invasion, and the Battle of Britain had been won by the British.

The War in North Africa and the Balkans (1941–1942)

In 1941, the war became a global conflict as Italian forces invaded North Africa, attempting to push the British out of Egypt. However, British forces routed the Italians; Germany responded by sending troops into North Africa and the Balkans. Germany had two objectives:

- Hitler coveted the Balkans for their rich supply of raw materials, especially Romanian oil.
- He also wanted control of the Suez Canal in Egypt, which was the vital link between Britain and its resource-rich empire.

The Germans successfully occupied the Balkans, as British efforts to make a last-ditch stand in mainland Greece and on the nearby island of Crete proved in vain. Italian regiments in Libya were reinforced by German divisions under General Erwin Rommel, and the ill-equipped British forces were driven back into Egypt.

German Invasion of the Soviet Union (June–December 1941)

The Nazi–Soviet Non-Aggression Pact had always been a matter of convenience. Both sides knew that war would eventually come; the question was when. Hitler answered the question late in the spring of 1941, launching Operation Barbarossa and sending three million troops into the Soviet Union. Hitler's decision was influenced by several factors:

- his desire to create an empire that dominated all of Europe
- his racialist view of the world, which told him that the "Slavic" peoples of the Soviet Union were an easier target that his "Teutonic cousins," the British
- his need to feed and fuel his war machine with the wheat of the Ukraine and the oil of the Caucasus
- his hope that, once Germany dominated the continent from the English Channel to the Ural Mountains, even the British would have to come to terms and that no invasion of Britain would be necessary

Germany's eastern army succeeded in conquering those parts of the Soviet Union that produced 60 percent of its coal and steel and almost half of its grain, and by December 1, it was within striking distance of Moscow. But as the Russian winter set in, the Russian Army launched a counterattack against German forces, which were ill-supplied for a winter war. The Russian Army suffered millions of casualties but turned back the German invasion.

Hitler's decision to attack the Soviet Union had one other great consequence: it forged the first link in what would become the *Grand Alliance* between Britain, the Soviet Union, and the United States, as Churchill (despite being a staunch anticommunist) pledged his support to the USSR. Publicly, he announced that, "Any man or state that fights against Nazidom will have our aid." Privately, he remarked that if Hitler invaded Hell it would be desirable to find something friendly to say about the devil. The final link in the Grand Alliance would come through a combination of Churchill's persuasion and a Japanese attack.

The American Entry and Impact (1942)

Churchill and the American president, Franklin Roosevelt, met in August of 1941 on a battleship off the Newfoundland coast. They composed the *Atlantic Charter*, a document setting forth Anglo-American war aims. It rejected any territorial aggrandizement for either Britain or the United States, and it affirmed the right of all peoples to choose their own form of government.

By 1939, a modernized and militarized Japan had conquered the coastal area of China, and its expansionist aims led it to join Germany and Italy in what came to be known as the Axis. When war broke out, Japan occupied the part of Indochina that had been under French control and began to threaten the Dutch East Indies. The United States responded with an economic embargo on all exports to Japan. On December 7, 1941, Japanese air forces launched a surprise attack on Pearl Harbor, Hawaii, hoping to cripple the U.S. naval presence in the Pacific Ocean. The United States immediately declared war on Japan, and within a few days, Germany and Italy had declared war on the United States.

Initially, America's impact on the war was through resources rather than soldiers, but its entry provided the third and final turning point (along with the Battle of Britain and Germany's decision to invade the Soviet Union) in the war. Throughout 1942, American productive capacities were being built up, and the American military force kept growing. In the autumn of 1942, American marines landed on the island of Guadalcanal; it was to be the first of many islands to be recaptured from the Japanese at great cost of human lives.

The Holocaust

In 1941, the embattled Hitler regime embarked on the "Final Solution," the deliberate and methodical extermination of the Jews of Europe. It began when SS troops under Reinhard Heydrich and Heinrich Himmler began executing Jewish and Slavic prisoners who had been gathered from around Europe and forced into concentration camps. At first, firing squads were used. Next, the process was speeded up through the use of mobile vans of poison gas. Eventually, large gas chambers were constructed at the camps so that thousands could be murdered at one time. In the end, an estimated six million Jews were murdered, along with an additional seven million gypsies, homosexuals, socialists, Jehovah's Witnesses, and other targeted groups.

Outside the Nazi inner circle, people and governments were slow to believe and to comprehend what was happening, and even slower to respond:

- Neighbors turned a blind eye when Jews were rounded up and put on trains.
- Collaborating governments from Vichy France to Croatia assisted in various ways with the rounding up and extermination of the Jews.
- British and American commanders refused to divert bombing missions from other targets in order to put the camps out of commission.

The Axis in Retreat (1942–1943)

In June and August of 1943, the tide turned against the Axis forces in the Soviet Union, the Mediterranean, and the Pacific. In June of 1942, the Germans resumed their offensive in the Soviet Union. By August, they were on the outskirts of Stalingrad on the Volga River. The mammoth Battle of Stalingrad lasted six months; by the time it ended in February of 1943, the greater part of a German Army had died or surrendered to the Russians, and the remainder was retreating westward.

In October 1942, the British Eighth Army under General Bernard Montgomery halted General Rommel's forces at the Battle of El Alamein, 70 miles west of Alexandria, Egypt, and began a victorious drive westward. In May of 1943, Germany's Africa Korps surrendered to the Allies. In November 1943, Allied forces under General Dwight Eisenhower's command landed in Morocco and Algeria and began a drive that pushed all Axis forces in Africa into Tunisia. Seven months later, all Axis forces had been expelled from Africa.

Allied victories in Africa enabled them to advance steadily northward from the Mediterranean into Italy and precipitate the overthrow of Mussolini and the signing of an armistice by a new Italian government. Germany responded by treating its former ally as an occupied country. German resistance made the Allied campaign up the Italian peninsula a long and difficult one.

Allied Victory (1944–1945)

On "D-Day," June 6, 1944, Allied forces under Eisenhower's command launched an audacious amphibious invasion of German-held France on the beaches of Normandy. The grand assault took the form of an armada of 4,000 ships supported by 11,000 airplanes. By the end of July, the Allied forces had broken out of Normandy and encircled the greater part of the German army.

By late August, Paris was liberated and Hitler's forces were on the retreat. Germany seemed on the point of collapse, but German defensive lines held, and the British people were exposed to a new threat: long-range *V-2 rockets* fired from the German Ruhr rained down on them for seven months. The last gasp of the German army came in December of 1944 with a sudden drive against thinly held American lines in the Belgian sector. In what has come to be known as the Battle of the Bulge, the Allies checked the German attack and launched a counteroffensive.

In early 1945, Allied troops finally crossed the Rhine River into Germany. In May, they successfully defeated German forces in the Battle of Berlin. On May 1, it was announced that Hitler was dead, and on May 7, the German High Command surrendered unconditionally. In the Pacific, the long and deadly task of retaking the Pacific islands was averted by the dropping of two atomic bombs on Japanese cities: one on Hiroshima on August 6, 1945, and another on the city of Nagasaki on August 8, 1945. Japan surrendered unconditionally on September 2.

Assessment and Aftermath of World War II

World War II was even more destructive than World War I, and civilian casualties rather than military deaths made up a significant portion of the 50–60 million people who perished in the conflict. Many of Europe's great cities lay in ruins from repeated aerial bombings.

Vast numbers of Europeans were displaced and on the move. Some were trying to get back to homes they had been driven from by the war, while others whose homes had been destroyed simply had no place to go. Russian prisoners of war were compelled, many against their will, to return to the Soviet Union, where they were greeted with hostility and suspicion by Stalin's regime; many were executed or sent to labor camps. Between 12 and 13 million Germans were moving west. Some were fleeing the vengeance of Soviet troops, while others were driven from their homes in the newly reconstituted Czechoslovakia and other Eastern European countries, and from parts of East Prussia that were handed over to Poland.

The war also produced a new power structure in the world. The traditional European powers of Britain, France, and Germany were exhausted. Their overseas empires disintegrated rapidly, as they no longer had the resources or the will to keep their imperial holdings against the desires of the local inhabitants. In the years immediately following the war, these countries became independent:

- India gained its independence from Britain.
- Syria and Lebanon broke away from France.
- The Dutch were dismissed from Indonesia.

Finally, it became clear that, in the new world order that emerged from World War II, the United States and the Soviet Union stood alone as great powers.

› Rapid Review

Europe in the 1920s was characterized by a fluctuating economy built on debt and speculation. With the Stock Market Crash of 1929, credit dried up and the Great Depression ensued. The economic problems added to a climate of social and cultural uncertainty and disillusionment. Political parties of the center lost support to socialists on the left and fascists on the right.

In the late 1930s, Adolf Hitler came to power in Germany and embarked on a policy of rearmament and expansion. France and Britain responded initially with a policy of appeasement, but when Hitler invaded Poland in September of 1939, World War II began.

Initial German success in the war was reversed in stages by three crucial turning points:

1. Britain's victory in the Battle of Britain in 1940
2. Hitler's decision to abandon an invasion of Britain and invade the Soviet Union instead
3. the entry of the United States into the war following the Japanese attack on Pearl Harbor on December 7, 1941

Germany surrendered on May 7, 1945, and Japan followed suit on September 2, 1945, following the dropping of two atomic bombs on the cities of Hiroshima and Nagasaki in August. In the end, between 50 and 60 million people lost their lives in World War II, including 6 million Jews who were murdered in the Holocaust, and the traditional powers of Europe, Britain, France, and Germany gave way to the new superpowers: the United States and the Soviet Union.

› Chapter Review Questions

1. Europe's post-World War I economy was inherently unstable because
   (A) Germany defaulted on its war reparations
   (B) the New York stock market crashed in 1929
   (C) governments tightened the money supply
   (D) it was built on a combination of U.S. loans and war reparation payments
   (E) governments were cutting expenditures

2. Which of the following was NOT a problem that contributed to the downfall of the Weimar Republic?
   (A) It was perceived to have been imposed by Germany's vengeful war enemies.
   (B) It was composed of a coalition of socialist parties that right-wing groups would never accept.
   (C) It was wrongly blamed for the humiliating nature of the Treaty of Versailles.
   (D) It was a liberal democracy, a form of government largely alien to the German people, whose allegiance had been to the Kaiser.
   (E) It was faced with insurmountable economic problems.

3. Lenin's New Economic Plan
   (A) was the first of a series of five-year plans
   (B) marked the transition to a state-managed economy
   (C) allowed peasants and small business owners to manage their own production and sell their own products
   (D) was a response to the Great Depression
   (E) was a failure

4. The end result of Stalin's purges was
   (A) the destruction of the traditional peasant culture in Russia
   (B) the abandonment of the Marxist vision of international revolution
   (C) the Hitler–Stalin Non-Aggression Pact
   (D) a culture of complete uniformity with the Communist Party vision as articulated by Stalin
   (E) Allied victory in World War II

5. The British economist John Maynard Keynes proposed that governments deal with the Great Depression by
   (A) increasing their expenditures and running temporary deficits
   (B) decreasing their expenditures
   (C) tightening the supply of money
   (D) raising tariffs on imported goods
   (E) going to war

6. Which of the following is an element of fascism?
   (A) a fanatical obedience to a charismatic leader
   (B) a professed belief in the virtues of struggle and youth
   (C) an intense form of nationalism
   (D) an expressed hatred of socialism and liberalism
   (E) all of the above

7. Support for Franco's military coup against the Spanish Republic came from
   (A) Germany
   (B) Italy
   (C) the Spanish monarchy
   (D) the Spanish Church
   (E) all of the above

8. Which of the following was a consequence of World War II?
   (A) the Treaty of Versailles
   (B) the emergence of the United States and the Soviet Union as the only world superpowers
   (C) the flourishing of democracy in Eastern Europe
   (D) a strengthening of the British Empire
   (E) the German invasion of Poland

› Answers and Explanations

1. **D.** The post-World War I economy was unstable because it was built on money borrowed from U.S. banks and because it counted on war reparation payments, so it was an economy dependent on money being moved around instead of constantly created wealth. Choices A and B are incorrect because Germany's default and the stock market crash brought on the *collapse* of the already unstable economy. Choices C and E are incorrect because both were measures that made the Depression *worse*, not preexisting elements that made the economy unstable.

2. **B.** The government of the Weimar Republic was not a coalition of socialist parties, but rather a coalition of liberal democrats from the center of the political spectrum. Choice A is incorrect because the liberal democratic government of the Weimar Republic was perceived by the German people to have been imposed by vengeful enemies at the Paris Peace Conference. Choice C is incorrect because the government was blamed for the humiliating nature of the Versailles Treaty when, in fact, the negotiators had no leverage with which to bargain or negotiate. Choice D is incorrect because the liberal democratic form of government was a form with which the German people had very little experience, and their loyalty was still with the Kaiser. Choice E is incorrect because the new government of the Weimar republic was faced with an economy that was dependent on U.S. loans and which needed to find a way to pay the huge sums of reparations required of it by the Versailles Treaty—an impossible task.

3. **C.** Lenin's New Economic Plan, launched in the early 1920s, was a temporary relaxation of state control of production that successfully stimulated the Russian economy. Choice A is incorrect because the first of the five-year plans was launched by Stalin in 1928. Choice B is incorrect because the NEP was a relaxation of, and not the transition to, a state-managed economy. Choice D is incorrect because the NEP was launched in the early 1920s, well before the Great Depression, which began in 1929. Choice E is incorrect because the NEP was successful in its goal of stimulating the Russian economy.

4. **D.** Stalin's purges of the late 1930s removed all independent thinkers and dissenters from the party system, creating complete uniformity with Stalin's own official Communist Party vision of the world. Choice A is incorrect because the destruction of the traditional peasant culture in Russia was accomplished in the early 1930s through Stalin's program of the collectivization of agriculture, not through the purges of the late 1930s. Choice B is incorrect because the abandonment of the Marxist vision of international revolution was marked by Stalin's policy of "socialism in one country" announced in the autumn of 1924. Choice C is incorrect because the Hitler–Stalin (Nazi–Soviet) Non-Aggression Pact, signed in August of 1939, was concerned with foreign, not domestic, Soviet policy. Choice E is incorrect because the purges concerned the removal of Stalin's internal opposition and occurred before the outbreak of World War II.

5. **A.** Keynes argued that governments should deal with the depressed economy by running temporary deficits to increase their expenditures, thereby pumping money into and stimulating or "jump starting" the stagnant economy. Choices B–D are incorrect because all are traditional measures that governments initially tried, and which only made the Depression worse; Keynes was the lone voice suggesting an opposite approach. Choice E is incorrect because, although going to war did ultimately help to end the Great Depression, it was not a suggestion made by Keynes.

6. **E.** All of the choices are correct. Fascist parties displayed: a fanatical obedience to a charismatic leader (e.g., Hitler in Germany, Mussolini in Italy, and Franco in Spain); a professed belief in the virtues of struggle and youth, as illustrated in the constant reference to struggle and in the organization of youth groups in all fascist countries; an intense form of nationalism as evidenced by the uniforms and constant dialogue about the enemies of "the nation"; and an expressed hatred of socialism and liberalism, as evidenced by their opposition to the existing liberal democratic governments and their constant rhetoric and violence against socialists.

7. **E.** All of the choices are correct. Franco garnered support from Germany and Italy because of their shared fascist ideals, and because the battles of the Spanish Civil War served as a sort of field test for the new German military weapons and tactics. He was supported by the Spanish monarchy and Church, because the socialists had abolished the monarchy and banished the king, and were likely to curtail the role and privileges of the Church in Spanish society.

8. **B.** The war effort exhausted the resources of the traditional European powers, Britain, France, and Germany, and left the United States, with its vast economy, and the Soviet Union, with the largest army in the world, as the two superpowers. Choice A is incorrect because the Treaty of Versailles was the treaty that concluded World War I. Choice C is incorrect because Eastern Europe was dominated after World War II by the Soviet Union; democracy did not flourish. Choice D is incorrect because World War II marked the beginning of the breakup of the British Empire, not a strengthening of it. Choice E is incorrect because the German invasion of Poland was one of the causes of World War II, not a consequence.

CHAPTER 22

The Cold War and Beyond, 1945–Present

IN THIS CHAPTER

Summary: The Cold War waged between the United States and the Soviet Union (1945–1989) and was followed by the abrupt disintegration of the Soviet Union and the Iron Curtain.

Key Ideas

✪ At the close of World War II, a division of East and West that was both strategic and ideological hardened into a Cold War between the two superpowers: the Soviet Union and the United States.

✪ In response to the Cold War, the western European nations plotted and maintained a course of economic integration that culminated in the creation of the European Union.

✪ Between 1985 and 1989, systemic economic problems and a bold attempt at reform led to the rapid disintegration of the Soviet Union, the destruction of the Iron Curtain, and the reunification of Germany.

✪ Following the collapse of the Soviet Union, two major trends affected life in Europe: the revival of nationalism and the emergence of globalization.

Key Terms

Manhattan Project	Truman Doctrine	Warsaw Pact
M.A.D.	Marshall Plan	Treaty of Rome
United Nations	Council for Mutual	Maastricht Treaty
Iron Curtain	Economic Assistance	Prague Spring
Berlin Airlift	NATO	*perestroika* and *glasnost*

Solidarity
Civic Forum

Velvet Revolution
globalization

Introduction

Following the Second World War, a Cold War developed between the two "superpowers": the Soviet Union and the United States. In response, the western European nations plotted and followed a course of economic integration that culminated in the creation of the European Union. In the decades that followed the collapse of the Soviet Union, Europe experienced both a revival of nationalism and the emergence of globalization.

The Nuclear Arms Race

In 1944, German physicists Otto Hahn and Fritz Strassmann published a paper (based on work they had done with Lise Meitner, a Jewish physicist who was forced to emigrate due to increasing anti-Semitism in Nazi Germany) that purported to show that vast amounts of energy would be released if a way could be found to split the atom. As World War II raged, the American government secretly funded an effort, known as the *Manhattan Project,* to build an atomic bomb. In 1945, the project's international team of physicists, led by American physicist Robert Oppenheimer, succeeded in building two atomic bombs. Those bombs were dropped on two Japanese cities: Hiroshima (August 6, 1945) and Nagasaki (August 9, 1945). The advent of those nuclear weapons forced Japan's unconditional surrender and created a nuclear arms race between the United States and the Soviet Union.

On August 29, 1949, the Soviet Union successfully exploded its first nuclear weapon. In the 1950s, both the United States and the Soviet Union developed ICBMs (intercontinental ballistic missiles), which assured that either superpower could deliver enough nuclear weapons to destroy the other. That situation evolved into a risky, but ultimately successful, strategy to avoid nuclear war that came to be known as mutual assured destruction.

The Cold War

The Settlement Following WWII

There was no formal treaty at the conclusion of World War II. The postwar shape of Europe was determined by agreements reached at two wartime conferences at Tehran, Iran (in December 1943) and Yalta, Crimea, which is now part of the Ukraine (in February 1945) and, where agreement could not be reached, by the realities of occupation at the war's end. These were the primary results of the eventual settlement:

- Germany was disarmed and divided into sectors, with the Western powers controlling the western sectors and the Soviet Union controlling the eastern sectors.
- Berlin, which lay in the eastern sector, was itself divided into West Berlin (controlled by the Allies) and East Berlin (controlled by the Soviet Union).
- Poland's border with Germany was pushed westward.
- The *United Nations* was created with 51 members to promote international peace and cooperation.

- Although the United States and Britain called for free elections in the eastern European nations that were physically under the control of the Soviet army, pro-Soviet governments were quickly installed by Stalin.
- By 1946, the world was speaking of an *Iron Curtain* that had descended over Eastern Europe (the phrase was first uttered by Winston Churchill in a speech given in the United States), stretching from the Baltic Sea in the north to the Adriatic Sea in the south and dividing Europe between a communist East and a capitalist West.

The Cold War in Europe

The phrase "the Cold War" refers to efforts of the ideologically opposed regimes of the United States and the Soviet Union to extend their influence and control of events around the globe, without breaking into direct military conflict with one another. The first showdown between the superpowers occurred from June 1948 to May 1949, when Soviet troops cut off all land traffic from the West into Berlin in an attempt to take control of the whole city. In response, the Western powers, led by the United States, mounted what has come to be known as the *Berlin Airlift*, supplying West Berlin and keeping it out of Soviet control. In 1949, the Western-controlled zones of Germany were formally merged to create the independent German Federal Republic. One month later, the Soviets established the German Democratic Republic in the eastern zone.

In 1947, the United States established the *Truman Doctrine*, offering military and economic aid to countries threatened by communist takeover. That same year, President Truman's secretary of state, George Marshall, launched what has come to be known as the *Marshall Plan*, pouring billions of dollars of aid into helping the western European powers to rebuild their infrastructures and economies. The Soviet Union soon countered with the *Council for Mutual Economic Assistance*, an economic aid package for eastern European countries.

In 1949, the United States organized the North Atlantic Treaty Organization (*NATO*), uniting the Western powers in a military alliance against the Soviet Union. The Soviet Union countered with the *Warsaw Pact*, a military alliance of the communist countries of eastern Europe. The one great military imbalance of the postwar period, the United States' possession of the atomic bomb, was countered by the development of a Soviet atomic bomb in 1949. From then on, the two superpowers engaged in a nuclear arms race that saw each develop an arsenal of hydrogen bombs by 1953, followed by huge caches of nuclear warheads mounted on intercontinental ballistic missiles. The overarching strategy of nuclear weapons became appropriately known by its acronym M.A.D. (mutual assured destruction), which "reasoned" that neither side would use its nuclear weapons if its own destruction by a retaliatory blast was assured.

The Global Cold War

Once the two superpowers had done what they could to shore up their positions in Europe, their competition spread across the globe. Major events in world history that are directly connected to the Cold War include:

- the *civil war in China*, where the Soviet-backed communist forces of Mao Zedong defeated, in 1949, the nationalist forces of Jiang Jieshi supported by the United States
- the *Korean War* (1950–1953) between Soviet- and Chinese-supported North Korean communists and UN and U.S.-backed South Koreans, which produced a stalemate at the 38th parallel (the original post-World War II dividing line between North and South Korea) at the cost of some 1.5 million lives
- the *Cuban Missile Crisis* of October 1963, in which Soviet attempts to install nuclear missiles in Cuba were met with a U.S. blockade of the island, bringing the world to the brink of nuclear war until the Soviets backed down and removed the missiles

- the *Vietnam War*, in which communist forces led by Ho Chi Minh battled an authoritarian, anticommunist government, increasingly reliant on U.S. military aid for its existence, throughout the 1960s until U.S. withdrawal in 1973

Although it was less in the headlines of world news, the Cold War also had devastating effects in Latin America and Africa where, for the better part of three decades, local and regional disputes were deformed by the intervention of Soviet and U.S. money, arms, and covert operations. Many of the difficulties faced by those regions today can be traced back to the Cold War.

Détente with the West, Crackdown in the East

In the late 1960s and lasting into the 1980s, U.S.–Soviet relations entered into a new era that has come to be known as the era of Détente. In this period, both sides backed away from the notion of a struggle only one side could win. The era of Détente was characterized by a number of nuclear test-ban treaties and arms-limitation talks between the two superpowers.

However, while Soviet–U.S. relations were thawing during this period, the Soviet Union demonstrated on several occasions that it still intended to rule the Eastern Block with a firm hand. The most dramatic occurred in 1968 in an episode that has come to be known as the *Prague Spring*. Czechoslovakian communists, led by Alexander Dubcek, embarked on a process of liberalization, stimulated by public demand for greater freedom, economic progress, and equality. Under Dubcek's leadership, the reformers declared that they intended to create "socialism with a human face." Dubcek tried to proceed by balancing reforms with reassurances to the Soviet Union, but on August 21 Soviet and Warsaw Pact troops invaded and occupied the major cities of Czechoslovakia; it was the largest military operation in Europe since World War II.

The Soviet regime also continued to demand conformity from its citizens and to punish dissent. A good example was the case of Alexander Solzhenitsyn, the acclaimed author who wrote novels which attempted to tell the truth about life in the Soviet Union. For writing novels like *The Cancer Ward* (1966) and *The First Circle* (1968), Solzhenitsyn was expelled, in November 1969, from the Russian Writers' Union. Much to the irritation of the Soviet government, his work was highly acclaimed in the West, and he was awarded the Nobel Prize in 1970. Following the 1973 publication of his novel *The Gulag Archipelago*, he was arrested. But in a sign that some concessions were being made to Western opinion, he was deported to West Germany rather than exiled to Siberia.

The European Union

The leaders of western Europe realized almost immediately they were going to need to function as a whole in order to rival the economic and military power of the two superpowers. Throughout the second half of the twentieth century, Europe embarked on a plan of economic integration that proceeded through several careful stages:

- In 1950, France and West Germany created the French–German Coal and Steel Authority, removing tariff barriers and jointly managing production in that industry.
- In 1952, the Authority expanded to create the six-country European Coal and Steel Community, adding Italy, Belgium, Luxembourg, and the Netherlands.
- In 1957, those six countries signed the *Treaty of Rome*, establishing the European Economic Community (EEC), sometimes referred to as the Common Market, to begin the process of eliminating tariff barriers and cutting restrictions on the flow of capital and labor.
- In 1967, the EEC merged with other European cooperative bodies to form the European Community (EC), moving toward a broader integration of public institutions.

- Between 1967 and 1986, the EC expanded to 12 countries, adding Denmark, the United Kingdom, and the Republic of Ireland (all in 1973), Greece (1981), and Portugal and Spain (both in 1986).
- In 1992, the 12 countries of the EC signed the *Maastricht Treaty*, changing the name from the EC to European Union (EU), creating the world's largest trading bloc, and moving to adopt a common currency (the euro).
- In 1995, Austria, Finland, and Sweden joined the EU.
- Following the breakup of the Soviet Union, the EU underwent a massive expansion, welcoming countries either newly freed or newly constituted. The addition of Cyprus, the Czech Republic, Estonia, Hungary, Latvia, Lithuania, Malta, Poland, Slovakia, and Slovenia in 2004, and Bulgaria and Romania in 2007, brought the total membership to 27 countries.

The Disintegration of the Iron Curtain and the Soviet Union

Between 1985 and 1989, the world was stunned as it witnessed the rapid disintegration of the Soviet Union, the destruction of the Iron Curtain, and the reunification of Germany. The causes of these dramatic events were rooted in the nature of the Soviet system, which had for decades put domestic and foreign politics ahead of the needs of its own economy and of its people. The result was an economic system that could no longer function. The trigger for its disintegration was the ascension of a new generation of Soviet leaders.

Gorbachev and the "New Man": 1985

While western Europe was creating the EC and dreaming of economic and political power that could match the superpowers, the big lie of the Soviet economy was coming home to roost. In 1985, Mikhail Gorbachev succeeded a long line of aging Stalinist leaders. At the age of 54, Gorbachev represented a younger and more sophisticated generation that had spent significant time in the West. Gorbachev believed that the Soviet Union's survival required a restructuring (*perestroika*) of both its economy and its society, and an openness (*glasnost*) to new ideas. Accordingly, Gorbachev challenged the people of the Soviet Union and its satellite countries to take on a new level of responsibility. However, such an invitation quickly fanned the fires of autonomy in satellite states.

Poland and "Solidarity": 1980–1990

There had been growing agitation in Poland since 1980, when workers under the leadership of an electrician named Lech Walesa succeeded in forming a labor union known as *Solidarity*. Pressured by numerous strikes, the Polish government recognized the union despite threats of Soviet intervention. By 1981, the movement had become more political, as some of Solidarity's more radical members began calling for free elections. As tensions grew, the Polish military, led by General Wojciech Jaruzelski, responded to the crisis by imposing martial law and a military dictatorship. However, with Gorbachev calling for reform, Jaruzelski tried, in November of 1987, to gain legitimacy for his rule through a national referendum. The majority of voters either voted against or abstained and in August of 1988, Jaruzelski ended his military dictatorship and set up a civilian government.

The new government attempted to retain the political monopoly of the Communist Party while simultaneously opening Poland up for Western business. It proved to be impossible, and Walesa and Solidarity took advantage of the new openness to push for political freedom. In January of 1989, Solidarity was legalized and, in April, the Communist Party gave up its monopoly on political power. In the first free election in Poland since before World War II, Solidarity triumphed and a noncommunist government was set up in September. In December of 1990,

Walesa was elected president, and Poland began to face the hard task of learning how to live in an unruly democratic society and to deal with the economic ups and downs of capitalism.

Czechoslovakia and the Velvet Revolution: 1989

Seeing Poland, and then Hungary (which held free elections in the summer and fall of 1989), shed their communist governments without Soviet intervention energized Czech resistance to communist rule. Student-led demonstrations in the fall of 1989 were met with tear gas and clubs by the Czech police, but the students were soon joined by workers and people from all walks of life. Leading dissidents, like the playwright Václav Havel, began a movement known as the *Civic Forum*, which sought to rebuild notions of citizenship and civic life that had been destroyed by the Soviet system. Soon Havel and other dissidents were jailed, but they became symbols of defiance and moral superiority.

What followed has come to be known as the *Velvet Revolution*. Faced with massive demonstrations in Prague (shown around the world on television) and urged by Gorbachev himself to institute democratic reform, Czechoslovakia's communist leaders resigned on November 24. After negotiations and maneuvers by both the Communist Party and the Civic Forum, Havel was chosen as president on December 25. Alexander Dubcek, who had led the original revolt of 1968, was brought home from exile and named chairman of the Czechoslovakian Parliament.

German Reunification: 1989–1990

West Germans had never accepted the division of Germany. The constitution of the German Federal Republic provided legal formalities for reunification. How the East Germans felt about the society of their Western relatives was hard to know. When reunification came, it came suddenly. East German dissidents organized themselves along the lines of the Civic Forum model pioneered in Czechoslovakia. In response to the pressure for reform, the communist regime rescinded its traditional order to shoot anyone trying to escape to West Berlin, and shortly thereafter issued "vacation visas" to those wishing to see their families in the West. There was little expectation of their return.

On November 9, 1989, protesters moved toward the Berlin Wall and, meeting almost no resistance from the soldiers, started to hammer it down. East Germans streamed into West Berlin where they were embraced by tearful West Germans who gleefully gave them handfuls of cash. The West German chancellor, the Conservative Helmut Kohl, moved quickly toward reunification. It was a reunification that amounted to East Germany being annexed by the West. Completely swept away in the pace of change were the original Civic Forum leaders who were not at all sure that they wished to be reunified with West Germany and its capitalist economy.

- In March 1990, elections were held in East Germany, creating a new government ready to negotiate with West Germany.
- By August 3, the official treaty of reunification had been drafted.
- The East German government approved it at the beginning of October and, on October 3, 1990, the Germans celebrated Reunification Day.
- On December 2, the first unified national elections resulted in sweeping wins for Kohl, "the Reunification Chancellor," and his party.

Yugoslavia—Fragmentation: 1989

Yugoslavia had been a fragile state of six ethnically self-conscious member republics. As the communist regime began to collapse, the ethnic rivalries of Yugoslavia quickly reasserted themselves.

- Albanians in the autonomous province of Kosovo revolted against Serbian rule.
- The Slovenes and Croatians (or Croats), both western Slavs, agitated for independence from Serbia.
- In 1989, the communist regime began to collapse, and the stronger republics were moving toward independence. A fragile multiparty system was put into place.

The Soviet Union Comes Apart: 1991

Caught between the hardliners who wished to slow down reform and a population that wanted it to come faster, Gorbachev's popularity began to slip. Determined to go forward, Gorbachev persuaded the Communist Party to give up its monopoly on political power and called for free elections. Sensing collapse, Party members resigned in large numbers.

The various "republics" that made up the Soviet Union now emulated the satellite states and began to agitate for independence. The Russian Republic led the way when its president and former Gorbachev ally, Boris Yeltsin, declared its independence from the Soviet Union. Ukraine followed suit, and Gorbachev was faced with a crisis. In the spring of 1991, Gorbachev proposed a compromise. He suggested that all the republics sign a "Treaty of the Union," declaring them all to be independent but also members of a loose confederation. In August of 1991, just as the treaty was about to take effect, hardliners tried to oust Gorbachev. For three days, there was confusion about who was in charge and what the military would do. Yeltsin seized the moment, positioning himself between the parliament building and military tanks. The military backed off and the coup attempt failed, but it was Yeltsin who was now the favorite. Gorbachev resigned late in 1991, and the Soviet Union, as the world had known it, disintegrated. Most of the republics chose to join a loose confederation known as the Commonwealth of Independent States, while a few, especially the Baltic States, opted for independence.

Nationalism and Globalization

Following the collapse of the Soviet Union, nationalism, which had been driven underground, came to the surface in Eastern Europe.

- In Czechoslovakia, Slavic nationalism split the country into halves, as the Slavic regions split off to form the republic of Slovakia, leaving the Czechs to form the Czech Republic.
- In Azerbaijan, Azerbaijanis and Armenians fought for dominance.
- In the Russian Republic, Chechnyans began a guerrilla war against Russian troops when their demands for independence were refused.
- In Yugoslavia, the fragile, multiparty system fell apart. Serbians and Slovenians fought over land and power; ethnic groups in Croatia, Bosnia–Herzegovina, and Macedonia followed suit as the situation degenerated into a vicious, multisided war with acts of genocide committed on both sides.

While politics in the post-Cold War era often seemed to regress, the unity of the world's economies, societies, and cultures continued to move forward. Near the end of the twentieth century, the term *globalization* became prominent to describe the increasing integration and interdependence of the economic, social, cultural, and even ecological aspects of life. The term not only refers to way in which the economies of the world affect one another, but also to the way in which the experience of everyday life is increasingly standardized by the spread of technologies which carry with them social and cultural norms.

❭ Rapid Review

During World War II, the American government secretly funded an effort, known as the Manhattan Project, to build an atomic bomb. In 1945, the project's international team of physicists, led by American physicist Robert Oppenheimer, succeeded in building two atomic bombs. Those bombs were dropped on two Japanese cities: Hiroshima and Nagasaki. The advent of those nuclear weapons forced Japan's unconditional surrender and subsequently created a nuclear arms race between the United States and the Soviet Union.

Following World War II, the Soviet Union solidified its control of Eastern Europe, creating an Iron Curtain that divided East from West. The two superpowers, the United States and the Soviet Union, engaged in a Cold War that had global implications. Meanwhile, the western European nations plotted and followed a course of economic integration that culminated in the creation of the European Union. Between 1985 and 1989, systemic economic problems and a bold attempt at reform led to the rapid disintegration of the Soviet Union, the destruction of the Iron Curtain, and the reunification of Germany. In the decades that followed, two major trends affected life in Europe: the revival of nationalism and the emergence of globalization.

›Chapter Review Questions

1. The settlement that followed World War II is best understood as
   (A) an implementation of Woodrow Wilson's 14-point plan
   (B) a solidifying of the realities that existed at the end of the war
   (C) a reconstruction of the settlement created by the Versailles Treaty
   (D) an outgrowth of globalization
   (E) a revival of nationalism

2. The significance of the Berlin Airlift was
   (A) its demonstration of the commitment of the United States to defend Western Europe from Soviet expansion
   (B) its effect on Hitler, causing him to abandon the invasion of Britain
   (C) that it signaled the end of the war in Germany
   (D) that it led to the division of Berlin into a western and eastern sector
   (E) that it demonstrated the resurgence of the German airforce

3. The plan for financial assistance to rebuild Western Europe after World War II was known as
   (A) the Warsaw Pact
   (B) the Truman Doctrine
   (C) the Council for Mutual Economic Assistance
   (D) the Marshall Plan
   (E) NATO

4. The softening of U.S.–Soviet relations from the late 1960s to the 1980s which led to a series of disarmament talks and missile-limitation treaties is known as
   (A) the Prague Spring
   (B) the Treaty of Rome
   (C) Détente
   (D) Socialism with a Human Face
   (E) globalization

5. The Maastricht Treaty, signed in 1992,
   (A) coordinated coal and steel production in six European nations
   (B) established the European Economic Community (EEC)
   (C) created the European Community (EC)
   (D) established the reunification of Germany
   (E) brought the European Union (EU) into being

6. *Glasnost* refers to
   (A) a social and economic restructuring
   (B) the attempt by Czechoslovakians to humanize socialism
   (C) the rise of nationalism in the former Soviet republics
   (D) an openness to new ideas
   (E) the Polish labor union which led a political revolt in the 1980s and 1990s

7. The movement that began in 1989 in Czechoslovakia and which sought to rebuild notions of citizenship and civic life that had been destroyed by the Soviet system was
   (A) the Velvet Revolution
   (B) the Prague Spring
   (C) the Civic Forum
   (D) Solidarity
   (E) *glasnost*

8. Which of the following is an example of the revival of nationalism in Eastern Europe after the disintegration of the Soviet Union?
   (A) the war between Chechnyans and Russia
   (B) the multisided war in Yugoslavia
   (C) the splitting up of Czechoslovakia
   (D) the war in Bosnia–Herzegovina
   (E) all of the above

❯ Answers and Explanations

1. **B.** The post–World War II settlement, with Germany divided into zones and the eastern European countries under the domination of the Soviet Union, was a solidifying of the reality that the Soviets occupied half of Germany and militarily controlled Eastern Europe. Choice A is incorrect because Wilson's 14-point plan, proposed at the conclusion of World War I, called for the growth of liberal democracy all over Europe; that did not happen behind the Iron Curtain. Choice C is incorrect because there are many differences between the settlement constructed by the Versailles Treaty and the settlement at the end of World War II, chief among them being the fate of Germany, which was shrunk and saddled with war reparations by the Versailles Treaty and divided between east and west and rapidly rebuilt by the superpowers after World War II.

2. **A.** The Berlin Airlift, in which the United States flew supplies into a Soviet-blockaded West Berlin from June 1948 to May 1949, demonstrated the commitment of the United States to defend West Berlin and all of western Europe from Soviet expansion. Choice B is incorrect because it was the Battle of Britain (not the Berlin Airlift) that caused Hitler to abandon his plan for the invasion of Britain. Choice C is incorrect because the chronology is wrong: the war had been over for nearly three years when the Berlin Airlift occurred. Choice D is incorrect because Berlin was already divided into eastern and western sectors prior to the Berlin Airlift. Choice E is incorrect because the Berlin Airlift was carried out by the United States Airforce, in aid of West Berlin (not the German Airforce, which had nothing to do with this).

3. **D.** The Marshall Plan, named after U.S. Secretary of State George Marshall, was the plan which called for pouring billions of dollars of aid into Western Europe to rebuild its infrastructure and economy. Choice A is incorrect because the Warsaw Pact was a military alliance of the communist countries of Eastern Europe. Choice B is incorrect because the Truman Doctrine offered military and economic aid to countries directly threatened by communist takeover (not countries in Western Europe). Choice C is incorrect because the Council for Mutual Economic Assistance was set up by the Soviet Union to counter the Marshall Plan by offering economic aid to eastern European countries (not western European countries). Choice E is incorrect because NATO, the North Atlantic Treaty Organization, united the Western powers in a *military* alliance against the Soviet Union; it had nothing to do with *financial* assistance to Western Europe.

4. **C.** The French term Détente was given to the softening of U.S.–Soviet relations that led to a series of disarmament talks and missile-limitation treaties from the late 1960s to the 1980s. Choices A and D are incorrect because the "the Prague Spring" refers to attempts by Czechoslovakian communists to resist Soviet domination and bring about a relaxation of state intervention in the lives of its citizens, a goal that came to be known as "socialism with a human face." Choice B is incorrect because the Treaty of Rome, signed in 1957, established the European Economic Community (EEC). Choice E is incorrect because globalization was a term coined in the late 1980s to describe the way in which the experience of everyday life is increasingly standardized by the spread of technologies which carry with them social and cultural norms.

5. **E.** The Maastricht Treaty, signed by the 12 countries of the European Community in 1992, created the European Union, the world's largest trading bloc. Choice A is incorrect because it was the European Coal and Steel Community, created in 1952, that coordinated coal and steel production in the six member nations. Choice B is incorrect because it was the Treaty of Rome, signed in 1957, that established the European Economic Community (EEC), sometimes referred to as the Common Market. Choice C is incorrect because it was the merger of the EEC and other cooperative bodies in 1967 that created the European Community (EC). Choice D is incorrect because

German reunification was accomplished by a treaty approved in October of 1990.

6. **D.** The term *glasnost* (or openness) refers to the call by Mikhail Gorbachev in the late 1980s for an openness to new ideas in Soviet society and government. Choice A is incorrect because the term for Gorbachev's call for social and economic restructuring was *perestroika*. Choice B is incorrect because the attempt by Czechoslovakians, in 1968, to humanize socialism was known as "socialism with a human face." Choice C is incorrect because the rise of nationalism in the former Soviet republics occurred as a reaction to *glasnost*. Choice E is incorrect because the Polish labor union which led a political revolt in the 1980s and 1990s was Solidarity.

7. **C.** The movement known as the Civic Forum sought to rebuild notions of citizenship and civic life that had been destroyed by the Soviet system. Choice A is incorrect because the phrase "the Velvet Revolution" refers to the entire process, of which the Civic Forum was only a part, by which civic opposition eroded the communist regime in Czechoslovakia. Choice B is incorrect because "the Prague Spring" refers to the uprisings of Czechoslovakians against Soviet domination in 1968. Choice D is incorrect because Solidarity is the name of the Polish labor union which led a revolt against Soviet oppression in Poland. Choice E is incorrect because *glasnost* refers to the openness to new ideas called for by Mikhail Gorbachev.

8. **E.** All of the choices are correct. The Chechnyan conflict arose because of Russia's refusal to accede to Chechnyan nationalist demands for independence. The multisided conflicts in Yugoslavia and in Bosnia–Herzegovina involved both ethnic tensions between and nationalist aspirations of the Serbs, Slovenes, Croats, Bosnians and several other groups. The splitting up of Czechoslovakia was the result of nationalist aspirations of the Slovaks.

UNIT 2 Summary: The Napoleonic Era to the Present

Timeline

1802	Napoleon becomes first consul for life in France
1804	Napoleon crowns himself emperor of France
1814	The Congress of Vienna creates the Concert of Europe
1815	Napoleon is defeated at Waterloo
1830	July Ordinances in France are followed by a revolution, which forces Charles X to abdicate
1839–1842	Opium War: British defeat Chinese, opening China to the West
1848	Year of revolution in Europe
June 1848	"June Days," Revolutionaries are beaten by the army in Paris
December 1848	Louis-Napoleon is elected president of the Second Republic in France
1848	Karl Marx publishes the *Communist Manifesto*
1851	Louis-Napoleon overthrows the Second Republic in France, becomes Napoleon III
1853	U.S. naval forces open Japan to the West
1857	Sepoy Rebellion: Britain replaces East India Company and governs India directly
1864	Marx founds the First International Working Men's Association
1866	Italian unification is mostly complete (Rome added in 1870)
1866	Austro-Prussian War: victorious Prussia organizes the North German Confederation
1867	Second Reform Bill passed in Britain, doubling the electorate
1869	Suez Canal opened
1870–1871	Franco-Prussian War
January 18, 1871	German unification is complete; Second Reich proclaimed
1876	Stanley sets up posts in the Congo for Leopold II of Belgium
1881	Tsar Alexander II assassinated in Russia
1882	Britain occupies Egypt
1884	Berlin Conference sets up guidelines for Africa
1884	Reform Bill in Britain grants vote to nearly all English men
1889	Second International Working Men's Association founded
1903–1905	Russo-Japanese War; victorious Japanese a modern power
June 28, 1914	Archduke Franz Ferdinand of Austria assassinated at Sarajevo
August 4, 1914	Germany invades Belgium
August 1914	Russians invade East Prussia and are defeated by Germans at Tannenberg
September 1914	First Battle of Marne saves Paris
February 1916	Germans fail to capture fortress town of Verdun
July–November 1916	Battle of the Somme
March 1917	Tsarist regime overthrown in Russia
April 6, 1917	United States declares war on Germany
November 1917	Bolsheviks, led by Lenin, take control of Russia
March 1918	Russia signs Treaty of Brest–Litovsk, withdraws from the war
March–June 1918	Germans launch last great offensive, advance to within 56 miles of Paris
August 8, 1918	British victory at Amiens

November 11, 1918	Germany signs armistice, ending World War I
January 1919	Paris Peace Conference
June 28, 1919	Germany signs Treaty of Paris
1921–1928	New Economic Plan in Russia
1922	Mussolini and fascists rise to power in Italy
1924	Lenin dies, succeeded by Stalin
1928	First of Stalin's five-year plans begins rapid industrialization of Russia
1929	Collectivization of agriculture in Russia
1933	Hitler becomes chancellor of Germany
1936–1939	Spanish Civil War
March 1938	Germany annexes Austria
September 1938	Munich Agreement; Hitler allowed to annex Sudetenland
March 1939	Germany invades Czechoslovakia
September 1939	Germany invades Poland, World War II begins
June 22, 1940	France surrenders
August–September 1940	Battle of Britain
June 1941	Germany launches offensive against the Soviet Union
December 7, 1941	Japan attacks Pearl Harbor; United States enters the war
1941–1945	Holocaust; Nazi regime murders six million Jews
1942	Tide of battle turns in Allies' favor
September 1943	Italy surrenders
June 6, 1944	D-Day, Allies land at Normandy
August 1944	Paris is liberated
January 1945	Soviet troops invade Germany
March–April 1945	Allies penetrate Germany
May 7, 1945	Germany surrenders
August 1945	United States drops atomic bombs on Hiroshima and Nagasaki; Japan surrenders
1947	Cold War begins; Truman Doctrine and Marshall Plan inaugurated
1949	NATO founded; Soviet Union acquires atomic bomb
1957	European Economic Community founded
1961	Berlin Wall built
1968	Prague Spring
1985	Gorbachev becomes leader of the Soviet Union
1988	Communist dictatorship in Poland ends
1989	Year of revolution in Europe; communist regimes ousted in Eastern Europe

KEY IDEA

Key Comparisons

1. Industrialization in Great Britain and on the continent of Europe
2. The development of mass politics in Great Britain and on the continent of Europe
3. The unification of Italy and the unification of Germany
4. German aspirations in World Wars I and II
5. The nature of war in World Wars I and II
6. Economic and political developments in Western and Eastern Europe after World War II

Thematic Change/Continuity

KEY IDEA

Economic changes
The Second Industrial Revolution and growth of the middle class
The creation and expansion of the British Empire
The rise of the United States and the Soviet Union as the dominant economic forces after
    World War II
Integration of the European economy

Economic continuities
British leadership maintained (until World War II)

Social/cultural changes
Death of the belief in progress in European culture
Rise and spread of globalization

Social/cultural continuities
Anti-Semitism

Political changes
Development of mass politics
Rise of extreme nationalism
Creation of the Soviet Union and the Iron Curtain
Dominance of the United States and Soviet Union after World War II

Political continuities
Western European leadership in progress towards democratization

STEP **5**

Build Your Test-Taking Confidence

AP European History Practice Test 1

AP European History Practice Test 2

AP European History
Practice Test 1—Section I

ANSWER SHEET

1 Ⓐ Ⓑ Ⓒ Ⓓ Ⓔ	31 Ⓐ Ⓑ Ⓒ Ⓓ Ⓔ	61 Ⓐ Ⓑ Ⓒ Ⓓ Ⓔ
2 Ⓐ Ⓑ Ⓒ Ⓓ Ⓔ	32 Ⓐ Ⓑ Ⓒ Ⓓ Ⓔ	62 Ⓐ Ⓑ Ⓒ Ⓓ Ⓔ
3 Ⓐ Ⓑ Ⓒ Ⓓ Ⓔ	33 Ⓐ Ⓑ Ⓒ Ⓓ Ⓔ	63 Ⓐ Ⓑ Ⓒ Ⓓ Ⓔ
4 Ⓐ Ⓑ Ⓒ Ⓓ Ⓔ	34 Ⓐ Ⓑ Ⓒ Ⓓ Ⓔ	64 Ⓐ Ⓑ Ⓒ Ⓓ Ⓔ
5 Ⓐ Ⓑ Ⓒ Ⓓ Ⓔ	35 Ⓐ Ⓑ Ⓒ Ⓓ Ⓔ	65 Ⓐ Ⓑ Ⓒ Ⓓ Ⓔ
6 Ⓐ Ⓑ Ⓒ Ⓓ Ⓔ	36 Ⓐ Ⓑ Ⓒ Ⓓ Ⓔ	66 Ⓐ Ⓑ Ⓒ Ⓓ Ⓔ
7 Ⓐ Ⓑ Ⓒ Ⓓ Ⓔ	37 Ⓐ Ⓑ Ⓒ Ⓓ Ⓔ	67 Ⓐ Ⓑ Ⓒ Ⓓ Ⓔ
8 Ⓐ Ⓑ Ⓒ Ⓓ Ⓔ	38 Ⓐ Ⓑ Ⓒ Ⓓ Ⓔ	68 Ⓐ Ⓑ Ⓒ Ⓓ Ⓔ
9 Ⓐ Ⓑ Ⓒ Ⓓ Ⓔ	39 Ⓐ Ⓑ Ⓒ Ⓓ Ⓔ	69 Ⓐ Ⓑ Ⓒ Ⓓ Ⓔ
10 Ⓐ Ⓑ Ⓒ Ⓓ Ⓔ	40 Ⓐ Ⓑ Ⓒ Ⓓ Ⓔ	70 Ⓐ Ⓑ Ⓒ Ⓓ Ⓔ
11 Ⓐ Ⓑ Ⓒ Ⓓ Ⓔ	41 Ⓐ Ⓑ Ⓒ Ⓓ Ⓔ	71 Ⓐ Ⓑ Ⓒ Ⓓ Ⓔ
12 Ⓐ Ⓑ Ⓒ Ⓓ Ⓔ	42 Ⓐ Ⓑ Ⓒ Ⓓ Ⓔ	72 Ⓐ Ⓑ Ⓒ Ⓓ Ⓔ
13 Ⓐ Ⓑ Ⓒ Ⓓ Ⓔ	43 Ⓐ Ⓑ Ⓒ Ⓓ Ⓔ	73 Ⓐ Ⓑ Ⓒ Ⓓ Ⓔ
14 Ⓐ Ⓑ Ⓒ Ⓓ Ⓔ	44 Ⓐ Ⓑ Ⓒ Ⓓ Ⓔ	74 Ⓐ Ⓑ Ⓒ Ⓓ Ⓔ
15 Ⓐ Ⓑ Ⓒ Ⓓ Ⓔ	45 Ⓐ Ⓑ Ⓒ Ⓓ Ⓔ	75 Ⓐ Ⓑ Ⓒ Ⓓ Ⓔ
16 Ⓐ Ⓑ Ⓒ Ⓓ Ⓔ	46 Ⓐ Ⓑ Ⓒ Ⓓ Ⓔ	76 Ⓐ Ⓑ Ⓒ Ⓓ Ⓔ
17 Ⓐ Ⓑ Ⓒ Ⓓ Ⓔ	47 Ⓐ Ⓑ Ⓒ Ⓓ Ⓔ	77 Ⓐ Ⓑ Ⓒ Ⓓ Ⓔ
18 Ⓐ Ⓑ Ⓒ Ⓓ Ⓔ	48 Ⓐ Ⓑ Ⓒ Ⓓ Ⓔ	78 Ⓐ Ⓑ Ⓒ Ⓓ Ⓔ
19 Ⓐ Ⓑ Ⓒ Ⓓ Ⓔ	49 Ⓐ Ⓑ Ⓒ Ⓓ Ⓔ	79 Ⓐ Ⓑ Ⓒ Ⓓ Ⓔ
20 Ⓐ Ⓑ Ⓒ Ⓓ Ⓔ	50 Ⓐ Ⓑ Ⓒ Ⓓ Ⓔ	80 Ⓐ Ⓑ Ⓒ Ⓓ Ⓔ
21 Ⓐ Ⓑ Ⓒ Ⓓ Ⓔ	51 Ⓐ Ⓑ Ⓒ Ⓓ Ⓔ	
22 Ⓐ Ⓑ Ⓒ Ⓓ Ⓔ	52 Ⓐ Ⓑ Ⓒ Ⓓ Ⓔ	
23 Ⓐ Ⓑ Ⓒ Ⓓ Ⓔ	53 Ⓐ Ⓑ Ⓒ Ⓓ Ⓔ	
24 Ⓐ Ⓑ Ⓒ Ⓓ Ⓔ	54 Ⓐ Ⓑ Ⓒ Ⓓ Ⓔ	
25 Ⓐ Ⓑ Ⓒ Ⓓ Ⓔ	55 Ⓐ Ⓑ Ⓒ Ⓓ Ⓔ	
26 Ⓐ Ⓑ Ⓒ Ⓓ Ⓔ	56 Ⓐ Ⓑ Ⓒ Ⓓ Ⓔ	
27 Ⓐ Ⓑ Ⓒ Ⓓ Ⓔ	57 Ⓐ Ⓑ Ⓒ Ⓓ Ⓔ	
28 Ⓐ Ⓑ Ⓒ Ⓓ Ⓔ	58 Ⓐ Ⓑ Ⓒ Ⓓ Ⓔ	
29 Ⓐ Ⓑ Ⓒ Ⓓ Ⓔ	59 Ⓐ Ⓑ Ⓒ Ⓓ Ⓔ	
30 Ⓐ Ⓑ Ⓒ Ⓓ Ⓔ	60 Ⓐ Ⓑ Ⓒ Ⓓ Ⓔ	

AP European History
Practice Test 1

Section I

Time—55 minutes

80 Questions

Directions: Each of the questions or incomplete statements below is followed by five suggested answers or completions. Select the one that is best in each case and fill in the circle for the letter that corresponds to your choice on the Answer Sheet supplied.

1. The most outstanding social effect of the development of a division of labor system of production was
   (A) increased volume of manufactured goods
   (B) unemployment or decreased wages for skilled craftsmen
   (C) increased profits for manufacturers
   (D) increased efficiency
   (E) decreased volume of manufactured goods

2. The development of the Bessemer process was significant because it
   (A) doubled cotton production
   (B) facilitated the move away from human and water power
   (C) shifted the balance of military power in the nineteenth century
   (D) allowed for the manufacture of iron and steel more cheaply and in larger quantities
   (E) doubled the speed with which goods could be transported

3. Throughout the Industrial Revolution, the country that held the lead in innovation and industrial production was
   (A) Russia
   (B) France
   (C) Germany
   (D) Great Britain
   (E) Holland

4. Of the nineteenth-century ideologies, the one that most staunchly defended the institution of monarchy was
   (A) conservatism
   (B) liberalism
   (C) socialism
   (D) communism
   (E) anarchism

5. The doctrine of *laissez-faire*, often attributed to the Scottish philosopher Adam Smith, argued that
   (A) people should be able to do whatever they want
   (B) Scotland should be free of English rule
   (C) governments should not try to interfere with the natural workings of an economy
   (D) welfare laws would retard the evolution of human society
   (E) imperial expansion was a necessary outcome of natural laws

6. Utilitarians differed from other liberals in their
   (A) support of tradition
   (B) emphasis on individual liberty
   (C) tendency to be more supportive of government intervention
   (D) call for the abolition of private property
   (E) advocacy of violence

7. Which of the following was a tenet of Martin Luther's theology?
   (A) salvation through good works
   (B) Church tradition as a source of knowledge about God
   (C) predestination
   (D) millenarianism
   (E) salvation by faith alone

8. The greatest significance of the Council of Trent for the history of Europe was
   (A) its triumph over Protestantism
   (B) its successful reform of the Roman Church
   (C) its pledge, on the part of the German princes, not to go to war over religion
   (D) that it signified a defeat for those who wished for reconciliation between Protestants and the Roman Church
   (E) that it served as an anti-Protestant force all over the globe

GO ON TO THE NEXT PAGE

9. The relative peace of the Restoration Period in England broke down when
   (A) Oliver Cromwell died
   (B) James II ascended to the throne
   (C) Charles II ascended to the throne
   (D) Elizabeth I ascended to the throne
   (E) a Protestant fleet invaded from the Netherlands

10. The degree of absolutism achieved by the seventeenth-century Bourbon monarchy in France is best explained by
    (A) the relatively low degree of religious turmoil in seventeenth-century France
    (B) the fact that seventeenth-century France was a republic
    (C) the series of "little ice ages" that characterized the climate of the 1600s
    (D) the availability of cheap housing for the rural poor
    (E) the brilliance of Louis XIV

11. The baroque style was popular in buildings built by
    (A) the aristocratic class only
    (B) all the classes of eighteenth-century Europe
    (C) absolute monarchs of seventeenth-century Europe
    (D) the lower classes
    (E) the bourgeoisie of nineteenth-century Europe

12. In early-twentieth-century Britain, the organization that advocated a broader notion of women's rights was the
    (A) Women's Social and Political Union
    (B) Fabian Society
    (C) Social Democrats
    (D) National Union of Women's Suffrage Societies
    (E) Zionists

13. In Britain, the political party that made the largest gains in the first decade of the twentieth century was the
    (A) Conservative Party
    (B) Liberal Party
    (C) Labour Party
    (D) British Union of Fascists
    (E) Democratic Party

14. Which of the following was a serious problem faced by the government of the Weimar Republic?
    (A) Its form was largely alien to the German people.
    (B) It was perceived to have been imposed on Germany by its vengeful war enemies.
    (C) It was blamed for the humiliating nature of the Treaty of Versailles.
    (D) It was faced with insurmountable economic problems.
    (E) All of the above.

15. Lenin's plan to allow small-scale private enterprise in order to stimulate the Russian economy was known as
    (A) the five-year plan
    (B) the New Economic Plan
    (C) the Soviet Constitution of 1923
    (D) socialism in one country
    (E) the collectivization of agriculture

16. Of the following, which is true of the fascists' rise to power in Italy?
    (A) They seized power illegally through a military coup.
    (B) They appealed to the working classes by promising to abolish private property and bring about a classless society.
    (C) They gathered massive public support by opposing the socialists and giving a sense of purpose to the disillusioned and unemployed.
    (D) They were opposed by the Church.
    (E) They were opposed by industrialists who feared that the fascists would nationalize industry.

17. The settlement which followed World War II differed from that which followed World War I because
    (A) It blamed Germany for the war.
    (B) It was a settlement imposed by the victors.
    (C) It dismantled the Hapsburg Empire.
    (D) It created national boundaries that ignored significant ethnic and nationalist differences.
    (E) There was no formal treaty or series of treaties signifying formal acceptance of the settlement.

GO ON TO THE NEXT PAGE

18. The *Risorgimento* failed because
    (A) it failed to attract intellectuals
    (B) it was not sufficiently nationalistic
    (C) it failed to win the support of the masses
    (D) it failed to win German support
    (E) the military was not strong enough

19. The successful nineteenth-century drive for unification in Germany differed from that in Italy in which of the following ways?
    (A) It was led by a conservative aristocrat.
    (B) It was free of direct foreign domination.
    (C) It sought to rally support around a popular monarch.
    (D) Its strategy was characterized by opportunism.
    (E) It required the provocation of war.

20. European imperialism in Asia differed from that in Africa in which of the following ways?
    (A) It lacked economic motives.
    (B) It was facilitated by technological innovations in weaponry and transportation.
    (C) It was connected to nationalism.
    (D) It was connected to the development of mass politics.
    (E) It was exerted through control of the local elite.

21. The term "Détente" refers to
    (A) the efforts of Czechoslovakian communists to reform their society in 1968
    (B) the post-World War II division of Europe into a West of United States–backed Western powers and an East dominated by the Soviet Union
    (C) the 51-member international organization created to promote international peace and cooperation
    (D) the U.S. mission to fly supplies into West Berlin in response to a Soviet shutdown of supply lines
    (E) a period of U.S.–Soviet relations characterized by a number of nuclear test-ban treaties and arms-limitation talks

22. The Warsaw Pact
    (A) was a military alliance among the countries of Eastern Europe
    (B) formed a military alliance between Poland and Russia
    (C) offered economic assistance to the countries of Eastern Europe
    (D) was a military alliance between the United States and western European powers
    (E) offered military and economic aid to countries threatened by communist takeover

23. The theory which came to be known as Copernicanism
    (A) argued that each piece of matter in the universe was attracted to every other particle of matter by a universally operating force.
    (B) promoted a geocentric model of the cosmos
    (C) declared that all matter was made up of four elements
    (D) promoted a heliocentric model of the cosmos
    (E) argued that the universe was infinite

24. Mary Wollstonecraft's criticism, in 1792, of the subjugation of women in European society on the grounds that the subjugation was irrational identifies her as
    (A) a conservative
    (B) an Enlightenment *philosophe*
    (C) a socialist
    (D) an anarchist
    (E) a suffragist

25. "Man is born free; and everywhere he is in chains." This quotation summarizes the view of human nature of
    (A) John Locke
    (B) Martin Luther
    (C) Jean-Jacques Rousseau
    (D) Voltaire
    (E) Jeremy Bentham

26. The Middle Passage refers to
    (A) Scripture
    (B) the shipping channel that connects the Mediterranean Sea and the Red Sea
    (C) the advent of rural manufacturing
    (D) the route to China that was the backbone of the silk trade
    (E) the transportation of African slaves across the Atlantic to the Americas and the West Indies

GO ON TO THE NEXT PAGE

27. Which of the following was NOT a way in which European armies changed in the eighteenth century?
    (A) They became larger.
    (B) The discipline and training became harsher and more extensive.
    (C) The officer corps became full-time servants of the state.
    (D) Troops came to consist predominantly of conscripts.
    (E) The officer corps were chosen and promoted on the basis of merit.

28. The decision by the representatives of the Third Estate to declare themselves, on June 17, 1789, to be the National Assembly of France signified
    (A) their intention to form a republic
    (B) their belief that political sovereignty belonged to the nation as a whole
    (C) their intention to overthrow the monarchy
    (D) their belief in democracy
    (E) their willingness to go to war with Germany

29. The agreement signed by Napoleon and the pope that stipulated that French clergy would be chosen and paid by the French state but consecrated by the pope is known as the
    (A) Concordat of 1801
    (B) Napoleonic Code
    (C) Consulate
    (D) Treaty of Tilsit
    (E) Continental System

30. The principle of "he who rules; his religion" was established by
    (A) the Edict of Nantes
    (B) the papacy in Rome
    (C) the Geneva Convention
    (D) the Peace of Augsburg in 1555
    (E) the Inquisition

31. Which of the following were part of the structure of Calvinist communities?
    (A) pastors
    (B) doctors
    (C) deacons
    (D) elders
    (E) all of the above

32. The period of British history 1649–1660, in which Britain was ruled without a monarch, is known as
    (A) the Restoration
    (B) the Glorious Revolution
    (C) the Commonwealth
    (D) the English Civil War
    (E) the Norman Conquest

33. Neoplatonism was an important component of the Scientific Revolution because
    (A) it encouraged the development of a tradition of chemical experimentation
    (B) it promoted the scientific method
    (C) it argued that scientific knowledge had practical implications
    (D) it denied the existence of God
    (E) it stimulated interest in a mathematical approach to the investigation of the natural world

34. In *Crime and Punishment* (1764), the Italian philosopher Cesare Beccaria extended the Enlightenment line of thought by arguing that
    (A) the purpose of punishment should be to rehabilitate and reintegrate the individual into society
    (B) an all-powerful ruler was necessary to keep order and prevent crime
    (C) the death penalty should be abolished
    (D) the punishment for crimes should be standard in all kingdoms
    (E) society corrupts human nature, which is naturally good

35. The significance of the Masons in eighteenth-century Europe was
    (A) their impact on the architecture of the period
    (B) their plot to assassinate the pope
    (C) that they provided a home for revolutionary plots
    (D) that their lodges formed a network for the communication for new ideas and ideals
    (E) the reform of currency they carried out

36. Which of the following were factors in the breaking of the traditional population cycle in eighteenth-century Europe?
    (A) the Black Death
    (B) the Hundred Years War
    (C) the development of heavy industry
    (D) the development of rural manufacturing
    (E) the advent of steam power

GO ON TO THE NEXT PAGE

37. Which of the following helps to account for the death of the liberal–nationalist alliance in nineteenth-century Europe?
    (A) the liberals' emphasis on individual liberty
    (B) the nationalists' tendency to mythologize the past
    (C) the liberals' emphasis on limited government
    (D) the failure of the liberals to hold and use the power they had seized at the beginning of 1848
    (E) all of the above

38. Bismarck's strategy of increasing Prussia's power by whatever means and strategies were necessary and useful has come to be known as
    (A) Détente
    (B) *Lebensraum*
    (C) *Realpolitik*
    (D) the Schlieffen Plan
    (E) the *Kulturkampf*

39. The radical break with tradition and convention ushered in by the French Revolution was experienced in the world of art through
    (A) the development of impressionism
    (B) a rejection of realism
    (C) the readoption of religious subject matter
    (D) the rejection of the dominant rococo aesthetic in favor of a neoclassical style
    (E) works like Caravaggio's *Calling of St. Matthew* and *Conversion of St. Peter*

40. Which of the following did NOT contribute to the outbreak of World War I?
    (A) the Anglo-German rivalry
    (B) the Alliance System
    (C) the rise of a unified Germany as an industrial and military power in Europe
    (D) German military planning
    (E) the remilitarization of the Rhineland

41. In late-nineteenth-century France, the Dreyfus affair illustrated
    (A) the weakness of French nationalism
    (B) the strength of ultranationalist and anti-Semitic sentiment in the French establishment
    (C) the subjugation of women in French society
    (D) France's lack of military preparation
    (E) France's desire for war with Germany

Source: Wikipedia (Public Domain Image).

42. The above propaganda poster from the period 1917–1920
    (A) depicts Germans mistreating Russian Army prisoners
    (B) illustrates Stalin's collectivization of agriculture
    (C) depicts Stalin purging his political enemies
    (D) depicts Trotsky as a Jewish devil and Bolsheviks as foreigners
    (E) illustrates the atrocities of the Holocaust

43. The most significant aspect of the social composition of the Renaissance art world was
    (A) the high degree of women's participation in it
    (B) its apprentice system
    (C) the large proportion of artists who came from the elite classes
    (D) the lack of a patronage system
    (E) the high degree of specialization that was demanded

44. In France, England, and Spain the Renaissance was centered in
    (A) the great independent city-states
    (B) the royal courts
    (C) small independent religious communities
    (D) the great universities
    (E) all of the above

GO ON TO THE NEXT PAGE

45. The Anglican Church, as created by Henry VIII, differed from other Protestant churches in that it
    (A) was congregational
    (B) remained loyal to Rome
    (C) had an episcopal structure
    (D) broke with Rome
    (E) abolished the sacraments

46. The landholding nobles of Central and Eastern Europe differed from those in Western Europe in the period 1600–1715 in that they
    (A) were drastically reduced in number
    (B) made an alliance with the middle classes
    (C) triumphed in their struggle with the monarchs
    (D) lost control of their lands
    (E) retained control of vast estates worked by serfs

47. The publication, in 1632, of the *Dialogue on the Two Chief Systems of the World* resulted in Galileo being called before the Inquisition because
    (A) it described the Copernican system
    (B) it blatantly ridiculed the Aristotelian system in the vernacular Italian
    (C) it denied the existence of God
    (D) it was a Protestant text
    (E) it claimed that the Copernican system was actually true

48. Enlightened despotism refers to
    (A) the idea that powerful rulers would act to reform and rationalize European society
    (B) Prussian militarism
    (C) the rule of law
    (D) the extensive, international correspondence network of the *philosophes*
    (E) a network of fraternities linked together by a Grand Lodge

49. The enclosure movement in Britain was most directly a result of
    (A) the development of the manorial system
    (B) the failure of mercantilism
    (C) the collectivization of agriculture
    (D) the development of the Bessemer process
    (E) the development of market-oriented agriculture

50. In the French Revolution, the March to Versailles that occurred in October of 1789 illustrates
    (A) the conservative nature of the *sans-culottes*
    (B) the power of the French army
    (C) the beginning of the radical phase of the revolution
    (D) the fact that the crowds of Paris did not yet look upon Louis XVI as their enemy
    (E) the brilliance of Napoleon as a military leader

51. The celebratory mood at the outset of World War I is best explained by
    (A) a fascination with militarism that pervaded European culture
    (B) feelings of fraternity or brotherhood that a war effort brought out in people who lived in an increasingly fragmented and divided society
    (C) a sense of romantic adventurism that cast war as an alternative to the mundane, working life of industrial Europe
    (D) expectations that the war would be short
    (E) all of the above

52. American entry into World War I was mostly triggered by
    (A) America's economic rivalry with Germany
    (B) America's desire to seize German colonies
    (C) the sinking of American vessels by German U-boats
    (D) the fall of Paris to the Germans
    (E) the Zimmerman Note

53. Abstractionist painters of the early twentieth century
    (A) sought to depict a world of emotional and psychological states
    (B) sought to accurately and honestly render the life around them in meticulous detail
    (C) sought to "analyze" the essence of perception and experience
    (D) sought to evoke the glory and power of ancient Rome
    (E) sought to reflect the grandeur of the aristocracy

GO ON TO THE NEXT PAGE

54. Which of the following helps to explain the British policy of appeasement of Germany during the 1930s?
    (A) The British public wanted no part of renewed hostilities.
    (B) Many of the British leaders privately agreed with the Germans that the Versailles Treaty had been unprecedented and unwarranted.
    (C) British leaders believed that a decision to pursue a military response to Hitler's demands was politically unwise.
    (D) Britain and her allies were not prepared militarily to back up any ultimatums they might give to Hitler.
    (E) All of the above.

55. Which of the following did NOT occur following World War II?
    (A) Germany was divided into western and eastern sectors.
    (B) Germany, in what came to be known as "the war guilt clause," was forced to accept full blame for the war
    (C) Poland's border with Germany was pushed westward.
    (D) The United Nations was created.
    (E) Pro-Soviet governments were installed in Eastern Europe.

56. The treatment received by Alexander Solzhenitsyn illustrated the Soviet regime's
    (A) preference for technocratic expertise
    (B) total immunity to pressure from the West
    (C) insistence on absolute conformity
    (D) new, more democratic policies
    (E) commitment to *glasnost*

57. The main motivation of the architects of the process of European integration that has culminated in the European Union was to
    (A) stand on more equal footing with the superpowers: the United States and the Soviet Union
    (B) end communism
    (C) rebuild a war-torn economy
    (D) increase iron and steel production
    (E) all of the above

58. The most prevalent form of religious belief among the *philosophes* was
    (A) Catholicism
    (B) Lutheranism
    (C) Islam
    (D) deism
    (E) atheism

59. Which of the following was NOT a component of the triangle of trade?
    (A) guns
    (B) silk
    (C) cotton
    (D) timber
    (E) slaves

60. The cottage industry or putting-out system that had a dramatic effect on European economic and social life in the eighteenth century primarily produced
    (A) steel
    (B) iron
    (C) cotton
    (D) guns
    (E) textiles

61. During the French Revolution, Robespierre asserted that terror was necessary because
    (A) there was no God
    (B) the revolution fought against genuine tyranny
    (C) the aims of the revolution were virtuous
    (D) the people were not loyal
    (E) the king had betrayed the people

62. The Frankfort Assembly's decision in 1848 to offer Frederick William IV of Prussia the crown of a united Germany illustrates
    (A) the power of parliamentary traditions in Germany
    (B) the weakness of the Germany monarchy
    (C) the role of liberalism in the unification of Germany
    (D) the tension between liberalism and nationalism in mid-nineteenth-century Europe
    (E) the charisma of Frederick William IV

GO ON TO THE NEXT PAGE

63. The advantage of electrical power over steam power that came to be exploited toward the end of the nineteenth century was the
    (A) speed of electricity
    (B) reliability of electrical power
    (C) greater versatility and ease of transportation of electrical generators
    (D) cheaper cost of electrical power
    (E) greater energy output of electrical generators

64. Which of the following was an outgrowth of the strain of thought known as social Darwinism?
    (A) eugenics
    (B) relief of the poor
    (C) workhouses
    (D) child labor laws
    (E) women's suffrage

65. In order to increase the power of the newly unified Spanish monarchy, Ferdinand and Isabella
    (A) instituted liberal reforms
    (B) bought the loyalty of the Spanish nobility by strengthening the institution of serfdom
    (C) allowed Protestantism to flourish in Spain
    (D) signed an alliance with Britain and France
    (E) used the Church to build national unity

66. The work of art that both captures the emphasis on human form and illustrates the last and most heroic phase of Renaissance art is
    (A) Giotto's *Life of St. Francis*
    (B) Picasso's *Guernica*
    (C) Donatello's *David*
    (D) Michelangelo's *David*
    (E) St Peter's Basilica

67. After the publication of Newton's *Principia Mathematica* in 1687,
    (A) mathematics became the "queen of the sciences"
    (B) people spoke of a universe instead of a cosmos
    (C) it was known that Jupiter had four moons
    (D) it was understood that the cosmos was geocentric
    (E) Newton was condemned by the Catholic Church

68. The *Encyclopedia* of the late eighteenth century was considered radical because it
    (A) was printed in English rather than Latin
    (B) was the first multivolume publication
    (C) labeled anything not based on reason as superstition
    (D) called for a revolution and overthrow of the monarchy
    (E) was a Protestant encyclopedia

69. Russia participated in the expansionist trend of the late eighteenth century by
    (A) defeating the Ottoman Turks in 1774
    (B) single-handedly conquering Poland in 1775
    (C) invading Prussia in 1770
    (D) enacting the Pragmatic Sanction
    (E) invading Finland in 1774

70. The event most responsible for turning the people of Paris against Louis XVI was
    (A) his attempt to flee Paris in June of 1791
    (B) his decision to execute Robespierre
    (C) his decision to raise taxes
    (D) his decision to crush the Paris Commune
    (E) his decision to issue the Civil Constitution of the Clergy

71. The Boulanger Affair in the late 1880s
    (A) testified to the strength of anti-Semitism in France
    (B) led to the fall of the Second Republic
    (C) was evidence of the radical nature of the French working class
    (D) led to the election of a socialist popular front
    (E) underscored the fragility of French democracy and the volatility of mass politics in France

72. The Sepoy Rebellion of 1857
    (A) was a vast nationalist uprising
    (B) demonstrated anti-Western sentiment in China
    (C) drove the British from Burma
    (D) led the British government to begin to rule India directly
    (E) led the British to concentrate on bringing liberal reforms to India

GO ON TO THE NEXT PAGE

73. The Taiping Rebellion is connected to European history because
    (A) the rebels were demanding Western-style reform
    (B) it was a result of the Russo-Japanese war
    (C) western encroachment undermined the power of the ruling dynasty
    (D) it was caused by fighting in World War II
    (E) the rebels were acting at the instigation of westerners

74. In the interwar years, the reconstituted nations of East-Central Europe, Hungary, Poland, and Yugoslavia,
    (A) flourished economically
    (B) became satellite states of the Soviet Union
    (C) ceased to exist
    (D) came to be ruled by right-wing, authoritarian regimes
    (E) were ruled by liberal-democratic parliaments

75. The German election of 1932 was significant because
    (A) it brought a socialist coalition to power
    (B) the Nazi Party won 35 percent of the vote
    (C) Hitler was elected Chancellor of Germany
    (D) a coalition of right-wing parties was elected
    (E) it was never held; Hitler seized power in order to prevent an expected socialist victory

76. The Marshall Plan of 1947 demonstrates that the United States was
    (A) an imperialist country
    (B) fearful of Soviet military expansion into Western Europe
    (C) mindful of the role that economic hopelessness had played in the rise of fascism
    (D) ready to enter World War II
    (E) fearful of Germany rising again

A BRUTAL FELLOW.

Policeman. "NOW MUM! WHAT'S THE MATTER?"
Injured Female. "IF YOU PLEASE, MISTER—I WANT TO GIVE MY WHETCH OF A 'USBAND IN CHARGE. HE'S ALLVAYS A KNOCKING OF ME DOWN AND A STAMPIN' ON ME!"

Source: *Punch* (public domain), the John Leech Archive.

77. Which of the following is connoted by the cartoon above?
    (A) support for the women's suffrage movement
    (B) skepticism about claims that marriage abuses many women
    (C) the need for child labor laws
    (D) the need for the protection of abused women
    (E) the need for a larger police force

78. Which of the following accurately illustrates the reciprocal nature of innovation in the Second Industrial Revolution?
    (A) the increase in the demand for coal created by the introduction of steam power
    (B) the demand for more and improved steam engines created by the development of the iron and steel industries
    (C) the need for a railway system to transport iron and steel
    (D) the increased demand for iron and steel created by the development of the railroad
    (E) all of the above

GO ON TO THE NEXT PAGE

79. In the first decades of the twentieth century, the "nationalities problem" referred to
    (A) the absence of an international organization to coordinate diplomacy
    (B) the Anglo-German arms race
    (C) the rise of ultranationalist parties
    (D) the agitation of linguistic and ethnic minorities within the Hapsburg Empire
    (E) the agitation of southern Slavs for independence from the Russian Empire

80. Fritz Lang's film *Metropolis* (1925) illustrates
    (A) the feeling of gaiety that permeated "the Roaring Twenties"
    (B) the futuristic style of architecture that was prevalent in the interwar years
    (C) the deep anxiety over the future that existed in the 1920s
    (D) the romantic sensibilities of the era
    (E) the year for the pastoral that characterized the films of the era

STOP. End of Section I

Section II

Part A

(Suggested writing time—45 minutes)

Directions: The following question is based on the accompanying Documents 1–10. (The documents have been edited for the purpose of this exercise.) Write your answer on the lined pages provided with the Answer Sheet.

This question is designed to test your ability to work with and understand historical documents. Write an essay that:

- has a relevant thesis and supports that thesis with evidence from the documents
- uses the majority of the documents
- addresses all parts of the question
- analyzes the documents by organizing them in as many appropriate ways as possible and does not simply summarize the documents individually
- takes into account both the sources of the documents and the authors' points of view

You may refer to relevant historical information not mentioned in the documents.

1. Compare and contrast the ideologies presented below concerning the proper form and role of government in society.

Historical background: From the late eighteenth through to the early twentieth centuries, Europe saw the development of mass politics and political parties. In response, nineteenth-century intellectuals codified their attitudes about society into ideologies which served as the basis of a political platform for their parties. Often, they were responding to each other.

Document 1

Source: Samuel Smiles, *Self-Help*, London, 1859.
Even the best institutions can give man no active aid. Perhaps the utmost they can do is to leave him free to develop himself and improve his individual condition. But in all times men have been prone to believe that their happiness and well-being were to be secured by means of institutions rather than by their own conduct. Hence the value of legislation as an agent in human advancement has always been greatly over-estimated.

Document 2

Joseph de Maistre, *Essay on the Generative Principle of Political Constitutions*, 1809.
One of the greatest errors of a century which professed them all was to believe that a political constitution could be created and written *a priori*, whereas reason and experience unite in proving that a constitution is a divine work and that precisely the most fundamental and essentially constitutional of a nation's laws could not possibly be written.

Document 3

Source: John Stuart Mill, *On Liberty*, London, 1859.
. . . the sole end for which mankind are warranted, individually or collectively, in interfering with the liberty of action of any of their number, is self-protection. That the only purpose for which power can be rightfully exercised over any member of a civilized community, against his will, is to prevent harm to others.

GO ON TO THE NEXT PAGE

throne of Austria. Choice E is incorrect because Russia did not invade Finland in 1774.

70. **A.** Louis's attempt to flee Paris in June of 1791 and head north to rally supporters, an event that came to be known as *the flight to Varennes*, was disastrous. He and the royal family were apprehended and forcibly returned to Paris. He was officially forgiven by the Assembly, but he had forever lost the trust of the people of Paris. Choice B is incorrect because Robespierre was taken to the guillotine by his fellow revolutionaries; Louis XVI had already been executed. Choice C is incorrect because the people of Paris had remained loyal to Louis XVI and did not blame him specifically for rising taxes. Choice D is incorrect because the Paris Commune was crushed by the French Army in *1871*. Choice E is incorrect because the Civil Constitution of the Clergy, decreeing that all clergy must take an oath to the state, was issued by the National Assembly, not by Louis XVI.

71. **E.** The attempted coup by General George Boulanger, which was supported by conservative nationalists who refused to accept the election of a liberal government, underscored the fragility of French democracy and the volatility of mass politics in France. Choice A is incorrect because it was the Dreyfus Affair that demonstrated the strength of anti-Semitism in France. Choice B is incorrect because the Second Republic fell in 1851. Choice C is incorrect because it was the Paris Commune of 1871 that gave evidence of the radical nature of the French working class. Choice D is incorrect because a socialist popular front would not be elected in France until the 1920s.

72. **D.** The Sepoy Rebellion of 1857 (sometimes known as the Sepoy Mutiny) was an organized, anti-British uprising led by military units of Indians who had formerly served the British. It led the British government to abolish the East India Company and to take direct control of India and its economy. Choice A is incorrect because, although there is considerable debate over the scope and meaning of the Sepoy Rebellion, it occurred in only parts of the continent and was not "nationalist" in any meaningful sense of the word. Choices B and C are incorrect because the Sepoy Rebellion took place in India, not China or Burma. Choice E is incorrect because the

period of liberal reform in India was actually *ended* by the Sepoy Rebellion.

73. **C.** The power and authority of the Manchu dynasty had been undermined by China's humiliation in the Opium War (1839–1842) and the resulting Treaty of Nanking, which ceded Hong Kong to Britain, created several tariff-free zones for foreign trade, and exempted foreigners from Chinese law; the Taiping Rebellion (1850–1864) was an attempt to overthrow the humiliated dynasty and free China from foreign interference. Choice A is incorrect because the rebels were trying to free China from Western influence, not imitate the West. Choice B is incorrect because the Russo-Japanese war occurred in the twentieth century. Choice D is incorrect because World War II was much later than the Taiping Rebellion. Choice E is incorrect because the West helped the Manchus ward off the rebellion.

74. **D.** In the years between World War I and World War II, liberal democracy failed to take root in Hungary, Poland, and Yugoslavia, as each came to be ruled by right-wing, authoritarian regimes. Choice A is incorrect because none of the countries of Europe enjoyed consistently flourishing economies in the interwar years. Choice B is incorrect because the states of East-Central Europe did not become satellite states of the Soviet Union until after World War II. Choice C is incorrect because none of the states mentioned ceased to exist in the interwar years. Choice E is incorrect because the liberal-democratic parliaments failed in those states during the interwar years.

75. **B.** In the elections of 1932, the Nazis won over 35 percent of the vote and refused to take part in a coalition government; the president, Paul von Hindenburg, responded by appointing Hitler Chancellor of Germany (the equivalent of prime minister). Choice A is incorrect because a socialist coalition was not brought to power in the election of 1932. Choice C is incorrect because Hitler was not elected Chancellor in 1932, but legally *appointed* by Hindenburg in the wake of the strong showing of the Nazi party. Choice D is incorrect because a coalition of right-wing parties was not elected. Choice E is incorrect because the election was held; Hitler did not seize power but rather used the powers of the

Chancellor to pass laws banning political opposition to the Nazis.

76. **C.** The Marshall Plan, which poured billions of dollars of aid into helping the western European countries to rebuild their infrastructures and economies, illustrates the fact that the U.S. government was mindful that fascism had arisen in a context of economic and social hopelessness and, therefore, that communism could well thrive in such contexts as well. Choice A is incorrect because it is too big a stretch to call the Marshall Plan imperialist; it did not and could not lead to either direct or indirect control of the governments or economies of Western Europe. Choice B is incorrect because NATO was created to counter possible Soviet military expansion into Western Europe; the Marshall Plan was motivated by the concerns expressed by choice C. Choice D is incorrect because the Marshall Plan was put in effect after World War II. Choice E is incorrect because the logic of the Marshall Plan was to rebuild, not hold down, the recovery of the countries of Western Europe, including West Germany.

77. **B.** The relative size of the small, frightened husband and the large assertive wife in this cartoon from *Punch* connotes skepticism of the claims of nineteenth-century British reformers that marriage was a brutal institution, especially for working-class women (note her working-class diction in the caption). Choice A is incorrect because suffrage, the right to vote, is not mentioned or alluded to. Choice C is incorrect because the little fellow in the woman's arms is not a child, but her husband. Choice D is not correct because the cartoon lampoons the notion that working class women are abused in the home. Choice E is incorrect because the size of the police force is not alluded to in the cartoon.

78. **E.** All of the choices accurately illustrate the reciprocal nature of the Second Industrial Revolution. Choice A is correct because steam engines required vast amounts of coal as fuel. Choice B is correct because the steam engines were needed to power iron and steel smelting. Choices C and D are correct because the railway system was required to transport iron and steel, but the development of the railway system simultaneously increased demand for iron and steel to build the engines, cars, and tracks.

79. **D.** "The nationalities problem" was the phrase that identified the presence of linguistic and ethnic minorities, such as Magyars, Czechs, and Slavs within the borders of the increasingly anachronistic Hapsburg Empire, and their agitation for greater autonomy or independence. Choice A is incorrect because the idea of such an organization was first proposed by Woodrow Wilson after World War I. Choice B is incorrect because, although there was an Anglo-German arms race in this period, it was not referred to as "the nationalities problem." Choice C is incorrect because the rise of ultranationalist parties was a response to the rise of socialist parties and was not referred to as "the nationalities problem." Choice E is incorrect because southern Slavs during this period tended to look to Russia as a "more natural" alternative to the Hapsburg Empire and its German-speaking ruling class.

80. **C.** Lang's *Metropolis* depicted a society in which humans are dwarfed by an impersonal world of their own creation, and is generally understood to reflect the deep anxiety for the future that constitutes the "darker" side of "the Roaring Twenties." Choice A is incorrect because Lang's *Metropolis* is devoid of the gaiety that was once understood to be the main cultural component of the 1920s. Choice B is incorrect because, although Lang's *Metropolis* is full of futuristic architectural images, they were visions of a future world and did not reflect the dominant architectural style of the 1920s. Choice D is incorrect because neither Lang's *Metropolis* nor the 1920s displayed romantic sensibilities. Choice E is incorrect because neither Lang's *Metropolis* nor the films of the era display a yearning for the pastoral.

Suggestions and Outline for the DBQ

Suggestions

Remember the five steps to a short history essay of high quality:

Step 1: As you read the documents, decide how you are going to group them.

Step 2: Compose a thesis that explains why the documents should be grouped in the way you have chosen.

Step 3: Compose your topic sentences and make sure that they add up logically to your thesis.

Step 4: Support and illustrate your thesis with specific examples that contextualize the documents.

Step 5: *If you have time*, compose a one-paragraph conclusion that restates your thesis.

A question about politics or political ideology almost always lends itself to the construction of a spectrum. Begin by grouping the documents according to ideology. Outline the shared aspects of each group of documents and explain how those shared characteristics identify a particular ideology. Construct a spectrum and organize the groups along it. Finally, note the differences in the documents within each group to note the variation possible in each ideology. For speed and brevity, refer to the documents by their number.

Outline

A possible outline to an answer to this DBQ looks like this:

Thesis: The documents illustrate a spectrum of political ideologies that run from conservatism through liberalism and socialism.

Topic sentence A: Documents 2, 4, and 7 are examples of conservatism.

Specific examples: In 2, de Maistre illustrates the conservative belief that written constitutions are unnatural. In 4, Metternich illustrates the conservative belief that traditional monarchy is the natural, time-tested and, therefore, proper form of government, and that monarchs must not yield to calls for reform. In 7, Pope Leo XIII reminds the ruling elite of their traditional responsibilities.

Topic sentence B: Documents 1, 3, and 6 are examples of liberalism.

Specific examples: In 1, Smiles illustrates the early liberal belief that only individual effort can better a person's social and economic position. In 3, J. S. Mill illustrates the liberal position that the only legitimate role in government is to protect individual liberty (note that later in his career, Mill would speak for the utilitarian position that there is a role for government in improving social conditions). In 6, Ricardo illustrates the liberal belief in laws of nature that govern human social and economic behavior.

Topic sentence C: Documents 8, 9, and 5 are examples of socialism.

Specific examples: In 8, Marx and Engels establish the position of scientific socialism, which argues that capitalism demands the exploitation of the working class, will inevitably crash, and that the workers should seize political power through violent revolution. In 9, Bernstein provides a corrective in the form of revisionism, arguing that capitalism's collapse is not imminent and that the workers should participate in politics. In 5, Shaw illustrates British Fabian socialism, a moderate form that calls only for the nationalization of key industries.

Topic sentence D: Document 10 is an example of anarchism and does not fit well on the spectrum.

Specific example: In 10, Kropotkin illustrates the position of anarchism that government corrupts humanity and must be disrupted and if possible destroyed. Because it is antipolitical, it does not fit neatly on a political spectrum.

Conclusion: The documents form a political spectrum from conservatism, through liberalism and socialism, with anarchism rejecting the notion of a political spectrum.

Suggestions and Outlines for Answers to the Thematic Essay Questions

Suggestions

Choose one question from each group for which you can quickly write a clear thesis and three topic sentences that you can illustrate and support with several specific examples. Then follow the five-step formula to constructing a short history essay of high quality:

Step 1: Find the action words in the question and determine what they want you to do.

Step 2: Compose a thesis that responds to the question and gives you something specific to support and illustrate.

Step 3: Compose your topic sentences and make sure that they add up logically to your thesis.

Step 4: Support and illustrate your thesis with specific examples.

Step 5: *If you have time*, compose a one-paragraph conclusion that restates your thesis.

And remember these writing guidelines:

- Avoid long sentences with multiple clauses. Your goal is to write the clearest sentence possible; most often the clearest sentence is a relatively short sentence.
- Do not get caught up in digressions. No matter how fascinating or insightful you find some idea or fact, if it does not directly support or illustrate your thesis, do not put it in.
- Skip the mystery. Do not ask a lot of rhetorical questions and do not go for a surprise ending. The readers are looking for your thesis, your argument, and your evidence; give these to them in a clear, straightforward manner.

Outlines

Part B
Question 2

Thesis: The approach to art as craft in the Renaissance produced an unparalleled period of artistic innovation and creativity.

Topic sentence A: The Renaissance art world was a world of commerce populated by craftsmen.

Specific examples: All art was commissioned: popes and Medici. Artists not from elite but craftsmen guilds and apprentice system.

Topic sentence B: Both the patrons and the artists of the Renaissance art world were imbued with humanism.

Specific examples: Motivations of patron popes and Medici. Emphasis on human psychology (Giotto) and form (Donatello's and Michelangelo's *David*).

Topic sentence C: The apprenticeship training and resulting craftsmanship enabled Renaissance artists to appropriate methods from one medium and apply them to another.

Specific example: Michelangelo's ceiling in the Sistine Chapel (sculpture-like qualities of painted figures).

Conclusion: The unparalleled period of innovation and creativity that characterizes Renaissance artistic achievement was due to its commercial and craftsmen qualities.

Question 3

Thesis: The approach to knowledge and accomplishments of the Scientific Revolution led directly to the Enlightenment and indirectly to the French Revolution.

Topic sentence A: The Scientific Revolution created an approach to knowledge that combined skepticism and empiricism and established the existence of natural laws in the universe.

Specific example: Galileo's observations in the *Starry Messenger*; Newton's laws.

Topic sentence B: The approach to knowledge forged in the Scientific Revolution and the belief in natural laws formed the foundation of Enlightenment thinking.

Specific examples: Locke's *Second Treatise*; Montesquieu's *Spirit of the Laws*.

Topic sentence C: In the radical Enlightenment, the skepticism and contrast between natural law and unnatural became political weapons.

Specific examples: *Encyclopedia*; *Declaration of the Rights of Man and Citizen*.

Conclusion: The approach to knowledge and belief in natural law forged in the Scientific Revolution led directly to the Enlightenment and indirectly to the French Revolution.

Question 4

Thesis: The revolutions of 1848 failed to alter the nature of political power in Europe and exhausted the appeal of liberalism for the masses.

Topic sentence A: The revolutions of 1848 attempted to force liberal reforms on continental Europe.

Specific examples: Second Republic in France; Frankfort Assembly in Prussia.

Topic sentence B: After initial success, all were crushed by a conservative reaction.

Specific examples: France, Prussia, Austria, Italy.

Topic sentence C: After 1848, the masses looked to the right and to the left of liberalism for leaders in whom to put their faith.

Specific examples: Successes of socialist parties in Germany and underground movement in Russia; Cavour in Italy; Bismarck in Germany; Louis-Napoleon and Boulanger Affair in France.

Conclusion: The failure of liberalism was the most significant lasting impact of the revolutions of 1848.

Part C
Question 5

Thesis: The settlement following World War I contained several unprecedented measures that contributed to the rise of fascism and World War II: enormous and open-ended reparations; severe limitations on the German Army; and the "assigning" of several hundred thousand Germans to newly created countries.

Topic sentence A: Fascism rose from the economic and social degradation caused, in part, by war reparations.

Specific examples: The appeal of the Nazis to the downtrodden; the role of war reparations in economic collapse; the Ruhr Valley occupation by the French.

Topic sentence B: The ban on the army created unemployment and humiliation, which were exploited by the Nazis.

Specific examples: Existence of Freikorps; Nazi militarism spread throughout the culture.

Topic sentence C: The creation of new nations out of Austria–Hungary "trapped" large numbers of German-speaking people and seemed to justify Hitler's early aggression.

Specific examples: The number of German-speaking people in the Sudetenland and the role it played in Hitler's expansionist program; policy of appeasement.

Conclusion: The ill-conceived settlement following World War I created several situations that were easily exploited by Hitler to justify the aggressive policies that led to World War II.

Question 6

Thesis: The desire to avoid domination by the two superpowers led to the creation of a process of integration in Europe.

Topic sentence A: Western European leaders recognized the need for integration soon after the war.

Specific examples: 1952, the six-country European Coal and Steel Community; 1957, the Treaty of Rome, establishing the European Economic Community (EEC).

Topic sentence B: Though most of the integration from 1952 to the 1980s was economic in nature, the issue of European autonomy from the superpowers was always present.

Specific examples: Quotes from leaders; 1967, greater social integration and transformation from EEC to the European Community (EC); 1992, the 12 countries, the Maastricht Treaty, creating European Union (EU).

Topic sentence C: After the fall of the Soviet Union, the EU proceeded more boldly toward its political objectives.

Specific examples: Expansion into Eastern Europe; drafting of an EU constitution.

Conclusion: Caught between two superpowers, the leaders of post–World War II Europe have followed a steady course of integration designed to build and protect European autonomy.

Question 7

Thesis: The French Revolution was a reaction against an oppressive regime that tried to resist the demands of an economically powerful commercial class that ended in a military dictatorship; the Russian Revolution was caused by the disintegration of an absolutist regime due to war and ended in a bureaucratic dictatorship.

Topic sentence A: The French Revolution began as a revolt of the Third Estate whose complaints were those of the commercial class.

Specific examples: What is the Third Estate; *cahiers*; social composition of the National Assembly.

Topic sentence B: The Russian Revolution began as a revolt of a professional revolutionary organization against a police state.

Specific examples: Lenin's "career," police-state tactics of the Romanovs.

Topic sentence C: Both revolutions gave way to dictatorships in the end.

Specific examples: Radicalization of the French Revolution; rise of the military following the Reign of Terror; Napoleon's coup; Russian Civil War; nature of the "Soviets"; rise of Stalin.

Conclusion: The two revolutions began for different reasons and had different aims, but both ended in dictatorships.

AP European History
Practice Test 2—Section I

ANSWER SHEET

1 (A) (B) (C) (D) (E)	31 (A) (B) (C) (D) (E)	61 (A) (B) (C) (D) (E)
2 (A) (B) (C) (D) (E)	32 (A) (B) (C) (D) (E)	62 (A) (B) (C) (D) (E)
3 (A) (B) (C) (D) (E)	33 (A) (B) (C) (D) (E)	63 (A) (B) (C) (D) (E)
4 (A) (B) (C) (D) (E)	34 (A) (B) (C) (D) (E)	64 (A) (B) (C) (D) (E)
5 (A) (B) (C) (D) (E)	35 (A) (B) (C) (D) (E)	65 (A) (B) (C) (D) (E)
6 (A) (B) (C) (D) (E)	36 (A) (B) (C) (D) (E)	66 (A) (B) (C) (D) (E)
7 (A) (B) (C) (D) (E)	37 (A) (B) (C) (D) (E)	67 (A) (B) (C) (D) (E)
8 (A) (B) (C) (D) (E)	38 (A) (B) (C) (D) (E)	68 (A) (B) (C) (D) (E)
9 (A) (B) (C) (D) (E)	39 (A) (B) (C) (D) (E)	69 (A) (B) (C) (D) (E)
10 (A) (B) (C) (D) (E)	40 (A) (B) (C) (D) (E)	70 (A) (B) (C) (D) (E)
11 (A) (B) (C) (D) (E)	41 (A) (B) (C) (D) (E)	71 (A) (B) (C) (D) (E)
12 (A) (B) (C) (D) (E)	42 (A) (B) (C) (D) (E)	72 (A) (B) (C) (D) (E)
13 (A) (B) (C) (D) (E)	43 (A) (B) (C) (D) (E)	73 (A) (B) (C) (D) (E)
14 (A) (B) (C) (D) (E)	44 (A) (B) (C) (D) (E)	74 (A) (B) (C) (D) (E)
15 (A) (B) (C) (D) (E)	45 (A) (B) (C) (D) (E)	75 (A) (B) (C) (D) (E)
16 (A) (B) (C) (D) (E)	46 (A) (B) (C) (D) (E)	76 (A) (B) (C) (D) (E)
17 (A) (B) (C) (D) (E)	47 (A) (B) (C) (D) (E)	77 (A) (B) (C) (D) (E)
18 (A) (B) (C) (D) (E)	48 (A) (B) (C) (D) (E)	78 (A) (B) (C) (D) (E)
19 (A) (B) (C) (D) (E)	49 (A) (B) (C) (D) (E)	79 (A) (B) (C) (D) (E)
20 (A) (B) (C) (D) (E)	50 (A) (B) (C) (D) (E)	80 (A) (B) (C) (D) (E)
21 (A) (B) (C) (D) (E)	51 (A) (B) (C) (D) (E)	
22 (A) (B) (C) (D) (E)	52 (A) (B) (C) (D) (E)	
23 (A) (B) (C) (D) (E)	53 (A) (B) (C) (D) (E)	
24 (A) (B) (C) (D) (E)	54 (A) (B) (C) (D) (E)	
25 (A) (B) (C) (D) (E)	55 (A) (B) (C) (D) (E)	
26 (A) (B) (C) (D) (E)	56 (A) (B) (C) (D) (E)	
27 (A) (B) (C) (D) (E)	57 (A) (B) (C) (D) (E)	
28 (A) (B) (C) (D) (E)	58 (A) (B) (C) (D) (E)	
29 (A) (B) (C) (D) (E)	59 (A) (B) (C) (D) (E)	
30 (A) (B) (C) (D) (E)	60 (A) (B) (C) (D) (E)	

AP European History
Practice Test 2

Section I

Time—55 minutes

80 Questions

Directions: Each of the questions or incomplete statements below is followed by five suggested answers or completions. Select the one that is best in each case and fill in the circle for the letter that corresponds to your choice on the Answer Sheet supplied.

Raw cotton consumption (metric tons)

	1830	1850
Belgium	5,000	20,000
France	40,000	60,000
German states	20,000	30,000
UK	170,000	260,000

1. 1. Which of the following is the most complete conclusion that can be drawn from the chart above for the period 1830–1850?
   (A) The United Kingdom was the largest consumer of cotton in both 1830 and 1850.
   (B) Belgium had the smallest population in Europe during this period.
   (C) The United Kingdom imported the most cotton during this period.
   (D) The United Kingdom led Europe in textile production.
   (E) The United Kingdom had both the greatest consumption of cotton and the greatest rate of increase in cotton consumption.

2. Which of the following can be understood as a result of the Seven Years War?
   (A) The French Revolution began.
   (B) Maria Theresa ascended to the throne of Austria.
   (C) Britain became the dominant imperial power in the world.
   (D) The Ottoman Turks were further weakened.
   (E) Prussia was weakened.

3. Which of following did NOT contribute to the radicalization of the French Revolution?
   (A) Austria and Prussia's declaration of war on the French Republic
   (B) the flight to Varennes
   (C) factionalizing of the Assembly
   (D) the execution of Louis XVI
   (E) the rise of the *sans-culottes*

4. The most significant, long-term result of the revolutions of 1848 was
   (A) the large-scale abandonment of liberalism by the masses
   (B) Hungarian independence
   (C) the rise of communism
   (D) the unification of Italy
   (E) the triumph of democratic reform

5. Which of the following is NOT true of the Second Industrial Revolution of nineteenth-century Europe?
   (A) It began in Great Britain.
   (B) It took place later farther east.
   (C) The pace slowed after an initial quick start.
   (D) It took place more quickly farther east.
   (E) There was more government involvement farther east.

6. Which of the following nineteenth-century ideologies stressed both individual freedom and government regulation?
   (A) socialism
   (B) utilitarianism
   (C) liberalism
   (D) conservatism
   (E) anarchism

GO ON TO THE NEXT PAGE

7. Which of the following is a combination of tactics used by both Cavour and Bismarck in their drive to unite Italy and Germany, respectively?
   (A) diplomacy and royal marriage
   (B) peasant revolts and military action
   (C) diplomacy and bribery
   (D) war and secret dealings with the pope
   (E) war and diplomacy

8. Fifteenth-century attempts to centralize and consolidate power were most successful in
   (A) France
   (B) England
   (C) Italy
   (D) Spain
   (E) Germany

9. Which of the following is true of humanism as it manifested itself in northern Europe?
   (A) It was less secular than Italian Renaissance humanism.
   (B) It pursued scholarship and learning in a tradition of religious piety.
   (C) It was critical of the notion that priests were required to understand and interpret scripture.
   (D) It formed part of the foundation for the Reformation.
   (E) All of the above.

10. Which of the following is particular to Calvinist theology?
    (A) Salvation is achieved through faith alone.
    (B) Scripture is the only reliable guide to salvation.
    (C) The Church must not be hierarchical in nature.
    (D) Some souls have been predestined for salvation.
    (E) The Bible should be printed in the vernacular.

11. Which of the following was accomplished by Peter the Great of Russia (1682–1725)?
    (A) He abolished serfdom.
    (B) He expanded the Russian empire.
    (C) He launched the industrialization of Russia.
    (D) He curbed the power of the nobility.
    (E) He provided tax relief for the peasantry.

12. Which of the following would be advocated by a follower of Descartes?
    (A) There are four elements in the terrestrial realm.
    (B) All true knowledge is derived from observation.
    (C) Seeing is believing.
    (D) One should always proceed from a clear and distinct idea.
    (E) Telescopic observations should be the basis of knowledge of the heavens.

13. An advocate of *laissez-faire*
    (A) advocates protectionist tariffs
    (B) argues that only natural laws are legitimate
    (C) argues that the government should refrain from trying to regulate the economy
    (D) argues that the government should act as an "invisible hand" to regulate the economy
    (E) argues that a monarch rules by the command of God

14. Which of the following was a result of the development of rural manufacturing in the eighteenth century?
    (A) the spread of capital throughout the population
    (B) a decrease in total agricultural output
    (C) the enclosure movement
    (D) urbanization
    (E) the formation of a working class

15. Which of the following precipitated the fall of the Second Republic in France?
    (A) France's defeat in the Franco-Prussian War
    (B) a coup and two plebiscites
    (C) the French Revolution
    (D) the Crimean War
    (E) the unification of Italy

16. The postimpressionists of the late nineteenth century are distinguished from their predecessors, the impressionists, by
    (A) their desire to create a more emotionally expressive effect
    (B) their use of visible brush strokes
    (C) their use of heightened color
    (D) their insistence on real-life subjects
    (E) their desire to capture the reality of the visual experience

GO ON TO THE NEXT PAGE

17. The Suez Canal episode in the early 1880s illustrates which of the following aspects of the "New Imperialism"?
    (A) the underlying economic motives
    (B) the willingness of Western governments to rule imperial holdings directly
    (C) the way imperial expansion demanded further expansion
    (D) the competitive nature of European expansion
    (E) all of the above

18. In which of the following ways did the Russian revolution affect the course of World War I?
    (A) It gave the Allies a new enemy.
    (B) Russia joined the Triple Entente.
    (C) Russia withdrew from the war.
    (D) It caused the Germans to launch a new offensive in the east.
    (E) None of the above.

19. Which of the following was NOT an element of fascism?
    (A) a fanatical obedience to a charismatic leader
    (B) an egalitarianism that extended to class and gender
    (C) a professed belief in the virtues of struggle and youth
    (D) an intense form of nationalism
    (E) an expressed hatred of socialism and liberalism

20. Successful resistance to communist rule in the 1980s was led by a labor union in which of the following countries?
    (A) Czechoslovakia
    (B) East Germany
    (C) Yugoslavia
    (D) Poland
    (E) Russia

21. Galileo's discovery of craters on the surface of the moon damaged the traditional view of the cosmos because it
    (A) demonstrated that the moon was not made of perfect matter
    (B) demonstrated the power of the telescope
    (C) contradicted the notion that the Earth was at the center of the cosmos
    (D) called into question the perfection of God's creative power
    (E) all of the above

22. Which of the following was argued by John Locke in the *Second Treatise of Government*?
    (A) Peace requires an absolute ruler.
    (B) A government must follow the "general will" of the people.
    (C) Democracy is the only legitimate form of government.
    (D) The government must always protect the people's right to property.
    (E) Monarchy must always be opposed.

23. The uncertainty principle was articulated as result of
    (A) efforts to prove that all human knowledge is relative
    (B) efforts to prove the existence of the ether
    (C) efforts to disprove Einstein's theory of relativity
    (D) efforts to develop an atomic bomb
    (E) efforts to reconcile quantum physics with the classical approach to physics

24. Which of the following explains the rapid development of technology in the textile industry in the eighteenth century?
    (A) a shortage of labor
    (B) the interconnected nature of technical innovation
    (C) the triumph of reason over superstition
    (D) the cotton boom
    (E) the invention of the steam engine

25. The War for Austrian Succession (1740–1748) was caused by
    (A) Prussian expansionist aims
    (B) a revolt of Austrian nobles
    (C) the Pragmatic Sanction
    (D) French aggression
    (E) all of the above

26. The most significant impact of the Civil Constitution of the Clergy on the course of the French Revolution was
    (A) the alliance it created between the clergy and the National Assembly
    (B) that it made the clergy subservient to the state
    (C) that it alienated much of the Catholic population from the revolution
    (D) its reaffirmation of the central place of the Church in the French government
    (E) that it made Catholicism illegal in France

GO ON TO THE NEXT PAGE

27. The larger significance of the British victory at the Battle of Trafalgar was that
    (A) the British navy defeated the combined French and Spanish fleets
    (B) Napoleon's Grand Army was destroyed
    (C) Napoleon had to call a halt to the Continental System
    (D) Napoleon was captured and sent to the island of Elba
    (E) it ended the threat of a French conquest of Britain

28. The Schleswig–Holstein affair is an example of
    (A) the *Risorgimento*
    (B) Russian conservatism
    (C) German liberalism
    (D) French imperialism
    (E) *Realpolitik*

29. The formation of the Indian National Congress in 1885 demonstrates
    (A) the successful colonization of India by Britain
    (B) the scramble for Africa
    (C) the formation of nationalism as a response to Western imperialism
    (D) the beginning of the New Imperialism
    (E) all of the above

30. Which of the following extended the right to vote to the adult, male middle class in Britain?
    (A) the Great Reform Bill of 1832
    (B) the Reform Bill of 1867
    (C) the Reform Bill of 1884
    (D) the People's Charter
    (E) the Midlothian Campaign

31. The organization that campaigned for women's voting rights in Britain was
    (A) the Fabian Society
    (B) feminism
    (C) the National Union of Women's Suffrage Societies
    (D) the National Women's League
    (E) the Women's Social and Political Union

32. Of the three main negotiators at the Paris Peace Conference of 1919, which one was most concerned to make sure that Germany could never threaten again?
    (A) David Lloyd George
    (B) Woodrow Wilson
    (C) Charles de Gaulle
    (D) Georges Clemenceau
    (E) none of the above

33. Pablo Picasso's *Guernica* (1937) depicts
    (A) the Impressionist style
    (B) the bombing of the town of Guernica by German planes
    (C) the savagery of the fighting between fascists and socialists
    (D) the valiant resistance of the socialists
    (E) Hitler invading Spain

34. The agreement which allowed Hitler to take the Sudetenland in return for his promise of no further aggression was known as the
    (A) Nazi–Soviet Non-Aggression Pact
    (B) Concert of Europe
    (C) Treaty of Brest–Litovsk
    (D) Treaty of Versailles
    (E) Munich Agreement

35. The military alliance between communist countries in Eastern Europe after World War II was known as
    (A) the Warsaw Pact
    (B) the Truman Doctrine
    (C) the Council for Mutual Economic Assistance
    (D) the Marshall Plan
    (E) NATO

36. Mikhail Gorbachev's attempt to "restructure" Soviet society and its economy was known as
    (A) socialism in one country
    (B) socialism with a human face
    (C) *glasnost*
    (D) *perestroika*
    (E) the New Economic Plan

37. In the fifteenth century, the Holy Roman Emperor was
    (A) appointed by the pope
    (B) dethroned in the Hundred Years War
    (C) elected by a seven-member council of German archbishops and nobles
    (D) the pope
    (E) Henry VIII

GO ON TO THE NEXT PAGE

38. The creation of a Spanish Empire in the New World had all of the following effects EXCEPT
   (A) economic inflation in Europe
   (B) the establishment of Roman Catholicism in the New World
   (C) the rise of a wealthy merchant class in Europe
   (D) the establishment of a hierarchical social structure in Europe
   (E) the establishment of a system of economic dependence between Europe and the New World

39. A traditional institution within the Catholic Church that was transformed in the sixteenth century to fight the spread of Protestantism was
   (A) the Reformation
   (B) the Counter-Reformation
   (C) the Inquisition
   (D) the Conciliar Movement
   (E) the Court of the Star Chamber

40. Which of the following is an example of the Cartesian approach to physical science popular in the late seventeenth and early eighteenth centuries?
   (A) Maupertuis's calculation of the exact shape of the earth based on observations of longitudinal measurement
   (B) Christiaan Huygens's explanation of the propagation of light by suggesting that it "flowed" like a fluid
   (C) Galileo's telescopic observations of the moon
   (D) Copernicus's hypothesis that the Earth is in the center of the cosmos
   (E) Linnaeus's creation of a system for the classification of living organisms

41. Which of the following best characterizes the Counter-Reformation?
   (A) a movement to reform the Catholic Church from within
   (B) a movement to stamp out Protestantism
   (C) a movement to create a "third theological way"
   (D) a movement to both reform from within and combat the spread of Protestantism
   (E) a movement to censure thinkers like Galileo

42. During the period from 1600 to 1715, the traditional social hierarchy of Europe came under pressure by all of the following EXCEPT
   (A) continuous warfare
   (B) climate change resulting in series of bad harvests
   (C) the rejection of religious practice by large numbers of people
   (D) increased trade and the diversification of the economy
   (E) the desire of monarchs to increase their power and authority

43. Which of the following is the best example of the method described by Descartes in his *Discourse on Method* (1637)?
   (A) True reality exists in the world of pure forms.
   (B) "I think, therefore I am."
   (C) A telescope reveals craters and mountains on the moon; therefore, matter in the celestial realm cannot be perfect.
   (D) The orbits of the planets can be calculated using calculus.
   (E) "Every particle of matter in the universe attracts every other particle with a force varying inversely as the square of the distance between them and directly proportional to the product of their masses."

44. Which of the following best explains the eventual defeat of Napoleon and his forces?
   (A) the inefficiency of the French army
   (B) flawed policies that exacerbated resistance to French rule
   (C) internal resistance by royalists and republicans
   (D) the British victory at the Battle of Trafalgar
   (E) tactical blunders

45. The source of Prussian power in the eighteenth century was
   (A) Bismarck's genius
   (B) Prussia's industrial strength
   (C) Prussia's diplomatic alliances
   (D) Prussia's geographical position
   (E) Prussia's powerful military

GO ON TO THE NEXT PAGE

46. The revolutions of 1848 are best understood as
    (A) the result of tension between liberal and nationalist aspirations of the people of Europe and the determined conservatism of their aristocratic masters
    (B) independence movements
    (C) large-scale attempts to redistribute wealth in European society
    (D) precursors to the French Revolution
    (E) democratic revolutions

47. Which of the following might be explained as a result of the introduction of steam power?
    (A) the creation of the factory system
    (B) the invention of the automobile
    (C) decreased demand for coal
    (D) an increased demand for coal
    (E) the collapse of the shipping industry

48. Conservatives opposed "constitutionalism" because they
    (A) were monarchists
    (B) believed that constitutions ignored reality
    (C) respected tradition
    (D) wanted to hold on to power
    (E) believed a government should protect private property

49. In the 1930s, Winston Churchill stood nearly alone in his
    (A) advocacy of socialism
    (B) support of the Soviet Union
    (C) opposition to the policy of appeasement
    (D) call for a coalition government
    (E) efforts to draw the United States into the war

50. Which of the following is an example of the revival of nationalist and ethnic tensions in eastern Europe after the disintegration of the Soviet Union?
    (A) the war between Chechnyans and Russia
    (B) the multisided war in Yugoslavia
    (C) the splitting up of Czechoslovakia
    (D) the war in Bosnia–Herzegovina
    (E) all of the above

51. Which of the following led an expedition that eventually circumnavigated the globe?
    (A) Vasco da Gama
    (B) Amerigo Vespucci
    (C) Martin Waldseemüller
    (D) Ferdinand Magellan
    (E) Christopher Columbus

52. All of the following help to explain why the Renaissance originated on the Italian peninsula EXCEPT
    (A) geography
    (B) political organization
    (C) religion
    (D) social structure
    (E) economic structure

53. All of the following posed difficulties for the Christian Church in Europe during the first decade of the sixteenth century EXCEPT
    (A) the pope's status as ruler of the Papal States.
    (B) the Church's use of Latin in the mass and in the printed Bible
    (C) an increasingly literate population
    (D) the Church's inability to tend to the emotional and spiritual needs of the population
    (E) the split in the Christian population caused by the Protestant movement

54. Which of the following would NOT be included in a list of the causes of the English Civil War (1642–1646)?
    (A) the religion of Charles I's wife
    (B) wars with Spain and France
    (C) the invasion of a Protestant army from the Netherlands
    (D) the invasion of England by the Scots
    (E) Parliament's refusal to fund the war with Scotland without reform

55. Which of the following is true of the Copernican model of the cosmos?
    (A) The planets orbit the Sun in uniform circular orbits.
    (B) The planets orbit the Earth in elliptical orbits with the Sun as one focus of the ellipse.
    (C) The universe is infinite.
    (D) The planets orbit the Sun in elliptical orbits with the Earth as one focus of the ellipse.
    (E) The moon orbits the Sun, not the Earth.

56. The book *System of Nature* (1770), by the Baron d'Holbach, was one of the most radical texts of the Enlightenment because of its
    (A) advocacy of revolution
    (B) materialism
    (C) liberalism
    (D) support for the French Revolution
    (E) advocacy of science

GO ON TO THE NEXT PAGE

57. The Diplomatic Revolution of the eighteenth century refers to
    (A) the invention of the "alliance"
    (B) traditional enemies becoming allies
    (C) the moderate phase of the French Revolution
    (D) the Revolutions of 1848
    (E) the Concert of Europe

My heart leaps up when I behold
  A rainbow in the sky:
So was it when my life began,
  So is it now I am a man,
So be it when I shall grow old
  Or let me die!

58. The nineteenth-century verse above is indicative of
    (A) neoplatonism
    (B) the Romantic movement
    (C) the impressionist school
    (D) conservatism
    (E) the Enlightenment

59. Charles Darwin, in *The Origin of Species* (1859), put forward the idea that
    (A) competition was natural and necessary for social progress
    (B) human nature was essentially cooperative
    (C) biological diversity was the product of a purely natural process
    (D) competition was the root of class conflict
    (E) human beings evolved from apes

60. Bismarck overcame south German reluctance to submit to Prussian leadership by
    (A) appealing to their Catholic faith
    (B) adopting their liberal reform agenda
    (C) appealing to their nationalism
    (D) appealing to their desire for a strong, authoritarian central government
    (E) allying with the Junker class

61. All of the following were effects of the Hundred Years War EXCEPT
    (A) a significant decrease in the population
    (B) a series of peasant rebellions
    (C) a more politically unified France
    (D) an economically weaker England
    (E) the rise of a Spanish Empire in the New World

62. All of the following were highly valued in the Renaissance EXCEPT
    (A) scholarly achievement
    (B) patronage of the arts
    (C) proficiency in the military arts
    (D) civic duty
    (E) study of ancient languages

63. All of the following are basic theological beliefs of Martin Luther EXCEPT
    (A) Salvation is attainable by faith alone.
    (B) Scripture is the only guide to knowledge of God.
    (C) The Church hierarchy was unwarranted and harmful.
    (D) Good works are essential to salvation.
    (E) All who have faith can and should read the Bible.

64. Which of the following is most true of the Glorious Revolution of 1688?
    (A) It represents the triumph of constitutionalism in Britain.
    (B) It brought democracy to Britain.
    (C) It began the Restoration Period in Britain.
    (D) It began the Commonwealth Period in Britain.
    (E) It ended the Commonwealth Period in Britain.

65. Isaac Newton is best described as working in
    (A) the Aristotelian tradition
    (B) the Scholastic tradition
    (C) the Hermetic tradition
    (D) the Platonic–Pythagorean tradition
    (E) the Copernican tradition

66. All of the following are examples of the philosophy of Jean-Jacques Rousseau EXCEPT
    (A) Humans are born essentially good.
    (B) The education of children should concentrate on developing the senses, sensibilities, and sentiments.
    (C) "Man is born free; and everywhere he is in chains."
    (D) The proper role of government is to protect individual property.
    (E) The virtuous citizen should be willing to subordinate his own self-interest to the general good of the community.

GO ON TO THE NEXT PAGE

67. All of the following transactions were part of the triangle of trade EXCEPT
    (A) slaves from Africa sold in the Americas and West Indies
    (B) tea from China sold in Europe
    (C) guns from Europe traded in Africa
    (D) cotton from the Americas sold in Europe
    (E) rum from the West Indies sold in Europe

68. The phase of the French Revolution known as "Thermidor" was characterized by
    (A) a reassertion of control by the nobility
    (B) the defeat of France by Austria
    (C) the restoration of the monarchy
    (D) the rule of the Committee of Public Safety
    (E) a reassertion of control by the moderate portion of the propertied bourgeoisie

69. Which of the following was an aim of the great powers represented at the Congress of Vienna in 1814?
    (A) to punish France
    (B) to divide and weaken Germany
    (C) to restore the traditional order and to create a new balance of power
    (D) to spread liberal reform more widely in Europe
    (E) to provide independent nation states for Italy, Hungary, and Czechoslovakia

70. Which of the following was a social effect of the Second Industrial Revolution?
    (A) a more even distribution of wealth
    (B) the development of a lower middle class
    (C) the creation of a class of poor people
    (D) the railway boom
    (E) gender equity

71. Which of the following is an example of the *Sturm und Drang* movement?
    (A) Michelangelo's *David*
    (B) Bismarck's *Kulturkampf*
    (C) the assassination of Franz Ferdinand
    (D) *Guernica*
    (E) *The Sorrows of Young Werther*

72. The best example of the power of nationalism in France in the mid-nineteenth century was
    (A) the two plebiscites that established the Second Empire and made Louis-Napoleon hereditary emperor
    (B) Louis-Napoleon's coup d'état on December 2, 1851
    (C) the Paris Commune
    (D) Louis-Napoleon's granting of universal manhood suffrage
    (E) the Directory

73. The Chartist movement (1837–1842) in Britain demonstrated
    (A) the power of the monarchy
    (B) the degree to which the lower middle and working classes desired further reform
    (C) the strength of nationalism
    (D) opposition to monarchy
    (E) the degree to which working people were opposed to the mechanization of industry

74. The atmosphere of "celebration" that accompanied the declarations of war in 1914 is partially explained by
    (A) feelings of brotherhood and glory
    (B) deep racial hatreds
    (C) Germany's strong desire to repudiate the humiliating conditions of the Versailles Treaty
    (D) deep resentment toward the Continental System
    (E) all of the above

75. In the context of World War I, the phrase "total war" referred to
    (A) the bombing of civilians in major cities
    (B) the total conversion of the economy to fulfill wartime needs
    (C) the refusal to take prisoners
    (D) the fighting of the war on multiple continents
    (E) all of the above

GO ON TO THE NEXT PAGE

76. Which of the following can be understood as a consequence of World War II?
    (A) the Treaty of Versailles
    (B) the emergence of the United States and the Soviet Union as the world's two greatest powers
    (C) the reunification of Germany
    (D) a strengthening of the British Empire
    (E) the German invasion of Poland

77. Following the collapse of the Soviet Union, the two major trends that most affected life in Eastern Europe were
    (A) the flourishing of individual liberty and democracy
    (B) the spread of corporate capitalism and a revival of religion
    (C) American isolationism and European integration
    (D) the revival of ethnic-nationalism and the advent of globalization
    (E) a widening gap in the distribution of wealth and increased poverty

78. Which of the following is true of the reunification of Germany?
    (A) It was the product of a long, lengthy process of negotiation and compromise.
    (B) Separate economic policies were set up to make the transition easier for East Germans.
    (C) The former East Germany was essentially annexed by the West.
    (D) It was led by East German members of the Civic Forum.
    (E) All of the above.

79. In "The Freedom of the Christian Man" (1520), Martin Luther
    (A) called for people to rise up against an unjust social system
    (B) appealed to the German princes' desire for both greater unity and power and to their desire to be free from the control of an Italian pope
    (C) established the principle of "whoever rules; his religion"
    (D) encouraged common men to obey their Christian conscience and respect those in authority who seemed to possess true Christian principles
    (E) all of the above

80. As the chief minister to Louis XIII of France, Cardinal Richelieu was able to
    (A) disband the private armies of the great French aristocrats
    (B) strip away the autonomy of the few remaining Protestant towns
    (C) build a strong administrative bureaucracy
    (D) strip provincial aristocrats and elites of their administrative power
    (E) all of the above

STOP. End of Section I

Section II

Part A

(Suggested writing time—45 minutes)

Directions: The following question is based on the accompanying Documents 1–10. (The documents have been edited for the purpose of this exercise.) Write your answer on the lined pages provided with the Answer Sheet.

This question is designed to test your ability to work with and understand historical documents. Write an essay that:

- has a relevant thesis and supports that thesis with evidence from the documents
- uses the majority of the documents
- addresses all parts of the question
- analyzes the documents by organizing them in as many appropriate ways as possible and does not simply summarize the documents individually
- takes into account both the sources of the documents and the authors' points of view

You may refer to relevant historical information not mentioned in the documents.

1. Discuss the changing attitudes and arguments regarding the basis for knowledge of the natural world in the following documents.

Historical background: Beginning in the sixteenth and culminating in the seventeenth century, an intellectual and cultural revolution took shape that has come to be known as the Scientific Revolution. At the heart of that revolution were changing attitudes and new arguments regarding the basis for knowledge of the natural world.

Document 1

Source: Nicolas Copernicus, *The Revolutions of the Heavenly Bodies*, 1543.
In the center of all rests the sun. For who would place this lamp of a very beautiful temple in another or better place than this, where from it can illuminate everything at the same time? As a matter of fact, not unhappily so some call it the lantern; others, the mind, and still others, the pilot of the world. Trismegistus calls it a "visible god"; Sophocles Electra, "that which gazes upon all things." And so the sun, as if resting on a kingly throne, governs the family of stars which wheel around.

Document 2

Source: Giambattista della Porta, *Natural Magick*, 1584.
There are two sorts of Magick, the one is infamous, and unhappy, because it has to do with foul spirits and consists of incantations and wicked curiosity; and this is called sorcery . . . The other Magick is natural; which all excellent, wise men do admit and embrace, and worship with great applause; neither is there anything more highly esteemed, or better thought of, by men of learning . . . Others have named it the practical part of natural philosophy, which produces her effects by the mutual and fit application of one natural thing to another. Magick is nothing else but the survey of whole course of nature.

GO ON TO THE NEXT PAGE

Document 3

Source: Galileo Galilei, "Letter to the Grand Duchess Christina of Tuscany," 1615.
[Copernicus] stands always upon physical conclusions pertaining to the celestial motions, and deals with them by astronomical and geometrical demonstrations, founded primarily on sense experiences and very exact observations . . . I think that in discussions of physical problems we ought to begin not from the authority of scriptural passages, but from sense-experiences and necessary demonstrations . . . Nature . . . is inexorable and immutable; she never transgresses the laws imposed upon her, or cares a whit whether her abstruse reasons and methods of operation are understandable to men.

Document 4

Source: Robert Bellarmine, "Letter on Galileo's Theories," 1615.
For to say that, assuming the earth moves and the sun stands still, all the appearances are saved better than with eccentrics and epicycles, is to speak well; there is no danger in this, and it is sufficient for mathematicians. But to want to affirm that the sun really is fixed in the center of the heavens . . . is a very dangerous thing, not only by irritating all the philosophers and scholastic theologians, but also by injuring our holy faith and rendering the Holy Scripture false.

Document 5

Source: Francis Bacon, *Novum Organum*, 1620.
There are two ways, and can only be two, of seeking and finding truth. The one, from sense and reason, takes a flight to the most general axioms, and from these principles and their truth, settled once for all, invents and judges of all intermediate axioms. The other method collects axioms from sense and particulars, ascending continuously and by degrees so that in the end it arrives at the most general axioms. This latter is the only true one, but never hitherto tried.

Document 6

Source: William Harvey, *On the Motion of the Heart and Blood in Animals*, 1628.
The heart, it is vulgarly said, is the fountain and workshop of the vital spirits, the centre from which life is dispensed to the several parts of the body. Yet it is denied that the right ventricle makes spirits, which is rather held to supply the nourishment to the lungs . . . Why, I ask, when we see that the structure of both ventricles is almost identical, there being the same apparatus of fibres, and braces, and valves, and vessels, and auricles, and both in the same way in our dissections are to found to be filled up with blood similarly black in colour, and coagulated—why, I say, should their uses be imagined to be different, when the action, motion, and pulse of both are the same?

GO ON TO THE NEXT PAGE

diversity was and is the product of a purely natural process which he termed natural selection. Choice A is incorrect because it was the so-called social Darwinist Herbert Spencer who put forward the idea that competition was natural and necessary for social progress. Choice B is incorrect because it was the French socialist Charles Fourier who argued that human nature was essentially cooperative. Choice D is incorrect because it was the communist Karl Marx who argued that competition was the root of class conflict. Choice E is incorrect because Darwin argued that both humans and modern apes were descended from some ancient ancestor that was neither human nor ape.

60. **C**. Bismarck appealed to the nationalist feelings of the south Germans by manufacturing a war with France in 1871. Choice A is incorrect because Prussia was a Protestant state. Choice B is incorrect because, although Bismarck was not above advocating the occasional liberal reform in order to strengthen his political position, it is too much to say that he adopted a liberal reform agenda, and because the south Germans were not won over by Bismarck's liberal overtures; they only joined Prussia when war broke out with France. Choice D is incorrect because the liberal south Germans had *no* desire for the strong, authoritarian central government favored by Prussians. Choice E is incorrect because the Junkers were the dominant aristocratic class *in Prussia*, and an alliance with them had no appeal for the south Germans.

61. **E**. The rise of a Spanish empire in the New World was the result of sixteenth-century voyages of exploration and the work of the soldier-adventurers who led them, a process unrelated to the Hundred Years War, which raged through the fourteenth and fifteenth centuries. The other four choices are incorrect because they *were* all effects of the Hundred Years War.

62. **C**. Proficiency in the military arts was valued highly by the traditional feudal lords of Europe. Because social status in the independent city-states of the Italian peninsula was determined by occupation, proficiency in the military arts was not highly valued there. The other four choices were all highly valued in the humanistic culture of Renaissance Italy.

63. **D**. Luther disagreed with the Church's traditional belief that good works were essential to salvation, arguing instead that salvation could only be a gift from God, given to those who have true faith. The other four choices are basic theological beliefs of Martin Luther.

64. **A**. The Glorious Revolution of 1688 represents the triumph of constitutionalism in Britain because it successfully ousted James II, the last of the Stuarts who claimed the right to rule as an absolute monarch, and replaced him with a monarchy that swore to rule as a "King in Parliament," that is, as a constitutional monarch. Choice B is incorrect because democracy, the notion of one person, one vote, came gradually to Britain, culminating in the enfranchisement of women in 1918. Choice C is incorrect because the Glorious Revolution ended the Restoration Period (1660–1688). Choices D and E are incorrect because the Commonwealth Period (1649–1660), where Britain was ruled without a monarch, preceded both the Restoration and the Glorious Revolution.

65. **D**. Newton is best described as working in the Platonic–Pythagorean tradition because he pursued and achieved its goal of identifying the fundamental mathematical laws of nature. Choice A is incorrect because Newton rejected the tradition of Aristotelian physics which relied upon an Earth-centered cosmos and the existence of different kinds of matter. Choice B is incorrect because Newton rejected the scholastic notion that all valuable knowledge was found in ancient texts. Choice C is incorrect because, although there are elements of the hermetic tradition in Newton's work, the search for fundamental mathematical laws which characterizes the Platonic–Pythagorean tradition is the most pronounced aspect of Newton's work. Choice E is incorrect because, although Newton was a Copernican in the sense that he advocated a Sun-centered model, he broke with almost every other aspect of Copernicus's approach.

66. **D**. The notion that the proper role of government is to protect individual property is a fundamental tenet of John Locke's philosophy, not of Rousseau's. The other four choices are all examples of Rousseau's philosophy.

67. **B**. Tea imported from China, in exchange for opium from British India, was sold in Europe, but this transaction was not part of the "triangle of trade," which involved Europe, Africa, and the Americas/West Indies. The other four choices describe transactions that did make up the triangle of trade.

68. **E**. In Thermidor (1794–1799), the bourgeois moderates who had begun the revolution by constituting a National Assembly came out of hiding and reasserted their control over a revolution that had briefly taken a more radical turn. Choice B is incorrect because France was not defeated by Austria, and would not be defeated until 1815. Choice C is incorrect because the French monarchy was not restored until after the defeat of Napoleon in 1815. Choice D is incorrect because the rule of the Committee of Public Safety occurred during the radical phase of the revolution (1791–1794).

69. **C**. The great powers at the Congress of Vienna were represented by members of the traditional, aristocratic ruling houses of Europe. Accordingly, their aims were to restore the traditional order of a Europe that the French Revolution had challenged and to create a new balance of power that would make another Napoleon impossible. Choice A is incorrect because the aims of restoring the traditional order and establishing a balance of power meant both the restoration of the Bourbon monarchy and of a reasonable economic and military power in France; France was not, therefore, to be "punished." Choice B is incorrect because Germany was not united in 1814 and a "weakening" of Germany would have made no sense in 1814. Choice D is incorrect because the aristocratic representatives at the Congress of Vienna were directly threatened by and, therefore, *opposed* to liberal reforms. Choice E is incorrect because the nationalist hopes of the Italians, Hungarians, and Czechs ran counter to the aim of restoring the traditional order.

70. **B**. The factory system that was characteristic of the Second Industrial Revolution required and produced a class of managers and clerks whose pay and status located them precariously at the lower end of the middle class. Choice A is incor-

rect because the Second Industrial Revolution did nothing to distribute wealth *more evenly* throughout the population; instead, it made a *relatively small number* of industrialists and entrepreneurs fabulously wealthy and made some workers better off than before. Choice C is incorrect because the poor had existed before the Second Industrial Revolution. Choice D is incorrect because, although the railway boom produced social effects, it is not itself a social effect. Choice E is incorrect because, although many women initially found work in the factories of the Second Industrial Revolution, they were not paid equally and were the first to be let go when increasing mechanization decreased the demand for labor.

71. **E**. Johann Wolfgang von Goethe's *The Sorrows of Young Werther* (1774) is an example of the German *Sturm und Drang* (storm and stress) movement of the late eighteenth century. Its glorification of the "inner experience" of the sensitive individual was a forerunner of nineteenth-century Romanticism. Choice A is incorrect because Michelangelo's *David* is an example of the late Renaissance period. Choice B is incorrect because Bismarck's *Kulturkampf* is an example of the political philosophy known as *Realpolitik*. Choice C is incorrect because the assassination of Franz Ferdinand is an example of ethnic nationalism. Choice D is incorrect because Picasso's *Guernica* is early cubist in style and dates from the twentieth century.

72. **A**. The fact that the French voters used their newly granted privilege of universal manhood suffrage to vote for the creation of a Second Empire (replacing the Second Republic) and to make Louis-Napoleon hereditary emperor demonstrates the degree to which nationalism (the desire to have a strong and powerful nation) had triumphed over all other ideologies in mid-eighteenth-century France. Choice B is incorrect because Louis-Napoleon's coup d'état simply illustrates his willingness to use force in order to rule; it was the overwhelming approval of this action by the public in the two plebiscites that demonstrates the power of nationalism. Choice C is incorrect because the revolt of the

working classes in Paris and their brief attempt to set up a Commune illustrates a development of class consciousness, not nationalism. Choice D is incorrect because Louis-Napoleon's granting of universal manhood suffrage illustrates his belief that he had the people's support; their use of that suffrage to bring into being an empire and an emperor demonstrates their nationalism. Choice E is incorrect because the Directory was a bureaucratic entity of eighteenth-century France.

73. **B.** The rise of Chartism (1837–1842), characterized by massive demonstrations in favor of the People's Charter, a petition that called for universal manhood suffrage and a democratic Parliament, demonstrated the degree to which the classes who had not been enfranchised by the Reform Bill of 1832, the lower middle and working classes, desired further reform. Choice A is incorrect because the Charter was ignored by Parliament; the monarchy played almost no role in the drama of Chartism. Choice C is incorrect because the Chartist movement was a reform movement; it was neither intrinsically nationalist nor antinationalist. Choice D is incorrect because the Charter called for a more democratic Parliament; it was not opposed to the monarchy. Choice E is incorrect because the Chartist movement did not involve opposition to the mechanization of industry; it was Luddism that offered organized opposition to the mechanization of industry.

74. **A.** In a European society increasingly devoted to the mundane proceedings of the business world and an accompanying sense of social alienation, war seemed to offer the possibility of a "brotherhood of arms" and the opportunity to do something glorious and worthwhile. Choice B is incorrect because while there was a racial component to the intense nationalism of 1914, a notion of "racial hatred" was not a strong component to the celebratory mood of 1914. Choice C is incorrect because Germany's strong desire to repudiate the humiliating conditions of the Versailles Treaty was a factor in German enthusiasm for war in 1939; the Versailles Treaty did not come into existence until the conclusion of World War I in 1918. Choice D is incorrect

because the Continental System was instituted by Napoleon in the early 1800s and was long gone by 1914. Choice E is incorrect because B, C, and D are incorrect.

75. **B.** In the context of World War I, the phrase "total war" refers to the marshalling of every sector of the economy to support the war effort and the abandoning the production of normal consumer goods that was required to win the war of attrition. Choice A is incorrect because the bombing of civilians in major cities was a development of World War II. Choice C is incorrect because both sides did take prisoners in World War I. Choice D is incorrect because World War I was fought in a long line of trenches in Flanders and France; war on multiple continents was a development of World War II. Choice E is incorrect because choices A, C, and D are incorrect.

76. **B.** The war effort exhausted the resources of the traditional European powers, Britain, France, and Germany, and left the United States, with its vast economy, and the Soviet Union, with the largest army in the world, as the two superpowers. Choice A is incorrect because the Treaty of Versailles was the treaty that concluded World War I. Choice C is incorrect because it was the division of Germany that was a consequence of World War II; German reunification did not come until 1990. Choice D is incorrect because World War II marked the beginning of the breakup of the British Empire, not a strengthening of it. Choice E is incorrect because the German invasion of Poland was one of the *causes* of World War II, not a consequence.

77. **D.** Following the collapse of the Soviet Union, nationalism which had been driven underground came to the surface in Eastern Europe, resulting in the split of Czechoslovakia and the advent of several ethnic-nationalist wars in the former Yugoslavia and in the former republics of the Soviet Union. The absorption of Eastern Europe into the European Union has brought the effects of globalization to eastern Europe. Choice A is incorrect because, although there was an undeniable increase in individual liberty following the fall of the Soviet Union, the degree to which either

individual liberty or democracy has flourished in eastern Europe in the subsequent decades is highly debatable. Choice C is incorrect because America has not become isolationist. Choice E is incorrect because the economic effects of the fall of the Soviet Union regarding the distribution of wealth and the effect on poverty varied greatly throughout Eastern Europe.

78. **C.** Following the breach of the Berlin Wall in November of 1989, the West German Chancellor, the Conservative Helmut Kohl, moved quickly toward reunification. In March 1990, elections were held in East Germany to create a new government ready to negotiate with West Germany; by August 3 the official treaty of reunification was drafted; on October 3, 1990, the Germans celebrated Reunification Day. It was a reunification that amounted to East Germany being annexed by the West. Choice A is incorrect because the process happened very quickly. Choice B is incorrect because there was nothing that could be called separate economic policies that were set up to ease the transition. Choice D is incorrect because the Civic Forum leaders, who were not at all sure that they wished to be reunified with West Germany and its capitalist economy, were swept aside in the reunification process. Choice E is incorrect because choices A, B, and D are incorrect.

79. **D.** Luther's "The Freedom of the Christian Man" (1520) was his message to the common people; no social revolutionary, Luther walked a thin line between encouraging the common people to "obey their Christian conscience" and assert their individual independence from the Church in Rome, but also to respect those in authority who seemed to possess true Christian principles. Choice A is incorrect because Luther was an opponent of social upheaval and the essay was specifically designed to discourage such uprisings. Choice B is incorrect because "The Freedom of the Christian Man" was Luther's message to the common people; to the nobility, he wrote an "Address to the Christian Nobility of the German Nation" (1520), which appealed to the German princes' desire for both greater unity and power and to their desire to be out from under the thumb of an Italian pope. Choice C is incorrect because it was not Luther, but rather the German princes who established the principle of "whoever rules; his religion" by signing the Peace of Augsburg (1555), which signaled Rome that the German princes would not go to war with each other over religion. Choice E is incorrect because choices A, B, and C are incorrect.

80. **E.** All of the choices are correct. Richelieu built a powerful royal army and used it to defeat and disband the private armies of the Great French aristocrats. He then turned the royal army on the Protestant towns, stripping them of their autonomy. In addition to the royal army, Richelieu also built a strong administrative bureaucracy and used it to strip provincial aristocrats and the elite of their administrative power by dividing France into some 30 administrative districts and putting each under the control of an *intendent*, an administrative bureaucrat, usually chosen from the middle class, who owed his position and therefore his loyalty directly to Richelieu.

Suggestions and Outline for the DBQ

Suggestions

Remember the five steps to a short history essay of high quality adapted to the DBQ:

Step 1: As you read the documents, decide how you are going to group them.

Step 2: Compose a thesis that explains why the documents should be grouped in the way you have chosen.

Step 3: Compose your topic sentences and make sure that they add up logically to your thesis.

Step 4: Support and illustrate your thesis with specific examples that contextualize the documents.

Step 5. *If you have time*, compose a one-paragraph conclusion that restates your thesis.

For this question, the documents display a wide array of positions; so a good strategy would be to try to identify a central dividing issue. In these documents, you can notice that all except Copernicus seem to take some sort of position on the senses and observation: some believe that all knowledge of nature must start with direct sense experience, while others argue that starting with sense experience is a mistake. Begin the essay by discussing that central divide and then see if you can form a few groups based on the similarities and differences between their approaches.

Finally, since Copernicus does not address the central issue, ignore the document. It is okay to ignore *one* document if it does not fit into your thesis, but never ignore more than one or two.

Outline

A possible outline to an answer to this DBQ looks like this:

Thesis: These documents show that arguments regarding the basis for knowledge of the natural world have often hinged on assumptions about the reliability of sense experience.

Topic sentence A: Documents 2 and 9 illustrate the faith in direct, trial-and-error experience that developed in the "alchemy" and "natural magic" traditions.

Specific examples: Della Porta's emphasis on "practical application"; Agricola's emphasis on handling the materials, making "dissolutions" and "combinations" and recording results carefully.

Topic sentence B: Documents 5 and 6 illustrate the emphasis on observation as the correct starting place for knowledge of the natural world.

Specific examples: Bacon outlines two approaches and argues for the superiority of the one that begins with observed particulars; Harvey *illustrates* how the method should work.

Topic sentence C: Documents 3 and 10 refine the process to include the goal of finding general laws.

Specific examples: Galileo—sense experiences and very exact observations; begin not from the authority of scriptural passages, but from sense experiences and necessary demonstrations; nature never transgresses the laws imposed upon her. Newton codifies the approach into "rules."

Topic sentence D: Documents 4, 7, and 8 dissent from the view that sense experience is a valid foundation for knowledge of the natural world.

Specific examples: Bellarmine: the dangers of contradicting scholastic and church authority; Descartes: the senses are easily fooled; an alternative method, proceed logically from a general distinct idea to particulars.

Conclusion: The variety of attitudes and positions regarding knowledge about the natural world depended upon the amount of faith one put in the reliability of sense experience.

Suggestions and Outlines for Answers to the Thematic Essay Questions

Suggestions

Choose one question from each group for which you can quickly write a clear thesis and three topic sentences that you can illustrate and support with several specific examples. Then follow the five-step formula to constructing a short history essay of high quality:

Step 1: Find the action words in the question and determine what it wants you to do.

Step 2: Compose a thesis that responds to the question and gives you something specific to support and illustrate.

Step 3: Compose your topic sentences and make sure that they add up logically to your thesis.

Step 4: Support and illustrate your thesis with specific examples.

Step 5: *If you have time*, compose a one-paragraph conclusion that restates your thesis.

And remember the writing guidelines:

- Avoid long sentences with multiple clauses. Your goal is to write the clearest sentence possible; most often the clearest sentence is a relatively short sentence.
- Do not get caught up in digressions. No matter how fascinating or insightful you find some idea or fact, if it does not directly support or illustrate your thesis, do not put it in.
- Skip the mystery. Do not ask a lot of rhetorical questions and do not go for a surprise ending. The readers are looking for your thesis, your argument, and your evidence; give it to them in a clear, straightforward manner.

Outlines

Part B

Question 2

Thesis: The success or failure of seventeenth-century monarchs to consolidate political power within their kingdoms rested on their ability to form an alliance with a rising commercial class.

Topic sentence A: The French monarchy built the most absolutist government by cementing an alliance with both the clergy and middle class, and by using the great administrative expertise of both to build a powerful centralized bureaucracy.

Specific examples: Richelieu divided France into 30 administrative districts, each under the control of an *intendent*, an administrative bureaucrat, usually chosen from the middle class.

Topic sentence B: In England, the Parliament successfully resisted the absolutist designs of the Stuart monarchy because the English Parliament of the seventeenth century was a pre-existing alliance of nobles and well-to-do members of a thriving merchant and professional class that saw itself as a voice of the "English people."

Specific examples: Social composition of the two camps in the English civil war—traditional landed nobility and high Church sided with the king; newer, commercial-based nobles and merchant class fought for Parliament.

Topic sentence C: In those areas where the commercial class was less developed, a political standoff between monarch and landed nobility was the norm.

Specific examples: Brandenburg–Prussia, the independent German states, Austria, and

Poland all lacked a well-developed commercial class and all had political compromise between monarchy and traditional elites.

Conclusion: The degree to which seventeenth-century European monarchs were successful in consolidating political power was directly related to their ability to build an alliance with the commercial class.

Question 3

Thesis: In the eighteenth century, a combination of the development of market-based agriculture, rural manufacturing, and increased demand shattered the traditional population and productivity cycles of western Europe.

Topic sentence A: Prior to the eighteenth century, changes in both population and productivity were cyclical and due to natural limits on agricultural productivity.

Specific examples: Population and productivity would rise together, as more hands meant more crops planted and harvested; eventually agricultural productivity would reach a maximum, causing food to become scarce and forcing population down.

Topic sentence B: In response to an increasingly commercialized economy due to trade with the colonies, eighteenth-century British land owners began to shift to cash-crop agriculture and the importation of food, removing the natural limit to agricultural productivity.

Specific examples: Shift to growing of grain and the enclosure movement.

Topic sentence C: The development of cottage textile industry spread capital throughout the economy and enabled the full-scale shift to commercial agriculture and food importation, removing the last check to population growth.

Specific examples: Development of the putting-out system; development of rural spinning, weaving, and carding industries.

Conclusion: The removal of the natural limit to agricultural production removed the limits to both productivity and population growth; increased demand led to an unprecedented era of technical innovation that continued to feed growth well into the nineteenth century.

Question 4

Thesis: The French aims and methods of the French Revolution evolved through three phases: the Moderate Phase (1789–1791), the Radical Phase (1791–1794), and Thermidor (1794–1799); the evolution can be explained by shifts in the social makeup of the revolutionary leadership.

Topic sentence A: The revolution was launched by the bourgeois leaders of the Third Estate who wished to curb the power and privilege of the aristocracy and clergy through economic pressure and the threat of mass violence.

Specific examples: Formation of the National Assembly, *Declaration of the Rights of Man and Citizen.*

Topic sentence B: Beginning in 1791, the politicized urban working class of Paris seized control and attempted to create a democratic republic and a more materially and socially egalitarian society by whatever means necessary.

Specific examples: Rise of the *sans-culottes*, Reign of Terror.

Topic sentence C: By 1794 the bourgeois faction reasserted its leadership and focused on restoring order, a process that led eventually to military dictatorship.

Specific examples: Death of Robespierre, Counter Terror, Directory and Napoleon.

Conclusion: The aims and methods of the French Revolution went from moderate to radical and back again as the leadership of the revolution went from the bourgeoisie briefly to the working class and back again.

Part C

Question 5

Thesis: The Second Industrial Revolution produced a western European society that was more urban, less family-oriented, and filled with uncertainty.

Topic sentence A: The rise of the centralized factory system that characterized the Second Industrial Revolution produced a western European society that was much more urban.

Specific examples: In the eighteenth century, the majority of British population lived in the countryside; by the end of the nineteenth century, the majority of British population lived in cities. Rise of Manchester, Sheffield, and Birmingham from small villages to industrial cities.

Topic sentence B: The Second Industrial Revolution created a western European society that was less family-oriented.

Specific examples: Eldest sons and daughters moved to cities to seek factory work; with the rise of industrial cities came the rise of working-class slums. Husbands, wives, and children often worked in different factories.

Topic sentence C: The Second Industrial Revolution destroyed the certainties of the traditional society.

Specific examples: In the agricultural economy, there was no such thing as unemployment; as more and more machines were introduced, the demand for labor went down and unemployment became a cyclical phenomenon; the workhouses and poor houses in Britain appeared.

Conclusion: The Second Industrial Revolution destroyed the traditional rural, family-oriented society of certainty and created a new urban, individualized society of uncertainty.

Question 6

Thesis: The development of mass politics contributed to the development of the New Imperialism in the late nineteenth century by creating a large group of nationalistic voters whose support had to be won by the political elite.

Topic sentence A: The second half of the nineteenth century saw the development of a large group of new voters.

Specific examples: In Britain, reform Bills of 1867 and 1884 created nearly universal manhood suffrage. In France, Louis-Napoleon granted universal manhood suffrage in 1848. In Germany, Bismarck promised universal manhood suffrage (though he never provided it) in return for popular support of his policies.

Topic sentence B: The newly politicized masses were enthusiastically nationalist.

Specific examples: Support for Crimean War and occupation of Egypt in Britain; plebiscites for Second Empire and making Louis-Napoleon emperor in France; support for Franco-Prussian War in Germany.

Topic sentence C: Politicians discovered that imperialism appealed to the newly politicized masses.

Specific examples: Disraeli makes conservatives the party of monarchy, church, and *empire* in Britain; Louis-Napoleon's decision to end the republic and proclaim the Second Empire in France; Bismarck's "blood and iron" unification of Germany; the popularity of the scramble for Africa.

Conclusion: The rise of a large, nationalistic constituency that politicians had to win over contributed to the New Imperialism of the late nineteenth century.

Question 7

Thesis: The methods of successful resistance to Soviet dominance in Eastern Europe in the 1980s and early 1990s can be divided into three categories: unionization, the Civic Forum model, and ethnic nationalism.

Topic sentence A: One successful method relied upon the building of a strong labor union.

Specific examples: Formation and politicization of Solidarity; legalization in 1989, and triumph with Walesa presidency in 1990.

Topic sentence B: Another successful method relied upon a rebuilding of civic life through Civic Forums.

Specific examples: Civic Forum in Czechoslovakia led by dissidents like Havel; eventual triumph and Havel presidency; Civic Forum model in East Germany; its success (but irrelevancy in Western-dominated reunification).

Topic sentence C: A third "successful" method involved the reinvigoration of ethnic-nationalist identities.

Specific examples: Albanians and Serbs in Kosovo; Slovenes and Croatians; complete fragmentation (successful in opposing Soviet domination, but disastrous in building stable post-Soviet society).

Conclusion: There were three models that were equally successful in opposing Soviet domination, but which produced differing long-term results.

Appendixes

Glossary of Terms
Bibliography
Web Sites

GLOSSARY OF TERMS

95 theses The 95 propositions or challenges to official Church theology posted by Martin Luther on the door of Wittenberg Castle in the autumn of 1517.

absolutism A theory of government that contends that a rightful ruler rules with absolute power over his or her subjects.

abstractionism An artistic movement of the late nineteenth and early twentieth centuries that sought to "analyze" the essence of perception and experience. Abstract painters of the period developed a system of seeing the world as composed of geometrical shapes.

almanacs Popular eighteenth-century texts which incorporated much of the new scientific and rational knowledge of the Enlightenment.

Anabaptists A sect of radical Protestant reformers prevalent in Europe in the sixteenth century who considered true Protestant faith to require social reform.

anarchism The nineteenth-century ideology which saw the modern state and its institutions as the enemy of individual freedom, and recommended terrorism as a way to disrupt the machinery of government.

Ancien Régime (also Old Regime) Term that refers to the traditional social and political hierarchy of eighteenth-century France.

Anglican Church The state Church of England, established by Henry VIII in the early sixteenth century when he decided to break from the Church in Rome.

Anschluss The annexation, in March of 1938, of Austria by Nazi Germany.

anti-Semitism The singling out of Jews as culturally, and sometimes racially, different for the purpose of discriminating against them.

appeasement Britain's policy, 1936–1939, of acquiescing to Hitler's demands in return for his promise of no further aggression.

Arc de Triomphe The most famous example of neo-classical architecture executed in Napoleonic France, the arch was commissioned by Napoleon in 1806 to honor those who fought for France in the Napoleonic Wars. It was designed by Jean Francois Chalgrin and built in the center of the Place de l'Étoile (now renamed the Place Charles de Gaulle) at the western end of the Champs-Élysées.

Atlantic Charter A document, drawn up in August of 1941, setting forth Anglo-American aims in World War II. It rejected any territorial aggrandizement for either Britain or the United States, and it affirmed the right of all peoples to choose their own form of government.

August Decrees Decrees passed by the National Assembly of France in August of 1789 renouncing and abolishing most of the traditional privileges of the nobility and the clergy.

Austro-Prussian War of 1866 Engineered by Bismarck as part of his master plan to unify Germany under the Prussian monarchy. Prussian troops surprised and overwhelmed a larger Austrian force, winning victory in only seven weeks. The result was that Austria was expelled from the old German Confederation and a new North German Confederation, completely under the control of Prussia, was created.

baroque The dominant artistic style of the seventeenth century characterized by its emphasis on grandeur and drama.

Bastille The prison-fortress of eighteenth-century Paris which symbolized the despotic power of the *Ancien Régime*. It was stormed by a revolutionary crowd on July 14, 1789.

Battle of the Somme (July to November 1916) World War I British offensive that produced enormous casualties: 400,000 British, 200,000 French, and 500,000 German soldiers perished.

Battle of Tannenberg A German victory over Russian troops in August of 1914 which led to the liberation of East Prussia and began a slow, steady German advance eastward.

Battle of Trafalgar The naval battle in which Great Britain's fleet, led by Lord Nelson, defeated the combined French and Spanish fleets on October 21, 1805, making Britain virtually unconquerable.

Battle of Verdun (February 1916) World War I battle in which French troops, led by Marshall Petain, repulsed a German offensive; 700,000 men were killed.

Battle of Waterloo Napoleon's last stand in 1815; he was defeated in Belgium by a coalition of forces led by Britain's Duke of Wellington.

Berlin Airlift The U.S.-sponsored airlift, from June 1948 to May 1949, which brought supplies to West Berlin; it was a response to Soviet troops cutting off all land traffic from the West into Berlin in an attempt to take control of the whole city.

Berlin Conference of 1885 A conference of the European powers to establish guidelines for the partitioning of Africa.

Bessemer Process A process, invented in the 1850s by the English engineer Henry Bessemer, that allowed steel to be produced more cheaply and in larger quantities.

Black Death A plague that first appeared in Europe in 1347 and recurred numerous times until it disappeared in 1352. It is estimated that between one-quarter and one-third of the population of Europe died during the plague years.

Blackshirts (also *squadristi*) Italian fascist paramilitary groups, largely recruited from disgruntled war veterans, commanded by Mussolini and increasingly relied upon to keep order by the Italian government in the 1920s.

Bolsheviks A party of revolutionary Marxists, led by Lenin, who seized power in Russia in November 1917.

Boulanger Affair An attempted coup by the French General George Boulanger in the early 1880s; it underscored the fragility of French democracy and the volatility of mass politics in France.

bourgeoisie In eighteenth- and nineteenth-century France, a term for the merchant and commercial classes. In Marxist social critique, the class that owns the means of production and exploits wage-laborers.

Boxer Rebellion (1899–1900) An attempted rebellion by Chinese Nationalists which aimed at overthrowing the Western-dependent Manchu dynasty; it was suppressed by European powers.

cahiers The official concerns and grievances of the three Estates that comprised the political orders of eighteenth-century France. Members representing each of the three Estates met in the Estates General to hear the problems of the realm and to hear pleas for new taxes. In return, they were allowed to present their cahiers.

Candide Voltaire's sprawling satire of European culture, penned in 1759; the classic example of Enlightenment-period satire.

Carbonari Secret groups of Italian nationalists active in the early part of the nineteenth century; in 1820, the Carbonari briefly succeeded in organizing an uprising that forced King Ferdinand I of the Kingdom of the Two Sicilies to grant a constitution and a new Parliament.

Cartel des Gauches A coalition of socialist parties swept into power in France in the elections of 1924; caused an ultranationalist reaction in France.

cash crops Crops grown for sale and export in the market-oriented approach that replaced the manorial system during the Agricultural Revolution of the eighteenth century.

celestial realm The realm, in the Aristotelian view of the cosmos, above the orbit of the moon.

Chartism (1837–1842) A movement in Britain in support of the People's Charter, a petition that called for universal manhood suffrage; annual Parliaments; voting by secret ballot; equal electoral districts; abolition of property qualifications for Members of Parliament; and payment of Members of Parliament.

city-states The independent cities of the Italian peninsula that were ruled by powerful merchant families; the unique political structure of the Italian peninsula that was a crucial factor in the advent of the Renaissance.

Civic Forum A movement in Czechoslovakia and East Germany in the 1980s, which sought to rebuild notions of citizenship and civic life that had been destroyed by the Soviet system; became an organizational and inspirational rallying point for opposition to Soviet domination.

Civil Constitution of the Clergy Legislation passed by the National Assembly of France in September of 1791 that turned clergymen into employees of the government and turned Church property into property of the state.

civil society The society formed when free men come together and surrender some of their individual power in return for greater protection.

class consciousness The sense of belonging to a "working class" that developed among European workers during the Second Industrial Revolution of the nineteenth century; a result of their working together in factories and living together in isolated slums.

collectivization of agriculture As an extension of his five-year plan (initiated in 1928), Stalin pursued a policy of destroying the culture of the peasant village and replacing it with one organized around huge collective farms. The peasants resisted and were killed, starved, or driven into Siberia in numbers that can only be estimated but which may have been as high as eight million.

Colloquies Dialogues written (beginning in 1519) by the most important and influential of the northern humanists, Desiderius Erasmus, for the purpose of teaching his students both the Latin language and how to live a good life.

Committee of Public Safety A 12-man committee created in the summer of 1793 and vested with almost total power in order that it might secure the fragile French Republic from its enemies.

Commonwealth, The (1649–1660) The period where England was ruled without a monarch, following the victory of the Parliamentary forces in the English Civil War and the subsequent execution of Charles I.

communism The ideology dedicated to the creation of a class-free society through the abolition of private property.

Compromise of 1867 The Austrian Emperor Franz Joseph's attempt, in 1866, to deal with the demands for greater autonomy from the ethnic minorities within the Hapsburg empire. The compromise set up a dual monarchy of Austria–Hungary, where Franz Joseph served as the ruler of both Austria and Hungary, each of which had its own parliament.

Concert of Europe The alliance created in November of 1815 that required important diplomatic decisions to be made by all four great powers—Austria, Russia, Prussia, and Great Britain—"in concert" with one another.

Conciliar Movement A fifteenth-century movement, composed of various councils of cardinals, which attempted to reform, reunite, and reinvigorate the Christian Church of Europe.

Concordat of 1801 An agreement signed by Napoleon Bonaparte and the Catholic Church of Rome, reconciling France with the Catholic Church by stipulating that French clergy would be chosen and paid by the state but consecrated by the pope.

Congress of Vienna Representatives from the four major powers that had combined to defeat Napoleon—Great Britain, Russia, Prussia, and Austria—met in Paris in November of 1814 to forge a peace settlement.

conservatism The nineteenth-century ideology which held that tradition was the only trustworthy guide to social and political action.

constitutional monarchy A theory of government that contends that a rightful ruler's power is limited by an agreement with his or her subjects.

Consulate A three-man executive body, established immediately following Napoleon Bonaparte's coup d'état in November of 1799. In 1802, Napoleon was acknowledged as the sole executive officer and given the title "first consul for life."

Continental System Established by Napoleon in order to weaken Britain, the system forbade the continental European states and kingdoms under French control from trading with Britain.

Copernicanism The theory, following Nicolas Copernicus, that the Sun is at the center of the cosmos and that the Earth is the third planet from the sun.

cottage industry (also putting-out system) A system in which rural peasants engaged in small-scale textile manufacturing that developed in the eighteenth century to allow merchants, faced with an ever-expanding demand for textiles, to get around the guild system.

cotton gin Machine invented in 1793 by an American, Eli Whitney, that efficiently removed seed from raw cotton, thereby increasing the speed with which it could be processed and sent to the spinners.

Council for Mutual Economic Assistance The Soviet Union's response to the Marshall Plan, whereby the Soviet Union offered economic aid packages to eastern European countries.

Council of Trent Reform council of the Catholic Church which began its deliberations in 1545. Despite its reformist aims, it continued to insist that the Catholic Church was the final arbiter in all matters of faith.

Court of the Star Chamber A judicial innovation of Henry VII (r. 1485–1509) of England, designed to curb the independence of the nobility, whereby criminal charges brought against the nobility were judged by a court of the king's own councilors.

De Revolutionibus Orbium Caelestum Nicolas Copernicus's astronomical book published in 1543. It proposed the shift from a geocentric (Earth-centered) model of the cosmos to a heliocentric (Sun-centered) model. Its theories contributed greatly to the Scientific Revolution in the seventeenth century.

"Declaration of the Rights of Man and of the Citizen" A declaration adopted by the National Assembly of France on August 27, 1789, espousing individual rights and liberties for all citizens.

Deism The belief that the complexity, order, and natural laws exhibited by the universe were reasonable proofs that it had been created by a God who was no longer active.

Dialogue on the Two Chief Systems of the World Galileo's treatise of 1632, where he dismantled the arguments in favor of the traditional, Aristotelian view of the cosmos, and presented the Copernican system as the only alternative for reasonable people.

Diplomatic Revolution The mid-eighteenth-century shift in European alliances, whereby the expansionist aims of Frederick II of Prussia caused old enemies to become allies. Specifically, Prussia, fearful of being isolated by its enemies, forged an alliance in 1756 with its former enemy Great Britain; and Austria and France, previously antagonistic toward one another, responded by forging an alliance of their own.

Directory A five-man board created to handle the executive functions of the government during Thermidor, the third and final phase of the French Revolution (1794–1799).

Discourse on Method René Descartes's treatise of 1637, where he established a method of philosophical inquiry based on radical skepticism.

dissenters The collective name for Protestant groups and sects that refused to join the Anglican Church in England.

Divine Right of Kings The theory that contended that monarchs received their right to rule directly from God.

division of labor A technique whereby formerly complex tasks that required knowledge and skill were broken down into a series of simple tasks, aided by machines.

doge The Italian word that refers to the military strongmen who ruled some of the Italian city-states, such as Venice, during the Renaissance.

Dreyfus Affair The protracted prosecution, beginning in 1894, of a young Jewish officer in the French Army, Alfred Dreyfus, for treason. His numerous trials divided the French nation, illustrating how strongly ultranationalist and anti-Semitic feelings were in the French establishment.

Edict of Nantes Royal edict which established the principle of religious toleration in France; proclaimed in 1598 and revoked in 1685.

elect, the The name given in Calvinist theology to the group of people who have been predestined by God for salvation.

elements The basic components of matter in Aristotelian physics; there were five: earth, water, air, fire, and ether.

Ems Telegram A diplomatic correspondence between Napoleon III of France and William I of Prussia, edited by Bismarck to make it seem like they had insulted one another. An example of *Realpolitik*.

enclosure The building of hedges, fences, and walls to deny the peasantry access to traditional farming plots and common lands which were now converted to fields for cash crops during the Agricultural Revolution of the eighteenth century.

Encyclopedia (1751–1772) Produced by the tireless efforts of its co-editors Denis Diderot and Jean le Rond d'Alembert, the entries of the *Encyclopedia* championed a scientific approach to knowledge and labeled anything not based on reason as superstition.

English Civil War (1642–1646) Forces loyal to King Charles I fought to defend the power of the monarchy, the official Church of England, and the privileges and prerogatives of the nobility; forces supporting Parliament fought to uphold the rights of Parliament, to bring an end to the notion of an official state Church, and for notions of individual liberty and the rule of law.

enlightened despotism The hope shared by many *philosophes* that the powerful monarchs of European civilization, once educated in the ideals of the Enlightenment, would use their power to reform and rationalize society.

Essay Concerning Human Understanding John Locke's treatise of 1689–1690, which argued that humans are born *tabula rasa* (a blank slate), contradicting the traditional Christian notion that humans are born corrupt and sinful, and implying that what humans become is purely a result of what they experience.

Estates General The representative body of eighteenth-century France. Members representing each of the three Estates met to hear the problems of the realm and to hear pleas for new taxes. In return, they were allowed to present a list of their own concerns and proposals, called cahiers, to the Crown.

eugenics A notion, first developed in the nineteenth century, that a progressive, scientific nation should plan and manage the biological reproduction of its population.

expressionism An artistic movement of the late nineteenth and early twentieth centuries that sought to depict a world of emotional and psychological states. Accordingly, expressionists turned away from the rules of realism and naturalism to produce images with distorted outlines and exaggerated color and form.

Fabian Society The socialist organization in Britain, beginning in the late nineteenth century, that counseled against revolution but argued that the cause of the working classes could be furthered through political solutions.

factory system A system of production created in order to better supervise labor. In the factory system, workers came to a central location and worked with the machines under the supervision of managers.

First Battle of Marne (September 6, 1914) A victory won by French troops that stopped the initial German advance in World War I.

First Battle of Ypres (October and November of 1914) Allied troops ended all hopes of a German advance, leading to a stalemate and the beginning of trench warfare.

five-year plans A series of plans initiated by Stalin, beginning in 1928, which rejected all notions of private enterprise and initiated the building of state-owned factories and power stations throughout the Soviet Union.

flight to Varennes Louis XVI's attempt to flee Paris in June of 1791 and head north to rally supporters.

Florentine Academy An informal gathering of humanists devoted to the revival and teachings of Plato, founded in 1462 under the leadership of Marsilio Ficino and the patronage of Cosimo de Medici.

flying shuttle Machine invented in 1733 by John Kay that doubled the speed at which cloth could be woven on a loom, creating a need to find a way to produce greater amounts of thread faster.

Frankfort Assembly Legislative body formed during the brief success of liberal reformers in Germany in 1848; they failed in their attempt to form a German nation.

Freikorps Regiments of German World War I veterans, commanded by old imperial army officers, that were used by the government of the Weimar Republic to defeat Marxist revolutionaries in the 1920s.

fresco Paintings done either on wet or dry plaster; an important medium of art during the Renaissance.

geocentric Earth-centered; the Aristotelian model of the cosmos.

Girondins Faction within the National Convention of France, during the French Revolution, whose membership tended to come from the wealthiest of the bourgeoisie; they opposed the execution of Louis XVI.

glasnost Russian term that refers to a new "openness" that Soviet premier Mikhail Gorbachev believed was required for the survival of the Soviet Union. Introduced in 1985, the concept of *glasnost* (along with *perestroika* or "restructuring") quickly fanned the fires of reform and autonomy throughout the Soviet Union and its satellite states.

globalization A term that refers to the increasing integration and interdependence of the economic, social, cultural, and even ecological aspects of life in the late twentieth and early twenty-first centuries. The term not only refers to the way in which the economies of the world affect one another, but also to the way that the experience of everyday life is increasingly standardized by the spread of technologies which carry with them social and cultural norms.

Glorious Revolution, The (1688) The quick, nearly bloodless uprising that coordinated Parliament-led uprisings in England with the invasion of a Protestant fleet and army from the Netherlands, and which led to the expulsion of James II and the institution of a constitutional monarchy in England under William and Mary.

Grand Alliance The alliance between Britain, the Soviet Union, and the United States to oppose the Axis powers of Nazi Germany, Italy, and Japan. Hitler's decision to attack the Soviet Union in June of 1941 forged the first link, allying Britain and the Soviet Union; the United States joined following Japan's attack on Pearl Harbor, December 7, 1941.

Grand Army The 600,000-strong army of conscripts assembled by Napoleon to invade Russia in June of 1812; 500,000 of them perished in the effort.

Great Depression A total collapse of the economies of Europe and the United States, triggered by the American stock market crash in 1929 and lasting most of the decade of the 1930s.

Great Fear, the Atmosphere of fear created in Paris in the summer of 1789 by the violence occurring in the countryside, as peasants raided granaries to ensure that they had affordable bread and attacked the chateaus of the local nobility in order to burn debt records.

Guernica (1937) Pablo Picasso's 25-foot-long mural depicting the bombing of the town of Guernica by

German planes in 1937, poignantly illustrating the nature of the mismatch between the German-supported Spanish fascist troops and the rag-tag brigades of volunteers defending the Spanish Republic.

guilds Exclusive organizations that monopolized the skilled trades in Europe from the medieval period until they were broken by the development of cottage industry in the eighteenth century.

gulags Work camps where Stalin sent Soviet citizens whom he considered to be enemies of the state.

haciendas The large, landed estates which produced food and leather goods for the mining areas and urban centers of the Spanish empire in the New World.

heliocentric Sun-centered; the model of the cosmos proposed by Nicolas Copernicus in 1534.

Hermeticism A tradition of knowledge which taught that the world was infused with a single spirit that could be explored through mathematics as well as through magic.

Historical and Critical Dictionary A dictionary compiled by Pierre Bayle in 1697; it included entries for numerous religious beliefs, illustrating why they did not, in his opinion, stand the test of reason.

Holy Roman Emperor The nominal ruler of the German states who, from 1356, was elected by a seven-member council consisting of the archbishops of Mainz, Trier, and Cologne, the Duke of Saxony, the Margrave of Brandenburg, the Count Palatine, and the King of Bohemia.

Huguenots The sixteenth- and seventeenth-century term for Protestants living in France.

humanism In the Renaissance, both a belief in the value of, and an educational program based on, Classical Greek and Roman languages and values.

Hundred Years War A dynastic conflict begun in 1337, pitting the armies and resources of the Norman kings of England and the Capetian kings of France against one another.

impressionism An artistic movement of the late nineteenth century. Impressionists desired to render the visual experience itself by creating images with visible brush strokes and heightened color.

Indian National Congress An organization of the Hindu elite in India, established in 1885 to promote the notion of a free and independent India.

indulgences Certificates of absolution sold by the Church forgiving people for their sins, sometimes even before they committed them, in return for a monetary contribution; the selling of indulgences was one of the practices objected to by Martin Luther.

industrial socialism A variety of nineteenth-century utopian socialism which argued that it was possible to have a productive, profitable industrial enterprise without exploiting workers. Its leading advocate was a Scottish textile manufacturer, Robert Owen.

Inquisition An institution within the Catholic Church, created in 1479 to enforce the conversion of Muslims and Jews in Spain; it was revived and expanded during the Reformation to combat all perceived threats to orthodoxy and the Church's authority.

intendent An administrative bureaucrat in Absolutist France of the seventeenth century, usually chosen from the middle class, who owed his position and, therefore, his loyalty directly to the state.

internal combustion engine Developed in 1886 by two German engineers, Gottlieb Daimler and Karl Benz, it burned petroleum as fuel and, when mounted on a carriage, was used to create the automobile.

International Congress of the Rights of Women (1878) Meeting, in Paris, of the political groups which campaigned for women's rights.

International Working Men's Association Founded in 1864, it was a loose coalition of unions and political parties whose aim was an international strategy for the advancement of working-class issues; the First International fell apart in the 1870s, but was replaced by the Second International in 1889.

invisible hand A phrase, penned by Adam Smith in *Wealth of Nations* (1776), to denote the way in which natural economic laws guided the economy.

Iron Curtain A phrase (first uttered by Winston Churchill in a speech given in the United States in 1946) that referred to the line which stretched from the Baltic Sea in the north to the Adriatic Sea in the south and divided Europe between a communist East and a capitalist West.

iron law of wages A theory promoted by nineteenth-century liberal economic thinkers which argued that competition between workers for jobs would always, in the long run, force wages to sink to subsistence levels.

Jacobins A faction within the National Convention of France, during the French Revolution, whose members came from the lower strata of the bourgeoisie; they were adamant proponents of the execution of Louis XVI.

July Ordinances Issued by Charles X of France in 1830, the ordinances dissolved part of the legislative branch of the government and revoked the voting privileges of the bourgeoisie. The result was a rebellion by the bourgeoisie, students, and workers that forced Charles X to abdicate.

Junkers A powerful class of landed aristocrats in nineteenth-century Prussia who supported Bismarck's plan for the unification of Germany.

Kepler's laws Three laws of planetary motion developed by Johannes Kepler between 1609 and 1619.

kinetic theory of gases A theory developed in the mid-nineteenth century, chiefly by Rudolph Clausius and James Maxwell, that envisioned gas pressure and temperature as resulting from a certain volume of molecules in motion. Such an approach allowed them to analyze, and therefore to measure and predict, pressure and temperature statistically.

Kulturkampf Bismarck's legislative assault, in the 1870s, on the religious freedom of Catholics in Germany.

laissez-faire The notion, promoted in Adam Smith's *Wealth of Nations* (1776), that governments should not try to interfere with the natural workings of an economy; a notion that became one of the basic tenets of liberalism in the nineteenth century.

Law Code of 1649 Legislation in Russia that converted the legal status of groups as varied as peasants and slaves into that of a single class of serfs.

Law of the Maximum Law passed by the National Convention of France in the summer of 1793 to cap the price of bread and other essentials.

lay piety A tradition in the smaller, independent German provinces, flourishing in the fifteenth and sixteenth centuries, whereby organized groups promoted pious behavior and learning outside the bureaucracy of the Church.

Leviathan Thomas Hobbes's treatise of 1651, which asserted that self-interest motivated nearly all human behavior and concluded that "without a common power to keep them in awe," the natural state of man was one of war.

liberalism The eighteenth- and nineteenth-century ideology which asserted that the task of government was to promote individual liberty.

Maastricht Treaty The treaty, signed in 1992, creating the European Union, the world's largest trading bloc, and moving to adopt a common currency (the euro).

M.A.D. The acronym for the risky, but ultimately successful, strategy (mutually assured destruction) that evolved between the United States and Soviet Union to avoid nuclear war by ensuring that neither side could survive one.

Maginot Line A vast complex of tank traps, fixed artillery sites, subterranean railways, and living quar-

ters built by the French, which paralleled the Franco-German border but failed to protect the border between France and Belgium.

Manhattan Project The project, secretly funded by the American government, that successfully invented and produced two atomic bombs in 1945.

manorial system The traditional economic system of Europe, developed in the medieval period, in which the land-owning elite (lords of the manor) held vast estates divided into small plots of arable land farmed by peasants for local consumption.

March to Versailles, the Following riots in Paris on October 5, 1789, a contingent of Parisian women organized an 11-mile march from Paris to the king's palace at Versailles. Along the way, they were joined by the Paris Guards, a citizen militia, and together they forced their way into the palace and insisted that Louis accompany them back to Paris.

Marshall Plan The plan, named after U.S. Secretary of State George Marshall, launched in 1947 which provided billions of dollars of aid to help the western European powers rebuild their infrastructures and economies.

Masonic Lodges Secret meeting places established and run by Freemasons whose origins dated back to the medieval guilds of the stonemasons. By the eighteenth century, the lodges were fraternities of aristocratic and middle-class men (and occasionally women) who gathered to discuss alternatives to traditional beliefs.

materialism A philosophical movement of the nineteenth century that argued that all natural phenomena could and should be understood as the result of matter and motion. First articulated by the German natural philosophers Karl Vogt, Jakob Moleschott, and Ludwig Büchner, materialism became a foundational assumption of the scientific view of the world by the end of the nineteenth century.

Meiji Restoration A successful rebellion by Japanese modernizers who were determined to preserve Japanese independence; it restored power to the emperor and reorganized Japanese society along Western lines.

Metropolis (1925) Film by Fritz Lang that depicts a world in which humans are dwarfed by an impersonal world of their own creation; illustrates the alienation and anxiety that permeated European culture in the 1920s.

Michelangelo's *David* Sculpted by Michelangelo Buonarroti (completed in 1504), this sculpture of the biblical hero is characteristic of the last and most heroic phase of Renaissance art; sculpted from a sin-